W9-AKU-805

5 ESSENTIALS FOR A WINNING LIFE

5 ESSENTIALS FOR A WINNING LIFE

THE NUTRITION, FITNESS, AND LIFE PLAN FOR DISCOVERING THE CHAMPION WITHIN

CHRIS CARMICHAEL

WITH JIM RUTBERG

RODALE

NOTICE

This book is intended as a reference volume only, not as a medical manual. The information given here is designed to help you make informed decisions about your health. It is not intended as a substitute for any treatment that may have been prescribed by your doctor. If you suspect that you have a medical problem, we urge you to seek competent medical help.

Mention of specific companies, organizations, or authorities in this book does not imply endorsement by the publisher, nor does mention of specific companies, organizations, or authorities imply that they endorse this book.

Internet addresses and telephone numbers given in this book were accurate at the time it went to press.

Rodale books may be purchased for business or promotional use or for special sales.
For information, please write to:
Special Markets Department, Rodale Inc., 733 Third Avenue, New York, NY 10017

Printed in the United States of America

Rodale Inc. makes every effort to use acid-free ♾, recycled paper ♻.

PHOTOGRAPHS BY Tom Kimmell

BOOK DESIGN BY Susan Eugster

Library of Congress Cataloging-in-Publication Data

Carmichael, Chris, date
5 essentials for a winning life : the nutrition, fitness, and life plan for discovering the champion within / Chris Carmichael with Jim Rutberg.
p. cm.
Includes index.
ISBN-13 978–1–59486–455–1 hardcover
ISBN-10 1–59486–455–1 hardcover
1. Health. 2. Health behavior. I. Rutberg, Jim. II. Title.
RA776.C37 2007
613—dc22 2006029145

Distributed to the trade by Holtzbrinck Publishers

2 4 6 8 10 9 7 5 3 1 hardcover

We inspire and enable people to improve their lives and the world around them

For more of our products visit **rodalestore.com** or call 800-848-4735

»«

To Paige, love you forever

»«

CONTENTS

PREFACE

The signed yellow jersey was the last straw. Lance Armstrong had just won his second Tour de France in 2000, and he gave me a yellow jersey that read "Happy 40th. Man, you're getting old!" Ten years earlier, I was a professional bike racer myself and fitter than 99 percent of the people on the planet, but it had been a long time since I'd fit into my skintight racing jersey. In fact, as I approached 40, I was unhealthy in a lot of ways. I was fat, out of shape, and dealing with the stress of starting my own business. My employees didn't know if I was going to hug them or fire them when they saw me marching toward them, and I was growing more disconnected from my wife and children. I became a slave to my cell phone. It was always on, and I stopped whatever I was doing, including having dinner with my wife or playing with my kids, to answer the phone or return an e-mail.

How did I get into this mess?! I wondered. My life had been about performance—achieving it myself and developing it in others. I still saw myself as someone who was only a few years removed from my racing career—still fast and strong but now more focused on performance in other areas: as a coach, business owner, and head of a family. Outwardly, I was very successful. I had been an Olympian, a professional athlete, the US Olympic Committee's Coach of the Year, and coach to a Cycling World Champion and two-time Tour de France winner; a husband and father; and a successful entrepreneur.

But in reality, I wasn't performing at a high level in any aspect of my life. In response to rising challenges and greater demands, I wasn't actually excelling at anything. I was, in fact, disgusted with myself. I didn't do all that work and make all those sacrifices to end up fat, out of shape, unpleasant, achy, and chronically tired.

Somewhere, I had lost contact with the high-performance aspects of life and replaced them with mediocre stand-ins. Instead of taking stairs two at a time, I took the elevator. Instead of relishing stimulating conversation over nutritious meals, I gobbled takeout on the drive home. Instead of participating in my kids' activities, I checked the family calendar so I knew what questions to ask about events I missed. The scariest part was that I didn't even know I had changed, because it occurred gradually. The hours I spent on my bike exercising, in the kitchen cooking, and in the backyard playing catch were slowly siphoned off as I spent more time building a career, providing for my family, tending to my home—you know the drill.

And that's just it. You know the drill the same way I do. You may have the great wife and kids, the high-paying job, the big house and fancy cars, but you're pulled in so many directions that you're putting in only the minimum amount of attention necessary to keep everything functioning. Somehow you ended up with an exhausting subsistence lifestyle instead of the high-performance, fully engaged lifestyle you started out with and still desire.

I knew I wasn't living the life I wanted to, but I also didn't have a clear picture of a high-performance lifestyle. So I looked back at my life and through the notes I'd compiled during years of coaching athletes and executives. I searched for common themes, actions, and feelings that characterized periods when they and I were living to the fullest. As a result, I determined that the following are indicators for high performance.

You're engaged. To be fully engaged, you need to possess the mental, emotional, and physical energy to keep up with a ton of information. People who aren't leading high-performance lifestyles struggle to connect meaningfully to their work and families; they're disengaged because they can't keep up with the pace of modern life, and their only choice is to step out of the game and watch from the sidelines.

You're in control. A sense of control is critical because it provides an energy reserve that allows you to handle an unexpected problem or sudden stressor without disturbing the balance of the rest of your life. Without this reserve, you can barely hold things together and don't have the capacity to take on one more thing—not even positive opportunities, like contributing to your company's exciting new project or taking a weekend off to go camping or fishing with your son or daughter.

You're looking beyond limitations. People are hindered most by self-imposed limitations. To navigate through obstacles, in cycling and in life, you have to keep looking at where you want to go instead of getting seduced by potential obstacles. The obstacles will always be there, and there will always be the chance you could fail, but high-performance individuals have the vision and perspective to see and stick with the route that takes them past obstacles instead of into them.

You're competitive. When you're leading a high-performance lifestyle, you want to win. When you're not leading a high-performance lifestyle, you shrink from competition because you already feel beaten. If you can't rise above everyday demands, you're stuck struggling with them while the people around you take steps to achieve greater rewards.

You're committed. High-performance individuals set valuable goals and commit to achieving them. You can change a high-performance individual's path, but only by presenting clear evidence that your way will work better. People who are not leading a high-performance lifestyle are easier to push around. They aren't committed to what they're doing, so they'll sway whichever way the wind blows.

You're respected. It's not that people won't respect you if you're not leading a high-performance lifestyle, but when you're consistently late or rushed, always fighting fires, and barely keeping it together, it's harder for people to put their confidence and trust in you.

You're proud. One of Lance's strongest qualities after beating cancer was his dedication to celebrating victories and facing defeats. When you're engaged and committed to achieving a personal goal, there's an emotional connection that has to be addressed, whether the goal is achieved or missed. High-performance individuals are connected to their lives, feel genuine joy from success, take credit for their work, and thank the people who helped them. They also take the time to acknowledge and learn from their defeats before moving on.

»«

Well, I wanted my high-performance life back, so I devised a plan to get it, which then turned into this book. It's based on the fact that it is never too late to rediscover high-performance living—the only things you may need to give up are things that have been holding you in check. The payoff is that you'll learn how to balance your life so you can focus your attention on making real and lasting achievements.

HOW THE 5 Essentials SAVED MY LIFE

—Spencer Aronfeld, Attorney

I WAS A STEREOTYPE AND ONE I WASN'T PARTICULARLY PROUD OF. I HAD A FLOURISHING law practice and more cases than I knew what to do with. With that came financial success, a faster car, a bigger house, and fancier suits. Meals went from Subway to steak houses.

I also started gaining weight, smoking two cigars a day, and drinking lots of wine. The pressures from clients, employees, judges, kids, and my wife were simply overwhelming. I felt depressed and hopeless and escaped my troubles by eating and drinking. By the time I turned 39, my body and marriage had starting giving out.

First I had repeated asthma attacks, which led to prescriptions for inhalers, pills, and things to squirt up my nose. Then I developed an abdominal bleed and spent 4 days in intensive care. The source of the bleeding was never found, and I was released—with a handful of new prescriptions. Later I started breaking out in painful hives during times of increased stress. I ended up in the hospital to have cortisone injections and, of course, left with more medications to take.

I kept gaining weight. I hired trainer after trainer at different gyms and even participated in a gymwide bet to see who could lose the most weight in a week. I gained 4 pounds and lost $100. I was so embarrassed, I changed gyms.

Each new trainer, tennis or boxing instructor, or yoga guru put me on a meal plan. The gym guys wanted me to drink protein shakes, take weight-loss pills, and eat tons of egg whites and chicken breasts. It didn't work. The yoga guru convinced me to eat only raw fruits and vegetables. After 3 months, I couldn't stand to see a raw carrot or do yoga. I heard about the Atkins plan and flew to New York to sit down with Dr. Atkins himself. I ate pounds of corned beef and cheese and never felt worse.

For my ninth wedding anniversary, we went to Key West. As we walked down Duval Street, I looked at my reflection in a store window and hated what I saw: big belly hanging over my pants, cigar in my mouth, yellow complexion. I was no longer me.

My marriage wasn't any better. My wife and I hardly spoke. I had no time or strength to listen to her, and we were drifting apart. Soon after we returned from Key West, she declared she was taking our two kids to visit her family overseas for the summer, against my wishes.

I knew I would be alone, so I decided to look into going to Europe to watch the Tour de France. I searched the Internet for different tours and came across one offered by Carmichael Training Systems. I called the toll-free number and explained to Sharon

Julia that it had been my dream to see the Tour, but I wasn't in shape for the rides on the trip. She suggested I speak to one of the Carmichael coaches.

I knew it wouldn't be Chris Carmichael; he was busy coaching Lance. I figured I would be assigned to some underling who wouldn't have a clue how to straighten me out. Nothing had worked before; why should this be different?

That afternoon, my coach, Jake Rubelt, called me. I told him my story: how I was afraid to eat sugar, how I had to buy custom suits because off-the-rack didn't fit right, and how I had tried every diet under the sun.

Jake asked, "Do you like to ride your bike?"

I said, "Yeah, I love it, but I haven't ridden in years." He said, "That's the first step. Go ride easy for an hour. No more."

That became very important: *No more.* He protected me from myself and taught me that I needed more rest to get stronger. He told me to stop weighing myself four times a day. He insisted that I take Mondays off. No matter how much I wanted to ride or how nice a day it was, I couldn't ride on Mondays. He also made me promise that family would come before training. If a conflict arose between family time and training time, family would always win.

My clothes started feeling looser, and I began looking through my closet for things I hadn't been able to wear for years. Yes, I worked a little less, but I was more productive at the office, and people, including friends, colleagues, and clients, noticed the positive changes.

I cut out all sodas and cut back on desserts. I also added fiber and lots of fresh fruits and vegetables and soon no longer required any medication to go to the bathroom. And speaking of medications, I no longer needed to take sleeping pills to fall asleep or use any allergy pills or inhalers for asthma.

I bought my wife a bike, and now we spend several mornings a week riding together, talking about our lives and kids. We've even planned to take a bike tour together.

I'm in the best shape of my life, and I'm mentally and emotionally more grounded, centered, and at peace. I only regret losing valuable time in my twenties and thirties, when I functioned far below my capacity.

Why did Chris's 5 Essentials approach work for me when everything else failed? It wasn't just about losing weight, looking different, or even getting stronger or faster. Jake guided me through lifestyle changes that helped me find balance and with it, greater personal performance. Chris may have started out helping athletes win races, but his greatest contribution to the world may very well be his methods for helping people lead winning lives. I am living proof, a transformed man, and I'm grateful to Chris and his 5 Essentials approach that I believe saved my life.

ACKNOWLEDGMENTS

Chris Carmichael

To my wife, Paige: Our life together is a wonderful and exciting journey, and I am happy we are going "hand in hand" together on this fantastic journey.

To my children, Anna, Connor, and little Vivian: You are all wonderful, sparkling balls of life for Paige and me.

I would like to thank all the people who make up Carmichael Training Systems for their dedication to making my vision a reality. You are the best. And to the members of the 5 Essentials Challenge Team in Colorado Springs, thank you for your dedication and your valuable feedback on the program. It has been a pleasure to watch you succeed.

Of course, many thanks to Lance Armstrong and all the athletes I have had the pleasure of coaching over the many years. I cannot imagine a career more fulfilling than this one.

To my mother and father, who were my first, and always my best, coaches: You have my eternal gratitude. The same is true for my brother and sister, who have always been there for me.

Thank you to Heidi Rodale and Emily Williams at Rodale for supporting this project from beginning to end.

And finally, a very special thank-you to Jim Rutberg, my close friend and colleague. I can't believe you attacked me during the last 5 miles of the Leadville 100 . . . Love ya.

Jim Rutberg

My thanks go to Chris Carmichael for his friendship, constant support, and leadership. Thank you for pushing me when I needed to be pushed and supporting me when the words weren't flowing and, most of all, for knowing the difference.

This project wouldn't have been possible without the tireless work of Tim Pelot, Kelly O'Boyle, and Alicia Kendig. Thank you for all your hard work in making sure the training program and meal plans were perfect. Special thanks to Mindy Fox and Allison Fishman for applying your creativity and expertise to the recipes. And this section would be incomplete without thanking Grant Davis for carefully editing every last piece of writing I put in front of him.

Other people who played integral roles in gathering information, reviewing material, talking through new ideas, and generally keeping me sane during this project include Jay T. Kearney, James Herrera, Jason Koop, Brian Delong, and the entire staff at Carmichael Training Systems.

Thank you to Heidi Rodale, Emily Williams, and Susan Eugster at Rodale for your support and guidance throughout this project.

Above all, my greatest thanks go to my wife, Leslie. Thank you for your support during the long days and late nights that always accompany big projects. And to Oliver, who arrived just weeks before this book hit the shelves: Welcome to the world, kid. Dad's trying to make it a better place for you.

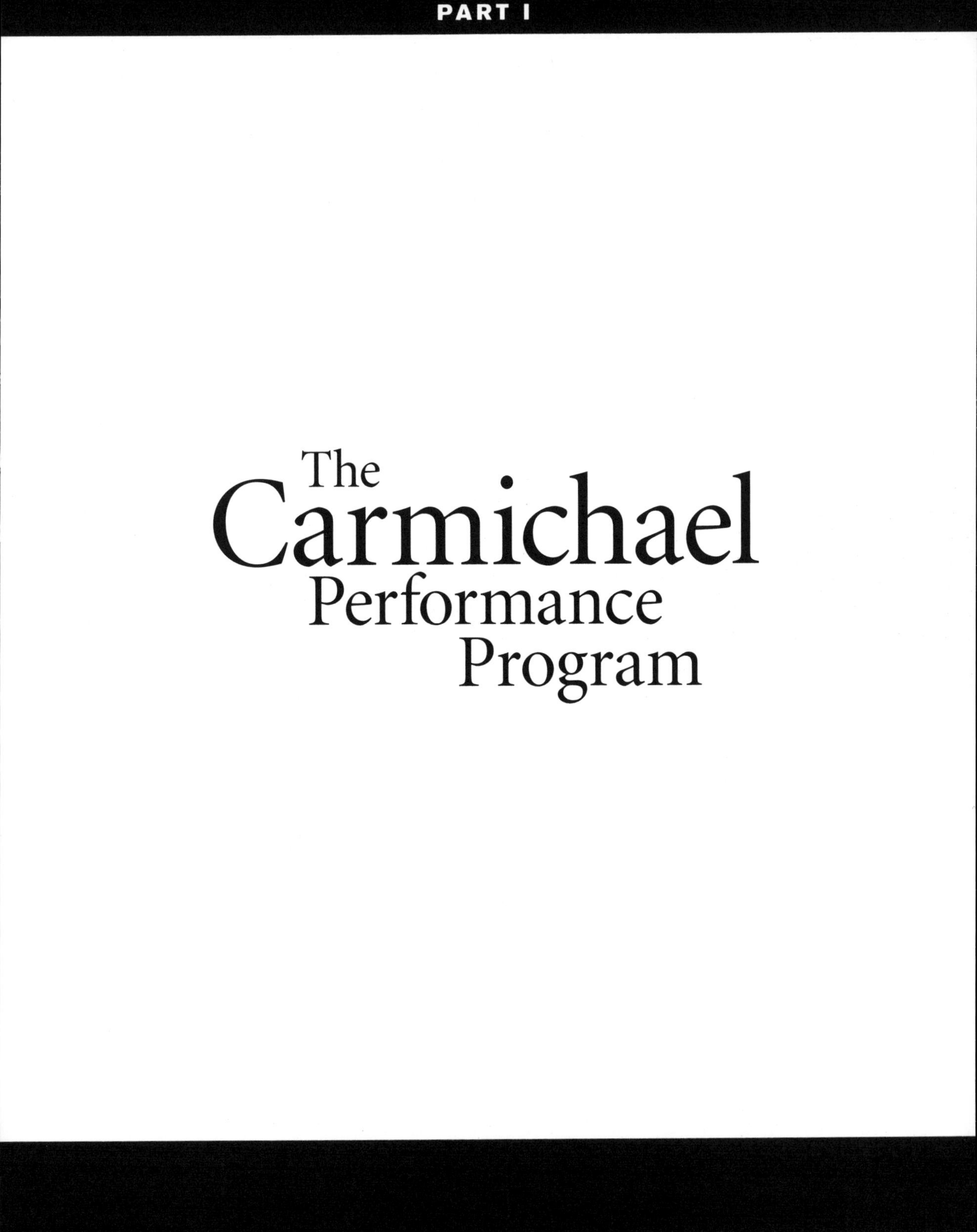
PART I
The Carmichael Performance Program

CHAPTER 1

5 Essentials for Having It All

I AM NOT SUBTLE. I'M BLUNT, TO THE POINT, HONEST, AND NOT AFRAID OF CONFRONTATION. Then again, that's a large part of being a coach, and it's the reason the athletes and executives I work with come to me in the first place. They come to me because I have a proven track record for pushing people's performance levels to all-time highs, for delivering all of the indicators of performance I mentioned in the Preface.

If you're feeling off-track or frustrated with where you are and you're looking to upgrade to a high-performance life, I'm here to cut through the wasteland of useless information and show you how to get there.

WHAT HAPPENED?

First of all, how did we go from having it all to wondering where it all went? It comes down to the idea of achievement. People with ambition, drive, and vision set their sights on achieving goals they find immensely valuable, but often they neglect other equally valuable aspects of their lives. Consider how many of the following you would say are true.

- Gaining weight is simply the cost of getting ahead in my career.
- I'm spending so much time at work so I can provide more for my family.
- My kids will understand my missing their soccer games when they're driving a car I paid for to a college I'm paying for.
- I don't weigh *that* much more than I did in college.

- I'm just gaining weight because I'm getting older and my metabolism is slowing down.
- I'm still too young to worry about heart disease, cancer, or high blood pressure.
- Everybody my age is on medication; it's part of life.
- Aches and pains are just a normal part of growing older.
- My family knows I love them even though they don't see as much of me as they'd like.
- I can probably still run 5 miles like I did when I was 25.
- We don't have sex as often anymore because sex drive declines with age.

You figured there were some sacrifices that simply had to be made to become successful, right? More than likely, you put your blinders on and went charging after the goal you valued, figuring that the eventual benefits would be so great that they'd make up for the cost. So, how's that been working out for you?

Everyone wants to be okay. You want to feel good about the relationships you have and the lifestyle you're leading, but how honestly are you looking at your life? If you answered "true" to more than five of the questions above, you're lying to yourself—and you're not on the road to having it all. More important, you're denying the fact that there's a problem, even though the evidence is right in front of your nose.

SAY IT OUT LOUD

Many people are afraid to reveal their personal goals, mostly because they are afraid the rest of us will laugh. In 1998, after coming back from advanced testicular cancer to place fourth at the 3-week Tour of Spain and fourth in two races at the Cycling World Championships just a few weeks later, Lance Armstrong started thinking seriously about the Tour de France. He didn't talk about it much, though, so I pressed him on the issue. Looking back after seven Tour de France victories, it's almost funny that the first threshold he had to cross—the one in his mind—was such a struggle.

All Lance had to do was state his goal out loud and with a straight face. He danced around it for hours. First, it came out as "I want to win a Grand Tour." (There are three of them: the Tour de France, the Tour of Italy, and the Tour of Spain, but the Tour de France is the sport's crown jewel.) Then it shifted to "I want to wear the yellow jersey in the Tour," referring to wearing the leader's jersey at some point in the 3-week race. "I want to try to win the Tour de France" was closer to the mark but not quite there. That was refined to "I want to win the Tour de France," and it became authentic when he said, "I am going to win the Tour de France."

You can tell your goal is authentic when it's hard to voice it to another person. Once others know about your goal, you feel committed, and if you're afraid you won't reach it, you'd rather keep it to yourself. That way, if you fail, no one knows but you.

BE AN ACHIEVER

Winning takes more than talent, skill, and a lot of preparation. Great athletes can find a path to the goal or finish line blindfolded on a moonless night. They can sense the precise time to apply their maximum speed, power, or best moves and, just as important, when to hang back and save energy. People who will achieve the most can read the playing field, find an opponent's weakness, or seize an opportunity in an instant. Most of all, winners don't hesitate; they see a path that could lead to victory, and even though they risk losing, they immediately launch themselves down that path.

Similarly, when I decided to start my own business, I had to find people with the skills and passion to build a company from the ground up. I was confident that the ideas and mission behind Carmichael Training Systems would be successful—so confident that I emptied my personal bank accounts and took out loans against my house to get my business off the ground. I immediately sought to surround myself with a small group of Achievers because I knew their skills, optimism, and commitment were my only chance of keeping my home.

In the late 1990s, an entire generation of companies failed, and one contributing factor was the way start-up founders and their investors made staffing selections. Carmichael Training Systems made it through the dot-com bust because I had an advantage: I had recruited a small staff of the best Achievers I could find; and they had the skills, outlook, perspective, and agility to navigate from dark and forbidding days to the big-sky success the company is experiencing today.

It's important to understand what being an Achiever means. While I have spent my life finding and selecting people who are already Achievers, I believe everyone has the potential to be one. I've coached athletes and businessmen across the spectrum of talent and ability level, from high Achievers like Lance Armstrong and Fortune 500 executives to fresh-off-the-couch exercisers and night-shift janitors and everyone in between. Being an Achiever has nothing to do with the amount of money you make, what you've won, where you live, the car you drive, or the colleges your children attend. Rather, it has everything to do with recognizing the tools you have to make positive changes in your life and having the courage to take your life into your hands and pursue the goals you find most valuable. This comes naturally for some, but for most of us it is a learned approach to living.

I've spent my life pursuing personal achievement and guiding others to theirs, one person at a time. Now, with the information and program in this book, I'm going to show you how you can use the same techniques to balance your life and create a strong platform from which you can reach for your dreams.

THE 5 ESSENTIALS FOR HAVING IT ALL

There are five essential aspects of life that must be balanced in order for a person to achieve his or her ultimate goals: fitness, nutrition, relationships, career, and health. When those five essentials are not balanced, you limit your ability to live life to its fullest.

Relationships: Learn skills and time-management techniques for reigniting the passion in your love life, maintaining meaningful relationships with your children, and building stronger bonds with friends and family.

Career: Get more done at work, regain your focus, become a more effective leader, and keep your career moving forward without letting it rule your life.

Fitness: Have more energy, increased strength and agility, consistent weight management, greater stability, and increased endurance.

Nutrition: Match your diet to your lifestyle for greater energy and easier weight management, reduce your need for supplements and medications, and protect your health.

Health: Follow simple, age-based guidance for protecting your health and reducing chronic-disease risks as you progress through adulthood.

When you are invested in healthy relationships, a period of increased career pressure causes fewer disruptions at home. Making fitness and nutrition consistent priorities enhances your health by reducing risks for developing heart disease, diabetes, cancer, back and knee injuries, and possibly even Alzheimer's. The five essentials are inextricably connected; to make progress in one, you must give attention to all.

I have learned lessons the hard way; from 1997 to 1999, I spent so much time focused on Lance's life that I lost sight of mine. As I optimized his fitness, mine declined. Lance's comeback from cancer was my passion and my career, but as I was supporting him emotionally, I neglected my relationships with my fiancée and family.

My own lack of balance really hit home when my father started forgetting things. For most of my life, he and I knew each other in passing. He was the chairman of the department of family medicine at the University of Miami and very active in the growth of family medicine as a specialty; as a result, he spent a lot of time at the hospital, at conferences, or traveling to speaking engagements around the country. Though I knew he loved me, I didn't see him much when I was growing up. He was driven and successful, but he also valued fitness and good nutrition; he cut back on saturated fat well before it was popular to do so and loved to go on long hikes whenever he could.

In the 1990s, my parents retired and bought a place on the same short dirt road I live on at the top of Cheyenne Cañon in Colorado Springs, Colorado. I was extremely fortunate to be able to spend more time with both my parents, but retirement had an unexpected impact on my father. His career had been so important to him and occupied so much of his time and focus that he seemed lost without it. He didn't have anything to replace the mental stimulation he'd relished for the previous 40 years, and he started to slow down considerably. This was particularly worrisome because there is a history of Alzheimer's disease in my family, and I remember watching as a child as my father dealt with the development of my grandfather's illness.

By the late '90s, it became apparent that my father's disease was progressing more rapidly. For a man who always enjoyed hiking the mountain trails around the cañon, his activity level dropped sharply. We had to curtail his walks even more as he started to have trouble remembering how to get home.

In the years since my grandfather first slipped into the grip of Alzheimer's, scientists have learned a great deal about the disease and its development. It turns out that my father's lifelong commitment to healthy habits may have helped delay the onset of memory loss. Research suggests that regular exercise increases the oxygen supply to the parts of the brain that control memory, which in turn helps keep those brain cells healthy. Diets rich in omega-3 and omega-6 fatty acids have also been shown to help preserve the integrity of brain cells. To me, the payoff for my father's healthy lifestyle was the opportunity he had to spend time with his grandchildren before his memory slipped away.

As I went through the same struggle my father had experienced with my grandfather, my own mortality came into sharper focus. My father, who was so active and took such great care of himself, turned into an old man in front of me, and I'm closer to his age than I am to the beginning of my life. Learning from the two generations before me, I realized that, for better and worse, I was following in my father's footsteps. I had his drive, but I had let my fitness and good nutrition habits lapse, and I also had the relatively narrow scope of interests that I believe kept my father from staying fully engaged once he retired.

After spending so much time optimizing performance for others, I was shocked to realize how far out of balance I'd let my own life become. Right then I made the decision to change. I decided that if there's any chance I can spare my children the experience of watching me descend into dementia, I'm going to pursue it. That led me to think beyond the subjects I knew best—exercise and nutrition—and recognize that I needed to properly balance them with my career, relationship, and health priorities.

It's never too late to make positive changes, and you owe it to yourself and the people you care about most to take an honest look at your life, celebrate the parts that are working, and rework the parts that aren't—right now.

YOU REALLY CAN HAVE IT ALL

In cycling, when everything is running optimally, we call it "being on top of the gear." You feel like your feet are just a fraction of a second ahead of the pedals; you can go as fast as you want with little or no effort. The opposite feeling is referred to as being "behind the gear"; it feels like you're pedaling through peanut butter. Many of my clients come to me when they feel like they are behind the gear in every aspect of their lives. The efficient, coordinated, and focused movements of their lives have broken down, and the harder they push, the farther they fall behind the gear.

The simple secret to getting back on top of the gear is to shift. On a bicycle, this literally means shifting gears to reduce the stress on your legs, allowing you to move your feet faster. Figuratively, it means you have to make some changes in the way you approach life's demands. You don't have to make sudden and wholesale lifestyle changes. In fact, spur-of-the-moment changes like deciding to never eat ice cream again typically are not successful in the long run. The best way to return to a high-performance life is to follow a coordinated series of smaller adjustments. The smallest movements have the greatest impact.

I started consulting with Saku Koivu, captain of the Montreal Canadiens NHL hockey team, after he was diagnosed with non-Hodgkin's lymphoma at the beginning of the 2001 season. He underwent successful chemotherapy and radiation treatments and then began the long process of recovery. He wanted to rejoin his teammates on the ice, but, as I had observed during Lance's comeback, he fatigued very quickly. The treatments had severely diminished the number of oxygen-carrying red blood cells in Saku's body, meaning that his body couldn't deliver enough oxygen to working muscles.

As he began getting stronger, he was able to practice for a total of 15 to 20 minutes on the ice. His presence was important to his teammates because the Canadiens were in the hunt for a place in the postseason Stanley Cup play-offs, but he didn't have the fitness to participate in a full-speed practice session. Instead, he focused on the small movements within the game, especially the details and timing of receiving, controlling, and then either shooting or passing the puck. He told me that it is in the fundamentals that the truly great hockey players excel, so if he was limited to working only on what mattered most, he would work on the same basics that kids in junior hockey practice every day.

As the regular season came to a close, the Canadiens were on the bubble and needed a few more wins to get into the play-offs. Saku made it back onto the ice—a major achievement by itself—and was determined to make the most of the opportunity. Even though he could play for only a couple of short shifts, his work in perfecting the smallest aspects of stick and puck control made him the Canadiens' leading scorer in the last 12 games; and through the goals he scored and the inspiration he provided to his teammates, the Canadiens made it to the second round of the Stanley Cup play-offs.

THE CARMICHAEL PERFORMANCE PROGRAM

I developed the Carmichael Performance Program by applying coaching methods proven at the highest levels of sports and business to optimize the activities of everyday life. When I started Carmichael Training Systems, my goal was to make elite-level coaching accessible to amateur athletes. But when I realized I needed to optimize my own life and that the program for doing this worked for everyone, especially nonathletes, I felt compelled to expand my original goal and guide as many people as possible to fully engaged, active, healthy, balanced, high-performance lives.

WHY 9 WEEKS?

My program for restoring your high-performance life has three periods that each last 3 weeks: long enough for you to see measurable improvements from the fitness and nutrition program and long enough to ingrain real changes in behavior related to your health, relationships, and career.

One of the first executives I worked with, an investment banker from New York City, had tried just about every program out there but still struggled with his weight. He was tired of being the pudgy guy in the office, and I remember that he kept asking me how long it would take him to lose 10 pounds. He asked so frequently in our first conversation that I finally stopped him and asked if he had to lose weight for some special event, like a wedding or graduation. That wasn't it. He had failed on so many programs that promised outlandish results through mere minutes of work that he just wanted to know where mine stacked up. I told him he needed to give me 9 weeks, not because it would take him that long to lose 10 pounds, but because that's how long it would take to make real and lasting changes in his life.

You see, I don't give people programs that they're either on or off. The trouble with a diet is that when you're on it, you're on a *diet.* Then at some point you're done, and you're off the diet and, hence, off-track again. Instead, over the course of 9 weeks, I guide clients to a new way of eating and exercising that's so seamlessly integrated into their lives, it's easier to stick with the changes than go back to old habits. The investment banker gave me 9 weeks, lost 12 pounds, and in the process developed the skills and understanding necessary to continue living a high-performance life.

I've found that shorter programs lack long-term effectiveness. The physical adaptations are not great enough to significantly impact your long-term health or performance. People don't quickly see the results they want, so even though they are making progress, they give up. Longer programs that last 6 months can be effective, but only if people can stick with them. The reality is, busy people have trouble committing to anything for 6 months, especially if their progress is barely perceptible.

The Carmichael Performance Program can restore your high-performance life and help you accomplish a lot in a relatively short period of time, but I'm not satisfied with stopping there, and you shouldn't be, either. I'll also show you how you can continue to use a progressive program to improve your long-term health, vitality, longevity, and relationships.

ON THE ROAD TO HIGH-PERFORMANCE LIVING

Some parts of the Carmichael Performance Program may add activities to your daily routine, and that means there has to be time to accommodate them. Many of us already feel overwhelmed by what we have to accomplish each day, and adding to that load won't help. Instead, I'm going to show you how you can maximize the impact of certain activities so you can accomplish more in less time and eliminate wasted effort.

The 9-week training and nutrition program in this book cuts out all the wasted effort found in most training programs and instead delivers impressive gains from short, targeted workouts you can fit into your busy days. The nutrition program is matched to the training program so you get the fuel you need for optimal performance without the excess that prevents you from losing weight. Unlike thousands of other plans out there, these fitness and nutrition aspects are linked from the beginning. For a program to be successful, nutrition and training cannot be separated.

There are some people who seem to be in constant motion and maintain amazing energy levels. To people running themselves ragged and struggling to keep up with the demands of daily living, it's all the more astonishing; you're chronically exhausted, and the other guy never seems to need any rest. The difference is that the other guy is working hard when he needs to and resting well between efforts. If, like him, you learn to focus and maximize the impact of your work, you'll accomplish a lot in a short period, which means you'll be less stressed about your progress when you leave work or the weekend is over. You may or may not actually have more time to relax, but when the quality of your downtime is greater, you reduce your overall stress level and recharge your physical and mental batteries more quickly.

The following chapters will take you through the simple progression of applying the Carmichael Performance Program to your unique life. Yet this is more than a simple follow-the-leader cookbook program. I am going to tell you how my program works and why I'm recommending certain activities but not others, because once you understand how to cause positive changes, you'll know how to keep the process going.

The three periods of the Carmichael Performance Program are Commit, Strengthen, and Perform. Each period focuses on a broad goal: committing to making changes in the right direction, strengthening your body and relationships, and performing at the top of your game. The exercises and activities within each period are all related to accomplishing those goals. By focusing on one broad goal in each period, you maximize the collective impact of all your activities, which subsequently enables you to take bigger steps forward.

Commit

The first 3 weeks of the Carmichael Performance Program focus on foundations, because you have to stand on solid footing to start reaching for your aspirations. This means clearing out the clutter in your nutrition program—the excess empty calories and junk that keep you from reaching your goals. It also means examining your priorities and schedule with the help of the Career and Relationships chapters, so you can allocate time for workouts.

The fitness program focuses on improving your endurance and preparing your body for more intense workouts in the second and third periods. You'll start with moderate aerobic (cardio) workouts and progress into interval training, and you'll start with light resistance training and progress to powerful movements. Be prepared for strenuous workouts (I told you I was going to be honest with you); as I'll explain in Chapter 2, they're strenuous because there is more to an effective training program than simply burning calories and fat.

The nutrition component of the first period not only prepares you for the second and third periods but lays the groundwork for dietary habits that should last the rest of your life. A big part of restoring your high-performance life is optimizing the fuel you're burning; and during the first period, I'll show you how to make some simple changes that will boost your energy level and make the food you eat work *for* you.

There are no complicated formulas or equations to master, because powerful nutrition is simple to achieve. In fact, most people are actually very close to eating a powerful diet right now; the biggest key to greater energy, more focus, a better mood, less fatigue, and lost love handles may be simply clearing out unnecessary clutter in what you're eating today.

Strengthen

The next period of the Carmichael Performance Program focuses on strength in its various forms, from improving your physical strength by adding more resistance training to strengthening the bonds you have with your significant other, friends, children, and coworkers.

Physical strength can be developed in numerous ways, but I'm particularly interested in the gains that will help you live a more productive and varied lifestyle. Remember, as part of a progressive program, all the activities in each period are related. The physical strength you develop will not only help you perform better in your chosen activity, but also improve the stability of your joints and the health of your bones. These benefits have far-reaching impacts on your overall lifestyle, including how active you can be with your children, how well you cope with stress from work, and even how long you will live.

The increased intensity of the exercise program in the Strengthen Period means making some changes to the nutrition program, as well. After all, the whole idea here is to make sure you have the energy necessary to build lean, metabolism-boosting muscle. Specific foods, including salmon, almonds, and low-fat dairy products, are incorporated into these crucial 3 weeks so you have the right amount of energy from protein and other key nutrients proven to build muscle and improve recovery as well as keep you mentally sharp and physically invigorated.

Perform

During the final 3 weeks of the program, you'll turn up the heat and apply the improvements you've made to real, specific actions. It's one thing to develop strength in a gym by moving a weight up and down, but what really counts is whether you can use that strength to make a difference in your life. The exercises in the Perform Period develop power, that elusive quality that combines strength and speed to let you dominate in basketball, football, tennis, hockey, and even endurance sports. Power is also important off the playing field; it provides the quickness you need to snatch your kid right before he falls, make the lunge for the closing elevator door, and hoist big bags of dog food, all without hurting yourself. You can develop power only after you've developed strength, which you can only build on an aerobic base. That said, I think of the first 6 weeks of the program as the process of forging the tools necessary to reap the greatest benefits from the Perform Period.

A foundation of endurance and strength training will enable you to develop power and speed in the Perform Period, but the revolutionary aspect of this program—the part that will have the biggest impact on your life—is the focus on agility in the final 3 weeks. Agility has been overlooked and forgotten in popular training programs over the past decade, and that's a shame. It's vital to your current performance and future health that we reintroduce physical agility, mobility, balance, and stability to your daily life. At first, you'll be shocked by how immobile you've become over the years and how much easier simple tasks, like bending to hoist a heavy computer bag or maneuvering through doorways while balancing coffee, a briefcase, and a cell phone, can be when you're more agile.

Regarding nutrition, this period focuses on specific foods that can improve performance in exercise, attention, mood, recovery, health, and weight management. Why are these foods so important now, whereas others took precedence before? Because the progress you have made in getting to this period of the program enhances the impact these foods can have on your system. Would you bother putting high-octane gasoline into a beat-up old clunker or wait until you've rebuilt the engine and restored the car to its original Detroit muscle-car status?

PROGRESSING TOWARD LASTING CHANGE

In orienteering, a navigation sport, you don't just pinpoint your destination on the map and start walking; you'd lose sight of it while crossing the valleys along the way. You need to establish landmarks, like a ridge or stream, that will let you know you're on the right path, even when your destination is still out of sight. Athletic coaches have long used a system of progressive achievement (called *periodization*) to keep athletes on track toward goals that may be years ahead of their current conditioning—and it's also a viable approach to life.

You can't pay down debt when you continue to spend more than you're bringing in, so you have to find ways to rein in your spending. You have to take the step to organize or consolidate your outstanding balances so you can minimize the additional costs of carrying debt. Only then can you take the step to start paying back the money you owe. And the process isn't necessarily over once you're out of debt. To keep yourself financially solvent and minimize the risk of going back into the red, you have to organize your spending and saving habits with budgets, investments, and professional guidance.

Progressive programs lead to lasting change because they help you take a step forward,

Progressive Motivation

FOR THE FIRST 3 YEARS OF Lance Armstrong's Tour de France reign, a large portion of his motivation came from the fact that many critics doubted both his abilities as a cyclist and his honesty about never using performance-enhancing drugs. He was driven by a desire to prove them wrong. After his third victory, however, he needed a new motivation. Instead of looking outside, Lance turned inside and focused on being better in every aspect of the race. He was already a great climber, but he wanted to perfect his technique going uphill. He was already the fastest in time trials, but he wanted to perfect his aerodynamic position and go even faster.

Progressive improvement can be a source of motivation that grows with you, but it has to be specific. Lance didn't just say he wanted to be better; in 2002, we worked on his climbing speed because there was an uphill time trial in the Tour de France that year. For 2003, we worked on his nutrition program so he didn't have to proactively lose weight in the weeks before the race. In 2004, we gave more attention to his sprinting and explosive power.

When you're motivated by the desire to make specific improvements, there's always room to keep getting better. On the other hand, when you're motivated purely by outcomes (like reaching a specific body weight or a 12-handicap in golf), it's easy to stagnate and grind to a halt instead of continuing to move forward.

and then—and this is critical—they provide time for you to get used to that step before moving on.

Massive and sudden changes in your exercise program, diet, relationships, and money management don't last because they make it easy to give up and return to old habits. The answer is to break important changes into smaller, more manageable pieces that allow you to capitalize on each success and minimize the negative impact of setbacks, all while staying on track toward your primary goal.

In athletics, progressive achievement (the concept of periodization) has been around in rudimentary form since the beginning of organized competition. In its simplest form, it is the process of breaking a big, intimidating goal into a series of smaller, easily achievable pieces. It became more organized in the mid-20th century with Eastern Bloc coaches—most notably, Tudor Bompa of Romania. To win Olympic medals every 4 years, the coaches started working backward. If they wanted an athlete to be ready for the 1972 Games, that athlete may have started a periodized training schedule to reach progressive performance markers as early as 1965.

In modern Olympics, professional sports, and even amateur athletics, periodization is the most widely recognized and accepted form of effective training. I've been using progressive training and nutrition programs with athletes for more than 15 years, and the programs I designed to prepare Lance for seven Tour de France victories were all based on a periodization model. In fact, his Tour de France reign was part of one long-term periodization program rather than seven individual programs.

For Lance, it started with a commitment. Once he was able to say "I am going to win the Tour de France," we started talking about how and when he was going to accomplish his goal. We decided his first win would be in 1999 and that he would focus on the Tour de France for a 5-year period. His training, therefore, was designed as a 5-year plan that recognized each Tour de France as both a goal event and a component of his training for the coming years. I have to admit that the original plan didn't aim for seven wins, but as we approached the 2003 Tour de France, Lance had so much power and energy that it was clear we could add a few more years to the program and surpass the entire world's expectations. That's the remarkable thing about progressive programs; you usually end up blowing past your original goals and achieving more than you ever dreamed.

I utilize the Carmichael Performance Program to guide my life and my clients' lives. Like them, you're an Achiever, and this program is designed for you. I'm not here to sugarcoat the realities of what you need to do or blame your childhood for the way you're living right now. This is about proven techniques that successful athletes and business professionals use every day to have it all. It's time for you to have it all as well, so turn the page and let's get going!

CHAPTER 2

Boost Your Fitness

FEW ATHLETES TRULY CHANGE THE FACE OF THEIR SPORT, BUT LANCE ARMSTRONG DID. Before 1999, riders didn't build their entire year around preparing for one specific race, and they certainly didn't spend part of the spring riding the key parts of the Tour de France. Yet there we were, on the back roads of rural France in April. Lance was on his bike, and I was following him in a station wagon with his team's *directeur sportif* (think head coach in football), Johan Bruyneel.

It was a cold and raw day, and I was happy to be in the car instead of on the bike. Lance was riding at a steady clip through intermittent rain showers. We were in the southern part of France near the Spanish border so Lance could take a look at some of the key passes in the Pyrenees Mountains. The showers were hanging at about 5,000 feet of elevation, so every time he descended into a valley, he was soaked by a cold rain. As he climbed back out, he ascended into the clouds, where the rain was replaced by a cold mist that reduced visibility to about 20 feet. Finally, as he climbed higher, he rode into air that was drier but also chilled by the elevation. And though he was above the rain clouds, an even higher cloud cover prevented the sun from warming his back. It was a wet and miserable day to be training, but Lance's legs kept ticking over like a metronome; the Tour de France was only a few months away, and he was busy absorbing information that would prove critical to his first victory.

While Lance's days were built around optimizing his performance, mine were gradually breaking me down. Lance woke up around 8:00 a.m., drank one or two small cups of coffee, performed some core strength and stretching exercises, and then came down to the hotel restaurant for breakfast. I, on the other hand, woke up with a headache from drinking too much wine the night before, and then I made and drank a pot of coffee in my room while working on my computer and e-mailing the States.

When I met Lance and Johan for breakfast downstairs, Lance would be eating a big bowl of muesli with fresh milk and fruit, a three-egg omelet with cheese and mixed vegetables, and 1 to 2 cups of rice. I indulged in a chocolate croissant and more coffee.

As we packed the car with food and drinks for the three of us, we knew that day would be particularly nasty for Lance. He would be on the bike for about 6½ hours and cover three monster climbs: the Col d'Aspin, Col du Tourmalet, and Luz Ardiden. Even riders who live to climb steep mountain passes groan when they hear those names. To get to each summit, Lance would snake up narrow and twisting roads for more than an hour; by the time he reached the tops, he'd be drinking the freezing spray coming up from his tires as he rode through corridors carved through melting snowbanks that were still nearly two stories high.

Two hours into the ride, as we approached the base of the first big climb, the power meter on Lance's bike revealed he had already burned 1,500 calories. Based on his power and heart rate, I knew he was burning 16 to 20 calories per minute as he pushed the pace on the ascent. By the time he reached the top, we were about 3 hours into the ride, and Lance had finished seven bottles of sports drink, water, and hot tea, along with three PowerBars and a few pieces of fruit—and he was only about halfway through the ride.

Lance didn't stop at the top of the Col d'Aspin; we just pulled up alongside him to hand him a jacket, warm gloves, a dry hat, and a bottle of hot tea as he started down into the valley that would take him to the start of the Col du Tourmalet. As Lance careened around wet and potentially icy corners, Johan followed behind so closely that he had to use the windshield wipers to clear the spray coming off Lance's tires. The car's external thermometer said it was 36 degrees outside, but we were nice and toasty in the car, eating baguettes with fabulous Brie supplied by our hotel.

On the next climb, the Col du Tourmalet, we pulled up alongside Lance so I could check the data on his power meter, and he was holding exactly the pace I wanted him to. His heart rate was in the 163-to-170 range, an intensity I knew he could maintain for the duration of the 11.4-mile-long ascent that rose 4,600 feet out of the valley.

By the time Lance climbed off his bike for the day, he had climbed more than 10,000 vertical feet and burned about 6,200 calories in nearly 7 hours. He had consumed 16 bottles (just over 2 gallons) of fluid and about 2,200 calories' worth of PowerBars, sports drinks, fruit, baked potatoes, and ham-Swiss-and-butter sandwiches. I, on the other hand, sat on my butt for nearly 7 hours, but a quick tally of the wrappers in the car told me I was only about 400 calories behind Lance. With breakfast, dinner, and, of course, more wine later that night, I was headed for a 4,000-calorie day.

Sure enough, after reviewing the data from Lance's power meter, making business calls from my room for about an hour, and a 15-minute call to my family, I joined Johan and some potential team sponsors for a wonderful dinner of filet mignon in béarnaise sauce, scalloped potatoes, crème brûlée for dessert, and (of course) red wine. Two glasses turned into five as we talked about bike racing late into the evening, long after Lance had gone to bed. He had to wake up for another day of training in the mountains; all I had to do was sit in the car.

By the end of that training camp, both Lance and I were exhausted, but for very different reasons. He had ridden through valleys and mountain passes for more than 30 hours in 6 days, burning an average of about 900 calories per hour. He had every right to be tired. I had gained 2 pounds and felt like crud. I hadn't slept enough, nor had I slept well; over 5 days, I'd finished off the equivalent of four bottles of wine and hadn't exercised at all. During the flight home, I realized I hadn't spent any time doing anything specifically for my health or well-being.

I could have exercised. I had my bike and gear, and there was room on the car's roof rack; I could have easily joined Lance for the final hour of his ride or gone out on my own for an hour after we got back to the hotel. I could have grabbed a snack and used the hotel gym or worked out in my room before breakfast. I was consumed by the couldas and shouldas all the way home. The simple truth was that I would have performed my job better and felt better while doing it if I had paid even a little attention to optimizing my own performance as well as Lance's on that trip.

YOUR BEST HIGH-YIELD INVESTMENT

For the time and effort you need to invest in improving your fitness, you'd be hard-pressed to find an activity that yields bigger benefits. Being fit makes you leaner, more energetic, stronger, and better equipped to handle whatever life throws at you. A long layover spent sleeping in airport chairs is a pain for anyone, but if you're fit, you'll bounce back faster. As a result, you'll perform better in the meeting you're traveling to and still have the energy to join your clients for dinner afterward. When you finally arrive home, you'll be more inclined to engage with your family as soon as you walk in the door instead of heading straight to bed.

But let's put this into hard economic terms: Fitness has become a deciding factor in executive advancement because bosses and clients know you're more prepared to handle the rigors of the workplace when they see that you're in shape. You won't find this stated in any employee handbook, and the human resources department will vehemently deny it, but physical fitness plays a role in getting and keeping your job. Studies performed at leadership conferences and workshops confirm that employers perceive a physically fit employee or job candidate to be more qualified as a leader, more likely to be successful at work, and more likely to stay with the company longer.

Exercise not only yields the career and social perks that come with a fit body, but prevents a cascade of interconnected consequences that quickly turn into declining health. When inactivity causes your muscles to deteriorate and weaken, they can't adequately support your joints. This leads to aches and pains when you try to increase your activity level, which in turn reinforces your aversion to exercise and, most likely, an aversion to movement of any kind. So you stop moving, your muscles atrophy, and your metabolism slows. Now you're burning fewer calories to support your bodily functions, and you're more likely to gain weight. That added weight further increases your hatred of exercise because it makes each attempted workout that much more difficult. Your fitness goals

Your Fitness Affects Your Kids

HAVING MORE STAMINA AND flexibility means you'll have more opportunities to spend quality time with your kids. Instead of spending the evening sacked out on the couch, silently watching television together, you can go for a walk, jog, or bicycle ride around the neighborhood. And as anyone with young children knows, they have no shortage of energy, so instead of just watching them run around or getting annoyed because they're interrupting your TV time, turn off the TV, get up, and get involved in their lives.

You determine the positive lessons your children learn from you, and one of the most beneficial ones you can teach them is how to enjoy physical activity. No generation of American teenagers and young adults has been as out of shape and unhealthy as the current one, and it's largely because their parents are equally inactive.

Our children take cues from what we do and how we approach the priorities in our lives. So ask yourself what you would like them to emulate—your skill with the remote control or the way you throw a football or baseball? What do you want them to remember about growing up with their father—that you worked very hard but were otherwise zoned out on the couch? Do you really want them to recall that they were stronger and faster than you by the time they were 12?

Making exercise a priority will improve your fitness and health and help your children see physical activity as a vital and enjoyable component of a balanced life.

seem further out of reach; you slow down more, lose more muscle, and gain even more weight—to the point that your lifestyle decisions start enhancing any genetic predispositions you have for chronic diseases. Now, instead of merely worrying about dropping belly fat and finding more energy, you have to think about avoiding heart attacks, strokes, type 2 diabetes, and any of a host of cancers.

As if the increased disease risk weren't enough, the more time you sit in the plush comfort of your couch, desk chair, and car, the less time you spend on your feet, carrying around your own body weight. Your bones and connective tissue get stronger or weaker in response to the amount of stress placed on them; if you're sitting on your butt most of the time, your bones figure you don't need all the calcium they stored up when you participated in more weight-bearing activities such as walking. Bone mineral density falls as the calcium is gradually sucked out of your bones, which become brittle and fragile decades before you feel old enough to worry about a shattered hip.

A growing body of research suggests there will be a massive increase in the number of men suffering from osteoporosis in the coming decades. Women may be at a higher risk for the bone-wasting disease because of hormonal changes that accompany menopause, but the plague of inactivity within the current population of adult men between ages 35 and 55 means we're seeing men in their 40s with the bones of a 70-year-old.

Why should brittle bones bother you? Because, statistically, if you break your hip, you will most likely die sooner than if you don't—years sooner.

THE NEXT MOVEMENT IN FITNESS

I agree with experts that the best thing Americans can do is move more, even if it's just a little more than they do now. But I don't think that message goes far enough. To me, it's like saying you can build a multimillion-dollar business by working 4 hours a day from your living room. The truth is, big gains require real effort. Now, that doesn't mean you have to rearrange your life to center on training or model your exercise habits on those of Olympians. Rather, you need to focus your attention on performing meaningful work when you're exercising—start with a goal, work toward it, and stop wasting time with low-intensity, no-impact, ineffectual training programs.

Hard work is necessary for success; it's the only thing that forces your body to make the positive changes that take you to a higher level of health. By definition, low-intensity, short-duration, nonimpact, sweatless exercise is not hard. As a result, it doesn't provide enough stimulus to improve endurance, strength, or power. But when you build fitness progressively, as you will with this program, you gain the ability to sustain exercise that's strenuous enough and lasts long enough to produce real results. In order to work hard, you have to be *able* to work hard, and that's where so many exercise programs fail. For long-term success, fitness has to be about more than the pursuit of a flat stomach; from now on, it needs to be about the pursuit of a new set of performance goals.

In developing the Carmichael Performance Program, I realized that there are three primary goals that define a new approach to fitness training.

Endurance: Endurance exercise improves the health and integrity of your heart, lungs, and blood vessels, and studies show that exercising at higher intensities helps even more. In other words, steady walking is good for you, but faster walking, running, riding, or rowing is even better. The key is not only to go faster but to go faster for longer. You have to be able to sustain moderate to intense exercise for 30 to 60 minutes to make real progress toward your performance and health goals.

Stability: You need the muscular strength to maintain control of your body while lifting and moving objects, but part of the reason we're seeing more and more joint-related injuries is because inactive people have muscles that are too weak to support their joints. This program, therefore, is designed to help you gain lean muscle using exercises that also strengthen the muscles and connective tissues that support your knee, hip, back (spine), and shoulder joints.

Agility: You need balance and coordination to maintain proper body position while exercising and performing daily activities, and because everybody stumbles occasionally, you need limber joints and quickness to catch yourself before you fall. People who are more agile consistently perform at a higher level and are at lower risk for injuries. The agility drills in this program also challenge your coordination, and improved coordination translates into better performance when strength training and quicker reaction times in everyday activities, and it may even aid in preserving the long-term health of your nervous system.

COMMIT PERIOD: ESSENTIAL ENDURANCE EXERCISES

The exercises featured in the Commit Period of the Carmichael Performance Program are essential for establishing the aerobic and strength-training foundations that the following two periods—Strengthen and Perform—are built upon. The primary focus is on aerobic conditioning at this point because it increases the amount of oxygen you can deliver to working muscles and your brain. This is critical because it governs how long you can sustain activity, which in turn determines the number of calories you can burn and the amount of progress you can make.

Though the Commit Period includes aerobic and strength workouts, the aerobic conditioning takes precedence because the gains made in these 3 weeks will enable you to reap greater rewards in the Strengthen Period. Your primary goals for the strength training in the Commit Period are to learn the movements and adjust to the ranges of motion so you're ready to do higher-intensity work in the next period. With this program, you'll save time and accomplish two goals simultaneously: improving your aerobic conditioning while preparing yourself for a focused and highly effective Strengthen Period.

The Commit Period features five targeted aerobic workouts each week. We're going to boost their effectiveness with intervals that challenge your body, boost your total caloric burn, and stimulate your body to start adapting. Two sessions will also incorporate strength-training exercises you can do at home or in a gym, and one session will include the first agility exercises of the program.

Your aerobic and strength sessions will start at 20 minutes each, and total workout times will range from 20 to 60 minutes. Since the longer workouts typically feature an aerobic

FITNESS MYTHS

Slower Is Better If you have the time to plod through a low-intensity activity for several hours, you can certainly burn a lot of fat. At about 30 percent of your maximum effort, about 70 percent of your energy comes from fat and the other 30 percent from carbohydrate. But when you increase exercise intensity to 50 to 60 percent of maximum effort, the fuel mixture shifts so you're burning about half fat and half carbohydrate. However, because your overall caloric burn rate is higher, you actually burn more total calories per minute and per hour than at the lower intensity. The result: More fat disappears from your body in less time.

Strength Training Is Dangerous People injure themselves when they perform strength training with heavier weights than they can safely handle and when they use improper technique. That's why it's important to start any strength program by learning the proper range of motion for each exercise and practicing with very little resistance or light weights until you have the movement dialed.

Back Pain Is Just Part of Aging Back pain is one of the leading physical complaints adults present to physicians, coaches, and trainers, but it's primarily due to muscle weakness rather than age. Strengthening your body's structural core with abdominal crunches and back extensions is one way to increase spinal stability, and we also have to address the musculature in the upper portion of your back with overhead lifts. If that musculature is weak, it places excess strain on lower-back muscles, which can lead to pain, no matter how many crunches and extensions you may do.

More Crunches Yield Six-Pack Abs If you're dead set that you must have a six-pack to feel like you're fit, the only way to get one is through a *combination* of full-body exercise and a good nutrition program. The fat will melt away and be replaced with lean muscle, and your six-pack will emerge from its hiding place behind your belly.

and strength or agility component, you can split them if necessary. For instance, you could do the strength workout in the morning and then walk or run at lunch or after work.

Interval Training: Big Gains in Less Time

Interval training alternates hard efforts with recovery (or "rest") periods to get more done in less time. Instead of running at a moderate pace you can sustain for 30 minutes, a 30-minute interval workout may include two 5-minute periods during which you run at a hard pace separated by 5 minutes of easy jogging or walking.

Incorporating intervals into your workouts is how you get faster and stronger, as opposed to going slow and steady. If you always run 9-minute miles in training, you'll never be able to run an 8-minute mile. To run faster, you need to increase your sustainable running speed, which burns more calories and leads to improved fitness and competitive performance. Running faster for shorter periods of time stresses the body, and the body does what it's supposed to do: It adapts.

In cycling, an individual time trial is an event in which racers ride alone as fast as they can over a set distance. Lance Armstrong was one of the best in this specialized discipline, winning 11 of the 19 individual time trials he competed in during his seven Tour de France victories. On flat ground in July, at the height of his fitness, Lance could ride at about 30 to 35 miles per hour for about 60 minutes. Five months earlier, he hadn't had the fitness to ride that fast for that long. Since I knew the race speed he had to sustain to win, I started Lance on shorter, 15-minute intervals at or above race pace in training. As he gained fitness, I made the intervals longer and the rest periods shorter, until he was finally able to complete one long interval of 60 minutes at race pace.

Strengthen Period: Strength Exercises for the Real World

The differences between the exercises in the Commit and Strengthen Periods are subtle yet extremely important—mostly changes in the number of sets and reps in the resistance and agility training workouts, as well as the number and length of intervals in the aerobic workouts. This change will improve your muscles' ability to produce maximum force, which is what strength is really all about.

During this 3-week period, you'll still work out five times a week, but because we're focusing on building strength and lean muscle mass, there will be three strength-training sessions instead of two. Since strength training takes a higher priority during this period, these sessions will be a little longer, taking up to about 40 minutes.

To keep your aerobic system in top shape, we're going to add intensity rather than volume. Your weekly endurance training time won't increase, but the amount of time you spend—and need to spend—at a higher pace or intensity will go up.

I designed the strength exercises in this program to improve your ability to successfully handle the varied physical demands of daily life and accomplish more in less time. As a result, you'll focus on exercises and movements that are proven to increase strength, stability, balance, and mobility. Everything else is a waste of time.

I'd be willing to bet that in the last year, you've hurt yourself more often during normal, everyday activities like lifting a child, moving furniture, or twisting while shoveling snow than during exercise sessions or while participating in sports. Many times it's not actual injuries that knock us out so much as debilitating stiffness and soreness from overusing muscles that are not accustomed to the strain or the range of motion. Take gardening, for instance. An afternoon of raking or clearing brush shouldn't leave your shoulders, back, and hamstrings sore and aching for days. But they will hurt if you haven't used

Overload and Recovery

IN MY 9-WEEK PROGRAM, A short regeneration period at the end of the Commit Period reinforces the positive adaptations of the previous 3 weeks. It is during these days of reduced training load that your body actually adapts the most. Training applies stress (overload), and rest turns it into fitness. No matter how great you feel, the last thing you should do is power through these short recovery periods. If you do, you will not reap the full benefits of the work you did during the preceding 3 weeks.

Overload without recovery leads to stalled progress. Some people make the mistake of starting an exercise program and working out really hard for several weeks in a row. They see improvement for a few weeks, but then their progress plateaus. Many people in this situation, especially type A executives, figure they simply need to work harder to push through. Unfortunately, nothing could be further from the truth. You stop making progress because you're too fatigued to complete quality workouts and too exhausted to adapt to the stress. You're in a hole, and continuing to push forward only makes the hole deeper.

Listen to your body and do your best to adhere to the overload and recovery principle built into my program. Hard training days are separated by at least 1 full day. If time constraints limit you to only 2 or 3 consecutive days to exercise in a given week, you can do hard training days, like interval work or strength training, back-to-back, but no more than 3 in a row. If you start a 60-minute training session and feel lethargic after 15 minutes or your heart rate is not rising as high as normal for a given effort level, back off. Your body's telling you that you need a break. Respecting your body's need for additional recovery doesn't mean you're lazy; it means you're smart.

those muscles in months. When you stick to a fitness program that incorporates movements that address the demands of daily living, you're better prepared to live pain free.

To understand why real-world exercises matter, think about what you need to do on a day-to-day basis. For example, when you pick up an object from the floor, you should bend your knees, lower your body, grasp the weight, and then contract the muscles in your torso to keep your back stable as you drive with your legs to rise back to standing. Your whole body is engaged in the work.

Spending 5 minutes doing seated dumbbell biceps curls won't prepare you for that job, but the following exercises will enhance your strength and stability and make lifting objects much easier and safer.

Medicine ball squats: This exercise simulates one of the most common actions of everyday life: picking up a box or child. Instead of bending at the waist and plucking the object off the ground, which can lead to a back injury, you squat, center your weight over your heels, and then drive with your legs to rise back up. Get good at this and you'll avoid the most common cause of back injuries.

Medicine ball pick-ups: Similar to the medicine ball squat, but with a slight twist. Since there are plenty of times when you have to lift objects while twisting your upper body, it's a good idea to develop the strength to do so without injuring yourself.

Reverse medicine ball lunges: Your hips are held in alignment by a lot of small but powerful muscles, and lunges are critical for building hip stability; when you lift your body weight with only one leg, the muscles have to work hard to keep your hips level so they can support your upper body and keep you from falling over. Strong muscles around your hips mean less excess strain on your back muscles.

Multijoint Exercises

Since most real-world movements involve more than one joint, you're better off replacing exercises that isolate muscles, like the seated biceps curl, with exercises that recruit multiple muscle groups at the same time. Multijoint exercises do just that. A squat, whether it's the classic barbell squat, a body-weight squat, or even a variation like a single-leg body-weight squat, involves muscles that cross the ankle, knee, and hip joints. This means they tie together major muscle groups that articulate the entire lower body. Strengthening each of these muscle groups individually doesn't provide anywhere near the amount of total strength, stability, and coordination you get from movements that utilize them all at once.

If you lack the strength and stability that result from multijoint exercises like squats, your body tries to make up for it by calling on muscles that aren't normally involved. Basically, you overcompensate for weak muscles by overexerting with other muscles. For example, if your legs aren't strong enough to lift you and the box you're picking up off the floor, you'll change your body position and call upon the muscles along your spine and shoulders to help keep your upper body upright. Your weakness in one area leads you to inadvertently transfer loads to other muscles, which can then overload them. Trained muscles, on the other hand, are conditioned to bear greater loads, which means you can complete your activities with the correct body position, thereby minimizing soreness and risk of injury.

This same approach holds for multijoint exercises for your upper body. Rows and overhead presses involve your shoulders, elbows, and wrists, and your entire core is engaged as you maintain your balance during overhead lifts. Some other examples of multijoint exercises include:

	ANKLE	KNEE	HIP	TORSO	SHOULDER	ELBOW	WRIST
Squat	✓	✓	✓	✓	✓	✓	
Squat press	✓	✓	✓	✓	✓	✓	✓
Overhead triceps press			✓	✓	✓	✓	✓
Forward lunge	✓	✓	✓	✓			
Reverse lunge with ball	✓	✓	✓	✓	✓	✓	✓
Core bridge (plank)			✓	✓	✓	✓	

Overhead Lifts

Lifting objects over your head is another common everyday movement, but it's been removed from many strength-training programs. Many people have a fear of this movement because the first image that comes to mind is of Olympic powerlifters straining under giant barbells and the possibility of all that weight crashing down on their heads. But it's important to include overhead movements; controlling a weight that's extended an arm's length above your head requires a concerted effort from the muscles in your feet, legs, hips, torso, shoulders, neck, and arms, which work together to lift the weight and stabilize your spine. Of the muscles being used, those around your spine are like your mobility police, there to protect and serve.

No concerns about lifting weight over your head are worse than the consequences of not doing these exercises—chronic back pain from weak muscles around your spine. The following exercises enhance your strength and stability for lifting objects over your head.

Squat and presses: Using an exercise cord or dumbbells, perform a squat. When you return to standing, extend your arms straight over your head. While this works your shoulders, you'll also feel your entire torso and your legs engage. You'll activate muscles throughout your body to maintain your balance and keep from bending too far forward or backward.

Overhead medicine ball wall tosses: You don't chuck the ball at the wall in this one. Rather, you stand within inches of the wall, holding the ball high above your head, then repeatedly bounce the ball off the wall at a fast pace. You'll work your legs, hips, core, chest, shoulders, and arms as you react to the momentum of the ball. This exercise also takes concentration; you don't want to drop the ball on your head.

Walking overhead lunges: In a more advanced version of conventional, one-leg-at-a-time lunges, you alternate legs so you walk across the room. Holding a stability ball over your head works your core and shoulders and challenges your ability to balance.

Twisting

Most lifting, pushing, and pulling is done with hingelike joints such as the elbows and knees. Even the hips, which can twist, are mostly used as a hinge when you're walking, running, cycling, sitting, and standing up. Twisting, on the other hand, doesn't typically occur around one particular joint. When you twist your upper body to the side to grab your child off the counter, you're utilizing muscles along the entire length of your body. This rotation contracts some of your muscles and stretches others before you even grasp the weight you're going to move. When you grab your child, a box, or a shovelful of snow, the added weight can overload the muscles holding you in a twisted state and lead to a back injury or soreness anywhere from your legs up through your shoulders and neck.

Twisting movements are absolutely necessary for any exercise program focused on performance or long-term vitality. Since there isn't a solid joint to help support the movement, you're almost entirely dependent upon muscular strength for stability. These exercises are among the best for enhancing your strength and stability for twisting.

Windshield wipers: These are done on your back for added support. Point your legs toward the ceiling, and keep your arms outstretched to the sides. Lower your legs to one side until they barely touch the ground, then lift them back to center and down to the other side. You'll feel it through your torso; as you get stronger, stop your legs just before they touch the ground.

Medicine ball wall touches: Stand with your back very close to a wall, holding a medicine ball straight out in front of you. Twist your upper body, trying to keep your hips facing forward, until the ball touches the wall on your left side. Then cross back over center and touch the ball to the wall on your right. This exercise engages muscles from head to toes; even if you can't twist far enough to reach the wall at first, keep trying. Your flexibility will improve in time.

Core-Strength Exercises

Core, or torso, strength has received a lot of attention over the past decade, and for good reason. There's no doubt that a strong torso is integral to reducing the chance of injuring your back and increasing your performance in any sport. It's important to remember, however, that there's more to core strength than stomach crunches. The overhead, twisting, and multijoint exercises already recommended will enhance your core strength, even before we add core-specific workouts to your training program. After all, every real-world strength-training movement contributes to improved core stability. The muscles of your torso wrap around your body in multiple directions—like plywood or woven carbon fiber, in a way—to provide support for nearly every movement you make. When you twist, bend to the side, bend forward to pet the dog, or get up out of a chair, you use your core. To improve the strength and stability of your core, you have to exercise it using the same twisting and bending motions—in addition to doing crunches.

For athletes, core strength is directly related to performance because it plays a huge role in transferring power between the powerful lower body and the upper body. When you step into a baseball pitch and swing the bat, you're relying on core strength to help you move the bat faster. With a weak core, bat speed falls; even if you manage to hit the ball, it will have less power behind it. The same is true when throwing a football.

When one of my coaches was working with NFL defensive backs Ken Hamlin and Bobby Taylor, he saw improving core strength as a way to make them better players. They were strong and fast, but their torso strength, in terms of both crunch-type and twisting movements, was relatively weak when compared with the power in their legs, chest, and shoulders. He boosted the amount of core-strength work in their programs in the late winter and spring and saw impressive results at the team training camp in late August. The men were as fast as ever in straight-ahead sprints, and they were quicker and more precise on sideways cuts because their powerful cores kept them stable as they turned their upper bodies and drove with their legs. As a result, they were more effective on the field because they could get to the receiver or rusher more quickly and make the tackle earlier.

I like to include additional exercises like the following in my plan.

Reverse crunches: This move is great for targeting the harder-to-engage lower abdominal muscles, although you need to be careful not to rely too heavily on your hip flexors. Lie on your back, arms at your sides, and curl your knees up toward your chest. Reverse crunches reduce strain on the neck and shoulders because you're not pushing your head forward and lifting it off the floor.

Wastes of Strength-Training Time

THE EXERCISE ADVICE BELOW isn't worth your time. The moves might make you sweat and cause some muscles to burn, but they won't lead to the positive adaptations you're looking for and need.

BAD IDEA: ISOLATE MUSCLES TO GET STRONGER.

Forget about hamstring curls, especially the highly specialized version done on a machine that isolates the hamstrings. In the real world, a hamstring is just one of the many muscles used simultaneously in flexing your knee and extending your hip. No matter how strong you make an individual muscle, it will never produce more power on its own than several muscles working together will.

Working muscles in isolation can also destabilize your joints and leave you prone to injury. An overly developed quadriceps (the muscle on the front of your thigh) coupled with an underdeveloped hamstring (the muscle on the back of your thigh) can pull the knee joint out of alignment and cause excessive wear and tear that leads to pain, swelling, and tissue damage, for example.

BAD IDEA: LIFT WEIGHTS SLOWLY TO BUILD GREATER STRENGTH.

Some trainers figured that if moving weight faster leads to increased power, then maybe moving the weight slower leads to increased strength—hence, the birth of slow-motion weight lifting. For example, a slow-motion version of the bench press has you gradually pressing the weight up, taking 5 seconds or longer to complete each extension. You then lower the weight back to your chest just as slowly.

Slow-motion weight lifting is a waste of time because your muscles fatigue before you have the chance to generate maximum force, which is what has to happen for you to gain strength. Remember, we're trying to eliminate wasted effort, save time, and direct your energy to the exercises that move you forward. When you're

Core bridge (plank): This is one of the best exercises for developing stability because it forces you to hold your body in a straight line. With your weight supported only on your elbows, forearms, and toes, raise your hips off the floor until your body is in a straight line from shoulders to heels. At first you may be able to hold a bridge for only 10 to 12 seconds, but with practice you'll extend this to 60 seconds or longer.

PERFORM PERIOD: ESSENTIAL POWER-TRAINING EXERCISES

The Perform Period of the Carmichael Performance Program is when you apply the improvements you've made in endurance and strength over the past 6 weeks. Endurance

shooting for strength gains, a single rep of a weight-lifting exercise should take less than 3 seconds, and the weight should move at a steady speed. You don't have to count; just lift and lower the weight at a natural pace. Some of the last reps of a tough set may take a few seconds longer, but only because you're working hard and starting to fatigue. When increased power is the goal, you add a speed component (as we will in the Perform Period) to the positive phase of the movement (pushing the bar away from your chest in a bench press). The recovery phase, when you return to the starting position, should still be done at a moderate speed.

BAD IDEA:
DO HIGH-REP, LOW-WEIGHT RESISTANCE TRAINING TO IMPROVE STRENGTH AND AEROBIC ENDURANCE.

In this type of training—HRLW, for short—you move very light weights many times instead of heavier weights fewer times. For example, you could bench-press either 50 pounds 30 times without stopping or 150 pounds 10 times. The idea behind HRLW training is that the total work of moving 1,500 pounds is the same, regardless of whether the work is divided into 10 parcels or 30. Therefore, the theory goes, you can get the same strength gains from HRLW lifting as you could from the more strenuous lower-repetition, higher-weight methods. Proponents also claim their method qualifies as an aerobic endurance exercise because it elevates your heart rate.

The trouble with HRLW lifting is that it doesn't provide the stimulus necessary to create real and lasting strength gains. Yes, people sweat and push and pull, but the quality of the work is so low that they see only slight improvements, and then their progress plateaus. Strength is the ability to exert maximum force against resistance, but HRLW training uses just a fraction of your strength to move a smaller weight until your muscles run out of gas and fatigue.

does you no good unless you utilize it to make a positive change in your life. Strength is of no use unless it is applied to purposeful action. In the final 3 weeks, you will see the most visible improvements in performance. You'll be running faster during intervals, completing long endurance workouts with less perceived effort, and performing resistance movements with speed and power.

There is a principle in exercise training known as specificity: The training you do in preparation for a particular activity or event needs to specifically address the demands of that activity or event. We have long applied the principle of specificity only to athletes working to improve performance within the tight confines of their sport. Lance is fond of running and swimming, but he rarely did either during his 7-year reign as Tour de France champion. Every workout he did related to a specific aspect of his Tour de France preparation, because the only way you get ready to race a bicycle for 3 weeks is to spend a lot of hours on a bicycle.

I apply the specificity principle to this program by using the exercises in the Commit and Strengthen Periods to prepare you specifically for the demands of the exercises in the Perform Period. You will have gained strength and stability from the strength-training exercises and learned to move more freely with some agility drills. You will now be ready for plyometric (bounding) exercises, which you weren't prepared for 6 weeks before.

You'll see that many of the key exercises for the Perform Period were also part of the first two periods of the program. But in this period it's time to turn up the volume, open the throttle, add more speed, and put everything together into powerful, coordinated, and continuous exercises that will hone your agility and balance and supercharge your muscles.

Plyometrics

Plyometrics is basically jumping. You use muscles to accelerate your body off the ground, then use them again to stop yourself when you land. As with many other exercises, plyometrics involves a range of complexity. With elite athletes like Olympic snowboarders and skiers, track and field athletes, and sprint cyclists, I've utilized box jumps and depth jumps of up to 4 feet. They represent the extreme application of plyometrics training, but you can obtain important benefits by jumping over much smaller heights.

Plyometrics offers a great way to accomplish multiple goals with a single exercise. You gain strength and power because you apply force to accelerate off the ground and again to stop yourself when you land. You promote balance and joint stability because you have to control your body as it moves through the air and lands. As a bonus, the moves help shore up your bone mineral density because of the amount of force you exert on your skeleton. When you land, your muscles and bones must support a force of about three times your body weight to overcome the forces of gravity.

Agility Drills

Football, hockey, and basketball players; sprinters; and even cyclists spend a lot of time working on foot speed. The faster they can move, the more likely they are to keep their feet under them as they train and compete. Keeping your feet under you is important; it keeps you from ending up on your butt. Most of us, however, haven't done any kind of agility training since high school gym class. Maybe you don't need catlike reflexes to be successful in your office job, but as you get older and the consequences of falling grow, having quick feet just may save your butt or hip or wrists.

Plyometrics and agility drills go hand in hand, and many exercises fall into both categories. If you incorporate these moves into your training program, your balance and body awareness will improve mightily. On top of everything else, plyometrics and agility drills can be fun—or at least more interesting than doing pushups. In fact, they're so much like games that you might even be able to get your kids involved.

GETTING STARTED

The Carmichael Performance Program is designed to produce measurable changes in your fitness—but to know how much you improve, you first have to gather some baseline information. In "Getting Started" (page 111), you'll find instructions for a four-part test that provides data on your current aerobic conditioning, flexibility, strength, and agility. By taking the Carmichael Fitness Tests at the beginning of the program and again at the end, you'll see how much progress you've made.

For instance, you'll complete the 1-mile walk faster at the end of the program because your aerobic system will be able to deliver more oxygen to your working muscles. You'll complete more pushups at the end because your upper body will be stronger and more squats because your lower body will be, too. And the progress you've made will help you complete the agility test more quickly.

What do test results have to do with real-world performance? Everything and nothing. Testing will show that you can perform better, but it's up to you to actually carry those improvements into your life. In my experience, however, positive results from field tests such as these help build the confidence people need to go out and make the moves that lead to real-world success.

CHAPTER 3

Master Your Nutrition

Over the course of the Tour de France in 1999 and the rest of that summer, my weight ballooned. I had gone to France to be with Lance Armstrong as he won his first yellow jersey, and when you travel with the Tour instead of riding in it, you don't get any exercise. You do, however, drink a lot of wine. With the excitement after the race victory and the launch of Carmichael Training Systems later that summer occupying all my time, it wasn't until fall that I realized how much weight I'd gained. That was when I tried on the warmer long pants that I hadn't worn since April and found I couldn't button them.

At about the same time, I was talking with a cable television channel about filming short fitness tips, Carmichael Training Systems was getting ready to film a series of exercise videos, and I was appearing on news programs to talk about Lance's recent Tour de France success. The camera adds 10 pounds, an old saying I learned to be absolutely true when I saw the tape of one of my first interviews. And now I actually *was* 10 pounds heavier, so I dreaded the idea of spending even more time on camera. Worse than that, I felt like I wasn't in control—like my weight was increasing, and there was nothing I could do about it.

I was genuinely angry that I'd been blind to what had been going on, angry about the effort it was going to take to lose the weight, and angry that I had to go out and buy new clothes. My wife, on the other hand, saw it as an opportunity to update my wardrobe.

I bought two pairs of pants so I could wear one while the other was in the laundry, and

I immediately made changes to my nutrition program that ended up forming the first period of the Carmichael Performance Program. I committed to cutting the junk out of my diet and refocusing on whole, natural, nutrient-heavy, and calorie-light foods. I simply didn't want a closet full of new clothes. Sure enough, after a few weeks of working on my new approach to eating, my old ones fit just fine, as I knew they would.

COMMIT PERIOD: CUT THE CLUTTER

Most everybody understands that fried pork rinds and snack cakes have no redeeming features, but there's another, more deceptive grade of junk out there, and it's so inconspicuous that even nutritionists and registered dietitians find themselves eating it. This category of junk includes sugar-added juices, trans-fat-laden baked goods, and calorie-loaded coffee drinks. Some, like orange juice, started out as high-quality, nutrient-dense foods and drinks but were swept into the junk aisle by added sugar, flavorings, and preservatives. Whole grain breads and crackers have experienced similar nutritional hijacking: We associate whole grains with wholesome nutrition, but crackers that say "whole grain" on the front may also say "trans fat" and "high fructose corn syrup" on the nutrition label.

When I looked at my own nutrition program and reviewed my clients' nutrition profiles, I realized that the majority of the junk—the excess calories that add no positive value—comes from five primary sources: soda, corn syrup, trans fat, fancy coffee drinks, and alcohol.

No More Soda

The average American drinks up to 55 gallons of sweetened soda each year, and it serves absolutely no good purpose in your diet. That's nearly one 20-ounce bottle of soda and 250 calories from sugar every day of the year. Simply cut out soda, and you'll drop 1,750 calories and half a pound each week.

No More Corn Syrup

Corn syrup and its evil twin, high-fructose corn syrup (HFCS), are cheap sweeteners used in thousands of products, from colas to condiments and most commercial baked goods, including some whole wheat breads (read the labels). Not only is HFCS a concentrated source of empty calories, recent research from the University of California, Davis, also suggests that it might convert more easily to body fat than other types of simple sugar, such as those derived from cane or beets. This is because fructose bypasses some of your body's normal mechanisms for controlling energy balance, basically allowing you to consume more energy than your body realizes. It's kind of like an accounting mistake that results in a warehouse full of goods you didn't know you bought and that don't show up on inventory lists.

Before HFCS, which is actually a mixture of fructose and glucose sugars (see "Sugar During Exercise: Great Fuel at the Right Time" on page 36), people didn't consume that much fructose because it was mostly found naturally in fruits and honey. Now fructose accounts for about 25 percent of the sugar the average American consumes—much more than the human body has evolved to be able to process. In 1966, Americans ate no HFCS, but in 2001, HFCS made up 42 percent—a full 63 pounds—of the 147 pounds of sugar eaten by the average American.

Fructose goes to the liver to be converted into glucose before your body uses it for energy. The liver is also where you produce fat and cholesterol, and recent research suggests that putting excess carbohydrate in such close proximity to fat-producing machinery makes it that much easier for your body to convert it to fat.

Beware of products marketed as low fat; although cutting fat is a good idea, manufacturers often replace the fat with loads of HFCS to make the product's taste and texture seem "normal" to you.

EAT THESE	ELIMINATE THESE
HFCS-free breads such as Orowheat Honey Fiber Whole Grain (read labels; most brands have HFCS)	White, cinnamon, and sweet breads
Honey, Smuckers Simply 100% Fruit spread	Sweetened jellies and jams
Dried fruit, nuts	Cookies
Ice cream	Frozen yogurt
Unflavored instant oatmeal (use fruit to add sweetness)	Flavored instant oatmeal
Nature's Path FlaxPlus Raisin Bran, Kashi 7 Whole Grain cereal	Sweetened cereals
Wasa Multigrain Crispbread	Processed snack crackers (Ritz, Wheat Thins, Cheese Nips)
Spectrum Naturals Omega-3 Raspberry Vinaigrette, Annie's Naturals Tuscany Italian Dressing	Commercial salad dressings (including products from Kraft, such as Miracle Whip, and Wishbone)
Northland 100% juice blends	Artificially sweetened fruit drinks
Prego Organic pasta sauce	Sugar-added tomato sauce

Sugar During Exercise: Great Fuel at the Right Time

WHEN COMBINED WITH exercise, simple sugar can be quite beneficial for performance. When used to fulfill a specific purpose at a specific time, easily digested sugars like dextrose and maltodextrin are best, and even HFCS can be a good choice because, despite the name, it is mostly glucose. "High"-fructose corn syrup is high in fructose only compared with regular corn syrup.

Energy bars and gels provide the clearest examples of an appropriate use of HFCS. I've eaten PowerBar Performance bars and worked with the company to develop their line of sports drinks and recovery drinks. When I exercise, I eat the bars and gels and drink PowerBar Endurance, and I recommend these products to my clients. When I need a midafternoon snack, I reach for a handful of almonds, dried or fresh fruit, or one of PowerBar's whole grain or nut bars that contain a variety of complex carbohydrates—and no HFCS.

Some people worry that simple sugar will cause a spike in insulin and lead to type 2 diabetes, but this is of little concern when you eat it during and immediately after exercise, because exercise changes the way your body transports and utilizes sugar. Exercise blunts the normal spike in insulin that accompanies the digestion of sugar; your body uses more direct transport methods to speed sugar to working muscles. As a result, sugar consumed during exercise doesn't contribute to the overproduction of insulin that can lead to hyperinsulinemia and insulin resistance, which are the precursors of type 2 diabetes.

No More Trans Fats

Only humans could create something worse for you than saturated fat. Trans fat is a product of the food industry, which takes heart-healthy unsaturated fats and chemically corrupts them into molecules that are more harmful to your health than the saturated fat dripping off the greasy bacon in a back-alley diner. For years, partially hydrogenated oils, those dreaded trans fats, have been used in commercial baked goods, chips, and fast food. If you see partially hydrogenated anything in a food's ingredient list, put it back on the shelf and walk away. If it's already in your house, give it away or toss it in the trash.

While saturated fat increases levels of LDL cholesterol—the heart-stopping "bad" cholesterol—trans fat takes you even a few steps closer to a heart attack. It not only increases LDL cholesterol levels, it also lowers blood levels of beneficial HDL cholesterol, the kind that helps strip plaque off your artery walls. If that weren't bad enough, trans fat can also contribute to the stiffening of arteries. In other words, you'd be better off eating the solid fat you cut off the edge of your steak (saturated fat) than an equal portion of stick margarine (trans fat).

The FDA now requires all manufacturers to list trans fat separately on nutrition labels. So take a second to look at the labels in the grocery store and find products without trans fat. One exception to the rule is commercial peanut butter brands; they use a minimal amount of trans fat to keep the oil from separating, but not enough to worry about.

EAT THESE	DON'T EAT THESE
Butter, cooking spray, I Can't Believe It's Not Butter! Fat-Free Spread, Benecol	Stick or tub margarine (though tub is better than stick)
No Pudge! brownie mix	Boxed cake, cookie, or brownie mixes
Cascadian Farm Spud Puppies	French fries
Nature's Path Lifestream Synergy Waffles	Frozen waffles
Guiltless Gourmet or Que Pasa tortilla chips	Fried potato and tortilla chips
Wasa Multigrain Crispbread	Processed snack crackers (Cheese Nips, Cheez-Its, Wheat Thins, Ritz)
Newman's Own Champion Chip Cookies	Cookies
Fig Newmans	Fig bars

No More Alcohol

For the first 3 weeks of this program, commit to cutting the alcohol out of your diet. People don't realize that alcohol itself is a source of empty calories: 7 useless calories in every gram, or about 98 in each 1½-ounce shot glass of spirits like vodka or whiskey. Liqueurs (such as Kahlúa and Bailey's) have even more calories per shot because of added sugar. Cocktails made with sugary mixes and colas push the calorie counts even higher, up to more than 200 calories per drink. Besides being a source of empty calories, alcoholic beverages are diuretics and contribute to dehydration, even if you have only one or two. When you drink a lot of alcohol and feel miserable the next morning, that pounding in your head, lethargy, and cottonmouth are primarily due to dehydration. Even though your Bloody Mary mix may contain tomatoes and your White Russian contains milk, for these 3 weeks I want you to stay away from alcohol, including beer and wine. I'm often asked questions such as the following regarding alcohol and the Carmichael Performance Program.

What about the benefits of red wine?

There is some evidence that regular consumption of red wine may help reduce your chance of developing heart disease, but the benefit seems to come from the antioxidants in the grape skins, not the alcohol. You can get those antioxidants from other sources, including 100 percent grape juice and a variety of fruits and vegetables.

Do I have to give up drinking forever?

During the Strengthen and Perform Periods of the program, you can return to drinking beer, wine, and cocktails, but I recommend sticking to no more than four drinks per week.

Is it okay to indulge at a party?

Even when you return to consuming the occasional alcoholic drink, it's best to keep it to four drinks or fewer each week. By alternating between a drink and a tall glass of water, you can reduce your alcohol intake at parties and keep yourself hydrated. Also, hold on to your drink longer—people are less likely to offer you another if you already have a drink in your hand.

No More Tobacco

When my wife and I went to our first doctor's visit after learning we were having a baby, I was surprised to hear that Colorado is one of the leading states for underweight newborns. When I asked for the reason, I silently wondered if it had something to do with altitude or the relatively high activity level of Colorado residents. I was shocked when the doctor said the lower birth weights were due to high rates of smoking and alcohol use. "Outside the big cities, it's still the Wild West out here," she said.

On the way home, I realized that I was surprised by the doctor's answer because smoking had become so far removed from my own life. I didn't originally include "No More Tobacco" in this book, since no one in my circle of friends, business partners, and athletes smokes. Until that wake-up call in the doctor's office, I mistakenly believed that smoking was a problem of the past. In reality, according to the US Centers for Disease Control (CDC), 45 million Americans (roughly 21 percent of the population) smoke and expose millions more to the health risks of secondhand smoke. Nearly another 7 million Americans, mostly men, use smokeless tobacco. Across the board, tobacco contributes to more than 400,000 deaths in this country every year, and even though that number is slowly falling, aggressive marketing is still replacing a higher percentage of those who quit.

According to the CDC, adult smokers die 13 to 14 years earlier than nonsmokers do, and here's the important lesson I want you to take away from this section: You can reverse some of the negative impact smoking has had on your lungs and overall health. Think of it as reclaiming years of your life that you had already surrendered. Your lungs begin repairing themselves within a few months of quitting, and after several years, your risk of dying from lung cancer may drop by more than 50 percent.

If you use tobacco, it's going to be much more difficult to quit smoking or chewing than it will be to stop drinking sugary soft drinks or eating fast food. The physical addiction to nicotine is strong, and many smokers have deeply ingrained social habits linked with lighting up (during their commute, while on work breaks, when driving home, after meals, with alcohol) that make it even harder to quit. There are many helpful programs available, including medical interventions, patches, counseling, and group therapy. And keep in mind, very few people successfully quit the first time they try. It may take a few attempts and a few different methods, but quitting is essential; any improvements in health and longevity that you might see from building fitness or losing weight are essentially negated as long as you continue using tobacco.

No More Fancy Coffee Drinks

Recent research confirms what we have believed for decades: Caffeine improves mental performance, including short-term memory. Researchers believe it may block the action of a chemical that normally slows brain function. A more active brain allows you to focus better, find solutions faster, and come up with better ideas. Heightened brain activity also excites the entire nervous system, which may be why *some* caffeine improves exercise and sports performance, but *too much* leads to the jitters.

I spent years living in Europe, where they have had a lot more time to come to grips with their coffee habits. On a typical morning in France or Italy, you'd have coffee with milk or a 4- to 6-ounce latte with breakfast; if you had coffee later in the day, it was a double shot of espresso. Meeting for coffee was about getting out of the office or trading stories with a friend; the coffee was small and just an excuse to go for a walk.

In America, it started out innocently with coffee, which has virtually no calories, but now you can walk away with 700 to 1,000 calories in a single cup, thanks to the milk, cream, and sugar dumped in. I'm not saying you have to go without coffee, nor am I saying you have to go without caffeine, but it's time to stop with the fancy coffee drinks. The following are the worst offenders.

- Lattes, mochas, macchiatos, and hot chocolates: These are rich and creamy because they're made with cream or whole milk and sugar and, therefore, loaded with excess fat and calories.

- White hot chocolate and white chocolate mocha: White chocolate is sweetened cocoa butter and milk solids, so it has more calories and fat than darker chocolate.

If you need a java jolt, have one of these instead.

- Espresso: A double shot delivers less caffeine than a regular cup of coffee (90 milligrams versus up to 200 milligrams).
- Americano: Espresso and hot water make a bolder-tasting cup of coffee.
- Cappuccino made with fat-free milk (the smaller, the better): Traditionally, a cappuccino is a 5- to 6-ounce drink; the espresso provides a bold flavor, and the steamed milk forms a foam with small, fine bubbles. It was never meant to be a 20-ounce glass of warm milk with some espresso in it.
- Small latte with fat-free milk: A smaller size brings out more of the coffee flavor and gives you nearly a cup of calcium-rich milk yet keeps the calories in check.

BEVERAGE	CALORIES IN 20 OZ MADE WITH:				
	CREAM	WHOLE MILK	SOY MILK	FAT-FREE MILK	NO WHIPPED CREAM
Starbucks White Hot Chocolate	1,070	720	650	590	Subtract 100 calories
Starbucks Caffé Mocha	770	490	440	390	Subtract 100 calories
Starbucks Caffé Latte	710	340	270	210	Not applicable
Starbucks Caramel Macchiato	690	380	330	280	Not available
Starbucks Cappuccino	430	210	160	130	Not available

Source: Nutrition data available on www.starbucks.com

SAY YES TO PERIOD ONE POWER FOODS

By eliminating soft drinks, high-fructose corn syrup, trans fats, alcohol, and fancy coffee drinks in the Commit Period, you're eliminating the clutter that gets in the way of optimal nutrition and performance. You may find that removing the clutter and useless calories from your diet reveals that you're already eating a wide variety of nutrient-dense, healthy foods—the size of your gut just made you think you weren't.

Sam, a sales manager at a large software corporation, came to me because his weight was getting in the way of his job. At 5 foot 10 and 220 pounds, he was overweight but not huge, yet his weight and lack of fitness made business travel torturous. When I looked at what he ate in a week, I noticed a lot of excellent choices: whole grains, fruit, vegetables, lean meat, and low-fat dairy products, but I also saw excess sugar from sodas, lattes, muffins, and fast food. When I took those items out of the equation, his caloric intake was right where it should be for a man of his size and activity level. It was fascinating to watch how, over the next 3 weeks, the only change he made was to cut out the items I listed previously in this chapter—and he lost 7 pounds.

Like Sam, you need to get rid of the clutter—that's the most important step toward putting your nutrition program on the right track. You'll know you're there if you're already eating the foods listed below. If you're not, or if these foods make up less than half of your daily calories, replace the bad foods with more nutrient-dense choices from the whole food options listed throughout this chapter.

Eat More Whole Foods

The fact that eating whole foods is better than eating processed ones isn't news, but knowing it and doing it are two completely different things. The fact is, too many Americans aren't doing it and it's time to start. Some people cry that it's too hard or too expensive to eat whole foods, but I'm not talking about shopping exclusively at an organic grocery store. I'm talking about eating more of the whole grains, fresh fruits and vegetables, and hormone-free meats and dairy products that are available everywhere. And I'm not talking about making everything from scratch but, rather, making better choices with packaged foods.

BEST WHOLE FOOD CHOICES	NOT THE BEST CHOICES
Quaker 100% rolled oats	Flavored instant oatmeal packets
Uncle Ben's Instant Brown Rice	Bleached white rice
Orowheat Honey Wheat Bread	Soft white bread
Graham crackers, animal crackers	Oreos, Chips Ahoy, Girl Scout cookies
Dry roasted nuts	Honey-roasted or candied nuts
Maple syrup	Artificially sweetened and flavored syrups
Cascadian Farm Hearty Morning cereal	Sweetened cereals
Northland 100% juice blends	Artificially sweetened fruit drinks
Smuckers Simply 100% Fruit spread	Sweetened jellies and jams

Eat More Fiber

There are a host of reasons to eat more fiber, and one is that doing so will almost certainly result in your eating more whole foods. If you go to the grocery store looking for fiber, you're going to walk out with whole grains, fruits, vegetables, nuts, and seeds. You won't come out with bleached rice, white bread, processed snack crackers, cookies, and sugary cereals.

Because you don't digest either soluble or insoluble fiber, it helps to rout out your intestines, bind harmful chemicals, keep you regular, improve nutrient absorption, and possibly reduce cancer risk.

Soluble fiber in oatmeal, apples, berries, and beans forms a viscous gel and slows digestion, thereby helping to keep your blood sugar level from rapidly spiking the way it can after you eat low-fiber carbohydrate sources like cookies and soda. Soluble fiber is also the type thought to be primarily responsible for lowering blood cholesterol levels. Your liver uses cholesterol to produce bile, a nasty yellow liquid that aids in the digestion of fat and releases it into your intestine. Soluble fiber traps bile and moves it on down the line, which means that your liver has to make more. And since it has to pull cholesterol out of your blood to do that, your blood cholesterol level, and hence your risks for developing hardened arteries and cardiovascular disease, falls.

Because of the evidence linking high-fiber diets and reduced risks for cardiovascular disease, diabetes, obesity, and possibly some cancers, the widely accepted recommendation for fiber intake is 25 to 30 grams a day. The Institute of Medicine of the National Academy of Sciences recommends an even higher amount—up to 38 grams per day—for men under 50 because dietary habits during these years are a major predictor for disease later in life. Yet according to the Harvard School of Public Health, the average American consumes only 14 to 15 grams each day.

Eat these high-fiber whole foods: split peas and split pea soup; kidney, black, pinto, and garbanzo beans; oatmeal; raspberries; brown rice; air-popped popcorn; whole grain breads, muffins, and crackers; high-fiber breakfast cereals (more than 5 grams per serving); bulgur and buckwheat; and nuts (almonds, walnuts, pecans, and pistachios).

Avoid these poor sources of fiber: refined white flour, white bread, bleached white rice, and fruit juice.

Drink More Water

I'll let you in on a secret I teach the coaches at Carmichael Training Systems: The simplest way to improve performance is to get an athlete to drink more water. The majority of Americans, active and sedentary alike, are chronically dehydrated. We simply don't consume enough fluid each day, and we've been living this way for so long that we don't even realize it. And so, when you increase your daily fluid intake, you see almost immediate results. You feel more energetic, your workouts are better, you focus better at work, and you're less irritable.

We know that as little as 2 percent dehydration hinders performance (you can't exercise as long, hold as fast a pace, or lift as much weight) by about 10 percent. When dehydration increases to 5 percent, performance declines by 30 percent. Here's the kicker: If you're already 2 percent dehydrated when you start a workout, there's a pretty good chance you'll be 4 to 5 percent dehydrated during it.

Now, here's the tricky thing: Instantly increasing the amount you drink won't instantly improve hydration in your body. Over decades, you've adapted to a chronic state of dehydration, and suddenly flooding the system will simply increase urine production. Don't worry about it. This will diminish after about a week as your body happily adapts to assimilating more fluid. You do, however, want to increase intake gradually, and it doesn't all have to be water, either. Your main concern is total fluid volume, which should eventually come up to about 3 quarts to 1 gallon a day (more active individuals, athletes, and people living in hot environments may need more).

HOW ¾–1 GALLON OF FLUID/DAY BREAKS DOWN
8–16 oz water upon waking
8 oz water or fruit juice with breakfast
8 oz coffee with breakfast
16–20 oz fluid with midmorning snack
16–20 oz fluid with lunch
16–20 oz fluid with afternoon or preworkout snack
8–20 oz water before dinner
16–20 oz water before bedtime
TOTAL: 96–132 OZ

STRENGTHEN PERIOD: FEEDING STRONG MUSCLES

Some very important changes happen in the second period of this program. After 3 weeks, you're on your way to building more lean muscle and stripping away fat faster than before. Why? Because the gains you made in the first period have given you the fitness tools to make even greater gains now. After the first 3 weeks, you can burn more calories and more fat per minute than when you started. You can run or ride faster and farther, complete more crunches, and move more weight. Your body is adapting, which is why both the fitness and nutrition programs are changing, too.

To build lean muscle, you need the right nutrients coursing through your body. This means eating foods that enhance your ability to build lean muscle without overdoing the calories. If you're taking in too many calories, you'll gain muscle, but you'll also keep the fat you have—and maybe gain even more. On the other hand, if you consume too few calories, it doesn't matter what you eat—you won't gain an ounce of new muscle.

Remember when you had to do your chores before you could go out and play? Basically, the same rules govern your body. First priority goes to keeping all systems running in perfect order, which takes energy. Once those tasks are taken care of, you're free to use whatever's left to build more muscle. When there's nothing left because you failed to eat enough, you've wasted your exercise time because your body can't respond and make you stronger. In fact, you'll get weaker and most likely come down with a cold.

Eat More Muscle-Building Foods

The Strengthen Period is when you build metabolism-boosting lean muscle, and that requires eating the right foods. While you should continue to eat a wide variety of whole grains, fruit, and vegetables (carbs), the protein in your daily nutrition program now takes on greater importance. The increased focus on resistance training in this period boosts the natural production of both testosterone and human growth hormone, the essential drivers for developing muscle. If these hormones are revving up your body's muscle-building machinery, it's critical that all the nutrition building blocks be ready and available.

Fresh Seafood (salmon, tuna, halibut, cod, clams, crab, shrimp)

Muscle builders: Complete, high-quality protein, iron, iodine, and zinc

MVP features: Boost testosterone; provide heart-healthy omega-3 and omega-6 fatty acids (salmon and tuna)

Eat them this way: Broiled, baked, grilled, seared, smoked, or canned (white albacore tuna in water); as sushi or sashimi

Don't eat them this way: Breaded and fried; canned in oil

Eating more seafood can improve your performance, help you live longer, and even keep your brain healthy. Salmon, cod, halibut, and other cold-water fish are rich in omega-3 and omega-6 fatty acids, essential unsaturated fats that reduce your risk of heart attack and stroke, keep brain cells healthy, and prevent age-associated degradation.

Seafood, including fish and shellfish, is a good source of iron and iodine, two minerals essential for building muscle. Crustaceans, including oysters, clams, crabs, and shrimp, are also very good sources of zinc, and fish contains unsaturated fat; these two nutrients play important roles in the production of testosterone, the primary muscle-building hormone that many men start running low on after their 20s.

Two servings of fish a week, or up to 8 to 12 ounces, provides the health and performance benefits you're after and will keep you within the current safety guidelines concerning mercury in fresh fish.

Hormone-Free Farm Animals (lean beef, turkey, lamb)

Muscle builders: Complete protein, iron, zinc, and creatine

MVP features: Build muscle; help transport more oxygen in the blood; increase muscular power

Eat these: Eye of round, top round, bottom round, sirloin, tenderloin, and white-meat chicken and turkey

Eat them this way: Grilled, roasted, or broiled

The Truth about Metabolism

PEOPLE COMPLAIN TO ME THAT they're fat because their metabolism automatically declines with age. Listen up: There is nothing magical about your chronological age that causes your metabolism to slow down. There is no switch that flips at age 30, 35, 40, or even 50 that suddenly calls fat to gather at your love handles and spill over your belt. It's not your age that controls metabolism, but the amount of muscle you have on your frame.

Muscle is the driving force behind metabolism because it is voracious and greedy. Where most cells in your body sip energy like a hybrid car, your muscles fry through it like your neighbor's Humvee. As you moved through your twenties and thirties, *you* slowed down, not your metabolism. And because of that, you are carrying around less muscle than you were when you were more active, burning fewer calories to support your body, and gaining fat (which is metabolically stingy).

Body fat is like a metabolic debt. It takes virtually no energy to support a fat cell, but it can grow to hold a tremendous amount of energy. To shrink and eventually get rid of that fat cell, you have to provide a reason for it to give up its energy and a furnace to burn it in. Lean muscle mass provides both.

For every pound of lean muscle you build, you will burn 50 additional calories each day, just to keep that muscle alive. And while that's all well and good, the even bigger benefit is that more muscle means more and bigger mitochondria (fat- and carbohydrate-burning furnaces), which means you can exercise longer and faster and burn more calories and fat, per minute, in the process.

Don't eat them this way: Fried, southern fried, or battered and fried

Don't eat these: Filet mignon, prime rib, rib eye, brisket, spare ribs, duck, dark-meat poultry, or self-basting (and some rotisserie) turkeys and chickens, which are injected with fat

Meat has long been associated with muscle growth. The protein and zinc in meat and poultry help build more lean muscle, which will make you both stronger and faster. Whenever possible, choose meat from animals that were raised without hormones. While the FDA has not yet concluded that these hormones are harmful to people, there is growing evidence that our hormonal balance may be upset by the hormones given to livestock and passed on to us at the dinner table.

Delivering more oxygen to muscles that are more ready to receive it is the cornerstone to improving fitness, and iron from meat and poultry is essential for making that happen. When you're low on iron, you're starving your muscles of oxygen. You feel fatigued and apathetic, have a short attention span, can't exercise at an effective level, and are more susceptible to illness.

Why iron from meat, poultry, and fish? Because the heme iron they contain is more biologically available than the nonheme kind in iron-rich vegetable sources like pumpkin seeds, sunflower seeds, nuts, raisins, oats, and whole grains. If you consume the same amount of each type of iron, more of the heme will actually be put to use. That's why the Recommended Dietary Allowance (RDA) for iron increases from 8 milligrams for omnivorous men to 14 milligrams for vegetarian men (and 18 milligrams to 33 milligrams for premenopausal vegetarian women).

Meat can either be great for you or clog your arteries, depending on how much saturated fat it contains. You want beef cuts that come from the back legs (eye of round, top round, bottom round, top sirloin), the more muscular area of the animal. Roasted leg of lamb is also a lean choice. With poultry, white meat from the breast is leanest, while dark meat from the legs and thighs is higher in saturated fat. Wings are usually a bad idea because they're prepared with the skin, which is very high in fat.

Low-Fat Dairy Products

Muscle builders: Complete protein, calcium, and vitamin D

MVP features: Build muscle; promote weight loss; increase muscle strength

Eat these: Low-fat milk, cottage cheese, plain yogurt, and fruit-and-yogurt smoothies

Don't eat these: Frozen yogurt, sweetened fruit-on-the-bottom yogurt, whole milk, half-and-half, or cream

There are more reasons than ever to drink your milk and eat other low-fat dairy products. They're a good source of protein, and most are fortified with vitamin D, which plays a huge role in developing and maintaining muscle strength. These are on top of the original reason for fortification, which was that vitamin D enhances calcium absorption. You can make all the vitamin D you need by exposing your skin to the sun, but in an ironic turn of events, increased use of sunscreen and less time spent outdoors means we're making less D; thus, we need to obtain more of it from our food.

Yet calcium is perhaps the most important nutrient in dairy products. Your muscles use it for every contraction; when you get enough from your diet, you're stronger, and your muscles don't have to steal the mineral from your bones. And even though the original studies linking low-fat dairy products to enhanced weight loss were paid for by the dairy industry, subsequent independent research confirms those findings. Most of the benefit seems to be related to calcium, and researchers have found that dairy products lead to more weight loss than nondairy calcium sources.

Shun Protein Shakes

YOUR BODY CAN'T STORE excess protein, and studies show that eating more than about 1 gram per pound of body weight doesn't provide any additional benefit. What happens to the excess? It's converted to carbohydrate, which, if it's not burned through exercise, ends up as fat.

Eggs

Muscle builder: Highest quality complete protein available

MVP features: Build muscle; promote recovery

Eat them this way: Poached, hard-cooked, scrambled, or fried in a pan coated lightly with olive oil

Don't eat them this way: Raw, deviled, or in egg salad

Eggs are back from purgatory and ready to once again take their place among healthy power foods. Yes, they still have cholesterol, but scientists have recently learned that blood cholesterol has more to do with genetics and dietary fat than with dietary cholesterol. In fact, even with the relatively high amount of cholesterol in yolks, reducing saturated and trans-fat intake is more effective for lowering blood cholesterol than cutting out eggs is.

Eggs are important for building lean muscle because they have the most biologically available protein of any food. Biological availability is simply a comparison between the amount of a nutrient a food starts with and the amount that ends up being utilized in your body. This is the reason that even a few eggs per week can have a big impact on your performance without adding a large number of calories: The vast majority of the protein gets used. And forget about eating raw eggs. It's not only a health risk, but cooking makes the protein in whites and yolks easier to digest.

Beans and Legumes

Muscle builders: Protein, iron, and folate

MVP features: High in fiber; cholesterol free; slow digestion

Eat these: Beans (black, pinto, white, kidney, lima, and garbanzo), edamame (soybeans), lentils, and peas

Eat them this way: Boiled or in hummus

Don't eat them this way: Refried (typically loaded with fat) or baked (high in sugar)

Beans are an example of the food industry serving the consumer's best interest. Since they have to be cooked, and you probably don't have the necessary 2-plus hours to spare, canned beans are a great way to obtain optimal nutrition conveniently. Beans don't lose any nutritive value in the process; just watch out for additional ingredients, like sugar and sodium.

Because of the amount of protein, complex carbohydrate, and fiber in beans and legumes, they're best eaten after training, especially if you're working out in the afternoon or evening. The protein and fiber help you feel full and help keep blood sugar levels from spiking, so you'll be less likely to feel hungry for a big snack right before bed. Beans also supply the carbohydrate and protein energy that can enhance the impact of the day's largest human growth hormone release, which happens after you're in a deep sleep.

PERFORM PERIOD: SUPERCHARGE YOUR MUSCLES

The third period of the Carmichael Performance Program is, as its name implies, all about performance. Over the first two periods, you made the shift to whole foods and learned to focus on high-quality sources of carbohydrate and protein. At this point in the program, most people I work with tell me they feel like they are "running cleaner." Some compare it to the difference between driving a car before and after a tune-up. The goal from here on out is to utilize key foods to maintain your edge, protect your health, and supercharge your muscles.

But strenuous exercise (and air pollution) also leads to oxidative stress, which can tear down your body. Most of the oxygen you breathe is processed normally through your system, but a small percentage of these molecules splits into unstable compounds known as free radicals. These rogue molecules can damage cell structures throughout your body, and elevated free radical exposure has been linked to a wide variety of conditions associated with aging, such as a gradual decline in muscle function, strength, and lean body mass.

But there's help available right now from foods that contain antioxidant compounds that neutralize free radicals in the body. Reducing free radical damage won't help you run faster next week, but it may play a crucial role in preserving your vitality as you grow older. There is no way to reverse the effects of aging, but antioxidants at least provide a chance to slow the process.

We also need to talk about fueling your best performance. The problem with telling people to eat more when their energy output increases is that it's so easy for them to overstuff themselves. You may be looking for 100 to 200 more calories from carbohydrate sources but end up consuming 400 to 600 calories because your food choices include protein and fat, as well. The key to performance is getting more from less, so many of the key foods in this period are concentrated energy sources—they contain clean-burning carbohydrate in small packages so you get the energy you need without a load of excess calories.

Even so, the main components of your daily nutrition won't change significantly as you move into the Perform Period. You should still be eating a wide variety of whole foods and focusing on quality sources of carbohydrate and protein. The main feature of this period is the addition of a few key ingredients that maximize the impact of your fitness training, the strength of your immune system, and your long-term protection against deterioration and aging.

Eat More Berries

Superchargers: Vitamin C, fiber, antioxidants, and salicylic acid

Eat these: Blueberries, raspberries, strawberries, blackberries, black currants, chokeberries, and elderberries

Eat them this way: Fresh out of the container; fresh frozen; and in salads, cereal, oatmeal, baked goods, fruit smoothies, or by the handful

Don't eat them this way: Packed in syrup, sweetened frozen, as pie filling, or in sweetened jellies and jams

Don't eat these: None

When you're looking for a concentrated source of energy without excess calories, look no further than berries. They're so sweet, juicy, and refreshing that there's no need to add sugar, and you can eat them right out of the container or add them to a wide variety of dishes. Berries are packed with antioxidant vitamin C and provide a phenomenal amount of fiber for the calories.

According to the USDA, elderberries, black currants, chokeberries, blueberries, raspberries, blackberries, and strawberries provide the greatest amount of antioxidants, per serving, of all the berries you'll find in the supermarket. Researchers believe anthocynanins—the same compounds that give berries their purple, blue, and red pigments—are responsible for the protective properties.

Berries are also a good source of salicylic acid, the active ingredient in aspirin. A steady intake of salicylic acid has been shown to reduce heart-attack risk; eating foods high in salicylic acid can help you stay out of the cardiologist's office, even if you're already taking low-dose aspirin under a doctor's supervision. A few quick notes on berries:

- Juice stains in the bottom of the container mean the berries are close to being overripe or rotten.
- The presence of a few rotten berries makes the others rot sooner.
- When you buy plastic containers of berries, cut off the tops and put the containers in a convenient place in the fridge, like the door. When you open the fridge to look for a quick snack, the fruit is the quickest and easiest choice.

Surprise Them All at Your Next Reunion

EVERY CLASS HAS ITS reunions, but for me it isn't a high school or college get-together I look forward to. Every few years, there's an occasion that brings together the original members of the 7-Eleven Professional Cycling Team—the first American professional cycling team to race in Europe. By 1986, we gained entry to the Tour de France, and my teammate Davis Phinney became the first American to win a road stage of the race. Twenty years later, the anniversary of his historic win brought us all together again.

The June 2006 "Drafting for Davis" fund-raiser benefited the Davis Phinney Foundation, founded by Davis and his wife, Connie, when he was diagnosed with early-onset Parkinson's disease at 41. Everyone was there—a pretty impressive group. Eric Heiden, better known for winning five Olympic gold medals in speed skating than being a professional cyclist, is now an orthopedic surgeon. Bob Roll parlayed his wit and experience in the gutters of European professional cycling into several successful books and a steady gig as a television commentator. Jim Ochowicz, our team director back then, is a two-time Olympian and president of the USA Cycling Board of Directors. Jeff Pierce won the final stage of the 1987 Tour de France in Paris, and Steve Bauer wore the yellow jersey for 11 days during his cycling career before founding Steve Bauer Bike Tours. Though we had all retired from professional racing at least a decade earlier, we're still very competitive, so showing up overweight and out of shape wasn't an option.

I had dreaded earlier

Eat More Almonds and Other Nuts

Superchargers: Magnesium and manganese

MVP features: Protein, monounsaturated fat, vitamin E, niacin, and fiber

Eat these: Almonds, walnuts, pistachios, and peanuts

Eat them this way: Dry roasted or lightly salted and in sugar-free nut butters

Don't eat them this way: Honey-roasted or candied

Don't eat these: Macadamia nuts, cashews, or Brazil nuts
(more fat, fewer nutrients)

When you're building muscle and training for power, almonds and other nuts are definitely your friends. Not only are they good vegetable sources of protein, they are also rich in magnesium, which plays important roles in protein synthesis. Studies show that the combination of fiber and unsaturated fat in almonds and other nuts helps lower LDL cholesterol (the bad kind). Two large epidemiological studies involving more than 110,000

reunions because I had become the most sedentary and overweight member of the old team. When we were all in our prime, I was one of the leanest guys on the squad, but by 2000, there was no way I could even zip up one of my old racing jerseys. I used the travel and hours devoted to coaching Lance Armstrong and opening a new business as excuses, but in reality, my old teammates were just coping better with the same kinds of stress while still maintaining fitness and nutrition as high priorities.

When I showed up for "Drafting for Davis," it had been a few years since the old gang had gotten together, and I was 20 pounds lighter than I was at the previous reunion. People noticed and were very supportive, noting especially that they wouldn't be able to use me as a landmark anymore: "To find the bar, go over to where that fat guy is standing and then take a left." I had taken my own advice and carved out time for exercise (early mornings work best for me) while addressing my nutrition needs and excesses. I exercised three or four times a week instead of maybe once, and I did interval work (like you'll see in the walking/running fitness programs in this book) to make the biggest improvements in the least amount of time.

"Drafting for Davis" was a huge success for the Davis Phinney Foundation, raising $350,000 in the fight against Parkinson's. It was also a giant success for me because instead of smiling through my teammates' jokes about the gut hanging over my belt, I happily accepted compliments about how healthy, lean, and fit I looked.

men and women found that eating about 5 ounces of nuts (one handful is about 1 ounce) per week lowered the risk for cardiovascular disease by up to 35 to 50 percent.

Including a handful of nuts in a carbohydrate-rich preworkout snack is a great way to maximize the impact of your training. Studies show that consuming 15 to 20 grams of protein (about two handfuls of nuts, or one handful mixed into a small container of yogurt) in the hour before a resistance-training workout significantly improves performance, adaptation, and recovery. Since performance is also dependent on carbohydrate energy, it's best to combine this with 35 to 50 grams of carbohydrate. The following chart outlines some ideal snack options.

POWER-PACKED PERFORMANCE SNACKS	PROTEIN (G)	CARBOHYDRATE (G)
6–8 oz low-fat yogurt with 1 oz almonds	15	46
PowerBar Nut Natural bar and 4–6 oz low-fat yogurt	16.5	50
2 Tbsp peanut butter on whole grain bread with 1 c low-fat milk	21	35
2 oz Cheddar cheese, 10 whole grain crackers, and a handful of walnuts or almonds	20	35

Eat More Seeds

Superchargers: Iron, magnesium, copper, manganese, calcium, and zinc

MVP features: High in fiber and heart-healthy unsaturated fat; cholesterol free; antioxidants from vitamin E

Eat these: Pumpkin, sunflower, flax, and sesame seeds

Eat them this way: Dry roasted, lightly salted, toasted, ground, baked into breads, tahini (sesame seeds), or sprinkled over cereal

Don't eat them this way: Oil roasted, heavily salted, or artificially flavored

Don't eat these: Watermelon seeds

Like the spark plugs in an engine, minerals like iron, magnesium, copper, manganese, calcium, and zinc play crucial roles in the machinery that produces energy and keeps your body operating properly. Ounce for ounce, seeds are one of the best ways to ensure you're firing on all cylinders.

Seeds are like nature's mineral supplement, because even though there are foods that are good sources of one or two minerals (meat for iron and zinc; dairy for calcium), seeds provide a wide range of minerals all at once. The table below shows the mineral content of 1 ounce (one small to medium handful) of seeds.

	RDA FOR MEN/WOMEN	SUNFLOWER	PUMPKIN	SESAME	FLAX
CALCIUM (MG)	1,000/1,000	20	12	279	72
IRON (MG)	8/18	1.1	4.2	4.2	1.6
MAGNESIUM (MG)	420/320	36.4	151	101	111
POTASSIUM (MG)	3,500/3,500	240	228	134	230
ZINC (MG)	11/8	1.5	2.1	2	1.2
MANGANESE (MG)	2.3/1.8	0.6	0.9	0.7	0.7
COPPER (MG)	0.9/0.9	0.5	0.4	0.4	0.3
SELENIUM (MG)	55/55	23	1.6	0.3	7.2

Most of the calories from seeds, like nuts, are from heart-healthy unsaturated fat that helps lower LDL cholesterol and increase levels of beneficial HDL cholesterol. To top it off, seeds are packed with antioxidants that help counteract the oxidative stress that can damage cell membranes throughout the body. This is particularly important as exercise intensity increases or if you live (and exercise) in an area with a lot of air pollution. Both exercise and pollution independently increase oxidative stress and together are a double whammy. Two medium handfuls of sunflower seeds (about 2 ounces) provide half the vitamin E and two-thirds of the selenium you need each day.

Flaxseeds and flaxseed oil deserve special mention because they're also good sources of the same omega-3 fatty acids that make salmon so good for your heart. You can grind them up in a coffee grinder and add them to baked goods, or pour flaxseed oil into salad dressings or smoothies. One word of caution: You can cook with the whole or ground seeds, but the nutritive benefits of flaxseed oil are destroyed by heat.

CHAPTER 4

Jump-Start Your Career

Fit people are more successful. Period.

If you're really looking to impress your boss, forget the long hours and late-night e-mails. Surveys completed at corporate leadership summits indicate that managers associate excessive work hours and a lack of extracurricular activity as warning signs of impending burnout and an inability to manage time.

In contrast, a fit person is seen as someone who takes care of himself and cares about his health, how he looks, and how he carries himself. It's part of the reason that when hiring, top managers rate fit candidates higher on scales of leadership potential.

Fit employees show up for work more often and get more done. They have bright ideas because their brains aren't cloudy from either a lack of fuel or too many happy returns to the all-you-can-eat lunch buffet. They don't get sick as often, they cost the company less in insurance premiums, and they're less likely to be injured on the job. They handle travel better than out-of-shape coworkers do and can walk through two airports, sprint through a third, and still have the energy to nail the critical presentation to seal the deal. In management's eyes, fit employees are better for the company because they can shoulder a bigger load.

FITNESS SEALS THE DEAL

During that period when I was traveling a lot but not exercising or eating well, I wasn't surprised that my weight increased and my fitness declined. I was surprised, however, by how much difficulty I had performing my job duties at a consistently high level. I was traveling to meet with coaching clients and prospective investors, and exhaustion was dragging me down. I lost some of my enthusiasm, quick wit, and ability to make rapid decisions. To get the job done and come home with money in the bank, I had to exude confidence and sell people on my ideas for modernizing the coaching industry, but I didn't have it, and I knew it. I got my company off the ground, but the process made me realize I had to realign my priorities and schedule to ensure that I had enough time to exercise.

The Carmichael Performance Program is designed specifically for people with full-time careers. This isn't a watered-down pro athlete program or one targeted to the extremists who get up at 2:00 a.m. to run on treadmills. It's designed for overworked and overcommitted professionals just like you.

CONSISTENCY IS KING

Time you can control is the key to a consistent exercise program because it helps you establish a routine. You already have some routines in your life, and building some of them around exercise ensures that the time doesn't get siphoned off for other activities or, worse yet, wasted altogether.

The Carmichael Performance Program works equally well for exercising anytime. People have long looked for the time of day that corresponds to the greatest fat-burning or muscle-building capability, but the reality is that consistency matters more. Working out at a time that fits seamlessly into your lifestyle increases the likelihood that you'll make exercise a permanent priority. In contrast, when exercise sessions don't fit into your lifestyle, it's nearly impossible to stay on a program.

You'll need to tweak your nutrition program if you are exercising before or after work. The overall amount of food you eat during the day will be roughly the same, but it's important to make minor adjustments to when and what you eat so you have the energy you need for high-quality workouts and the fuel you need for optimal recovery.

Exercising Before Work

Many busy professionals have more control over their time in the morning, before the day gets complicated by either planned or unexpected events. And what many people value most from a morning workout is the fact that they accomplished something at the beginning of the day. Some days may be stellar and others seem to unravel before your eyes, but at least your workout's in the bag, checked off the list, a mark in the win column.

One of my clients, Jim, runs a successful software development firm and is the perfect example of someone who benefits from working out in the morning. By nature he's an early riser, and he values watching the news. He set up a television in a spare room so he can catch the early reports while riding a stationary bicycle. When he wakes up, he eats a small snack—typically, a PowerBar and some juice—while he prepares lunches for his elementary school–aged son and daughter. He has time to fit in a 45-minute workout, shower, and dress before his kids meet the school bus and his wife heads off to work. In the evening, he reads with the children while his wife gets out for the run she enjoys. Exercising before work gives Jim a productive start to his day, fits well into family routines, and allows him to separate his workday from his home life.

Yet there was a time when Jim struggled to stick with his morning workout routine because he read somewhere that he would burn more fat by exercising on an empty stomach. He knows better now, but thousands of other morning exercisers believe that myth and continue to struggle through ineffective workouts because of a simple lack of fuel.

When you get up, it's likely been 10 to 12 hours since you last ate. During sleep, your body is busy burning calories to keep you alive, as well as to build and repair muscle as a result of your training. At the same time, your brain feeds off the carbohydrate stores in your liver. By the time you wake up, those stores are about 80 percent depleted. Since carbohydrate from your liver is a major source of blood sugar and you will burn through the remaining 20 percent very rapidly once you start exercising, it's important to pay careful attention to energy early in the morning.

Jump-Start Your Morning

On the Carmichael Performance Program Meal Plan, the days begin, naturally, with breakfast. If you choose to work out in the morning, you should add a carbohydrate-rich preworkout snack to speed fresh energy into your bloodstream and supplement what's left of your energy stores. Otherwise, you'll struggle to fully engage in your training session. A simple snack containing about 50 grams of carbohydrate—perhaps a small bowl of oatmeal topped with blueberries and almonds or a PowerBar Nut Naturals bar and a glass of orange juice—will put enough carbohydrate into your bloodstream to ensure a powerful and productive morning workout. Follow these guidelines for eating before morning workouts.

- Keep the fat and protein content of your preworkout snack relatively low; carbohydrate is the nutrient you need in the morning. Fat and protein now will just add calories and may make you feel too full to exercise.
- Eat as soon as you get out of bed rather than just before starting to exercise. Since it takes about 10 to 15 minutes for the food to start entering your bloodstream, eating when you first get up gives you more time to digest the snack and have the fuel available for use.

- A cup of coffee is fine, but stick to a conventional mug (6 to 8 ounces); it's enough to give you the caffeine boost you're looking for.
- Aim to polish off 16 to 20 ounces of fluid, which can be a combination of water, coffee, and juice, between when you wake up and when you start exercising.
- Put your training clothes near your bed so you put them on first thing. If you throw on something else to walk around in because your training clothes are in the basement, it's too easy to just get comfortable with coffee and the paper and never get into your workout gear.
- Give yourself a few more minutes to warm up. Before getting to the meat of your workout, spend 10 to 15 minutes burning off the morning haze by running or riding at a moderate pace or going through some strength-training movements without added resistance.

If you're not a morning person, getting out of bed is an unpleasant experience, and there will be mornings when your grumpier side tells you to screw the workout and stay under the covers. This is where a good, loud alarm clock comes in handy, especially one you can't reach from the bed. The upside is that once you experience the satisfaction that comes from completing the day's workout before most people get out of bed, the 15-second struggle to extricate yourself from the covers will seem inconsequential.

Make the Most of Your Workout Time

All right, so you hauled your rear end out of bed, got right into your workout clothes, and grabbed an energizing snack. Congratulations—you're on your way to a great day. Some mornings, however, you're going to run a little short on time. You can blame the alarm or a slow coffee machine, but the inescapable truth is that you may not always have time to complete every exercise in the daily program. So what do you keep and what do you cut?

During the endurance-conditioning portions of the workouts in all three periods, the intervals are more important than the total endurance time. If you're limited on time, warm up for 5 to 10 minutes, do the intervals (with the appropriate recovery times), and then move on. The intervals apply the most stimulus to your aerobic engine and burn the most calories per minute.

If you're running short on strength-training time, focus on the biggest muscle groups. Keep the squats, lunges, overhead lifts, and core work, which recruit more muscles to do the work, but skip the triceps extensions and dips. All of the movements in the program are valuable, but when push comes to shove and you have to get to work, something has to give.

Finally, if you're faced with the decision of doing either endurance training or resistance training (which includes the agility portion of the program), shorten or eliminate the aerobic part and get the resistance work done. It's not that resistance training is more important than aerobic training but, rather, that you have more opportunities to incorporate some aerobic exercise into your day. For instance, you could walk or run the stairs at work or take a brisk walk for a couple of blocks to get coffee. It's more difficult to fit the resistance portion into your normal daily activities.

Eat a Power-Packed Recovery Breakfast

Don't make the mistake of rushing out the door without eating; within hours, you'll pay dearly for such a transgression against your fuel stores as your system grinds to a halt. And please don't mistake your small preworkout snack for a meal big enough to get you through both training and morning meetings. That was just a splash-and-dash stop to put enough sugar in your blood and brain to get a great workout out of the way. You're running on empty again, my friend, and it's time to fuel up for recovery and energy for the day.

Carbohydrate and protein play key roles in postworkout recovery. Though you don't burn much protein during exercise, and we all have plenty of fat to use for fuel, we burn through carbohydrates quickly. If you don't start replenishing immediately after exercising, your energy levels will fall dramatically in the middle of the morning. You will put yourself in a situation where you are constantly trying to catch up on carbohydrate intake, which will have you on an energy roller-coaster ride for the rest of the day.

For a successful transition from training to your workday, make sure to:

- Include a high-energy carbohydrate source in your postworkout recovery breakfast, such as oatmeal, whole grain bread or cereal, potatoes, low-fat dairy products (and you thought they were just for protein), or fruit.
- Consume protein in the form of one to three eggs, low-fat yogurt, or cottage cheese. Meats typically eaten at breakfast—ham, sausage, bacon—are typically very high in fat and sodium.
- Increase the Meal Plan portion sizes by about 100 calories. This means an additional ½ to 1 cup of cereal or oatmeal, a handful of nuts or berries, half a cup of yogurt, two slices of whole grain bread, or an additional piece of fruit.
- Drink plenty of fluids. The more rapidly you replenish the fluids you lost through sweat, the better off you will be. Coffee counts, but you should also have 16 to 20 ounces of water, milk, or juice.

Energy for the Rest of the Day

After breakfast, the only other change you want to make is to reduce the size of the afternoon snack in the Meal Plan. Essentially, part of it moved to the preworkout snack. Since you're not exercising after work, the midafternoon snack can be smaller, but don't cut it out completely; you need it to boost your energy levels for the last few hours of the workday and get you through to dinner.

Exercising after Work

I have a friend in Denver named Taylor who works in finance; because the New York Stock Exchange operates on eastern time and he lives in mountain time, he has to be in the office before 5:30 in the morning. There's no way he's going to get up even earlier to exercise, and there's no reason to. While he has to go to work at an obscenely early hour, he's out of the office by 4:00 p.m. Even in winter, he can get in a bike ride or run while the sun's still out.

A whole host of careers call for predawn starts and early afternoon departures, and many other people find they simply get more work done early in the morning. For example, executives who spend several hours each day in meetings may prefer to devote the early morning hours to important projects, before the phone starts ringing and people start popping in for "just a quick second."

I have found that people who have trouble putting an end to their workday often benefit from working out in the afternoon or evening. It gives their workday a tangible stopping point and provides the opportunity to vent workday frustrations through sweat instead of taking them home. By focusing on training—even for as few as 15 to 20 minutes—you can make a clean break from the day's earlier stresses. If you still have to tackle work that you brought home, at least you'll have done something good for your fitness and health, and you'll have a clear mind to help you concentrate.

Boost Your Workout Performance with the Midafternoon Snack

If you exercise in the afternoon or evening, your midafternoon snack is critical. In addition to keeping your energy level steady through the afternoon so you remain productive and alert, it is your source of preworkout fuel. In the Meal Plan, the afternoon snack is about 200 to 300 calories, and it's best to eat it 1 to 1½ hours before your training session. This is a time when energy bars can make a solid contribution to your performance. They are a concentrated source of carbohydrate, featuring a mix of quickly available simple sugars and longer-burning complex carbs. Most bars, including PowerBar Performance and Harvest bars, include a little fiber and protein to moderately prolong digestion, which keeps your energy levels from spiking and then crashing.

Fluid is another big consideration for this p.m. snack. You want to consume about 20 ounces (one standard-size water bottle) in the 60 to 90 minutes before you begin exercising, in order to ensure you're properly hydrated before you start sweating. Water, juice, or tea are great choices. A cup of coffee or tea or a double shot of espresso is fine, but follow it up with the full water bottle.

Here are some good afternoon preworkout snacks (more are listed in the Meal Plan).

- 6 ounces low-fat or fat-free yogurt mixed with a sliced banana and 1 tablespoon flaxseed
- A whole wheat bagel with 2 tablespoons fruit spread, peanut butter, or both
- A 12-ounce fruit smoothie (2 cups fruit of choice, 6 ounces fat-free yogurt, ¼ cup fat-free milk, 1 tablespoon wheat germ, and ice)
- An energy bar, such PowerBar Harvest or Nut Naturals
- ½ cup hummus with mixed vegetables (carrots, peppers, celery, etc.)
- Snack Mix with Toasted Pecans, Sesame Seeds, Flaxseeds, and Dried Fruit (page 254)
- A 6-ounce container of fat-free or low-fat yogurt, ¾ cup whole grain cereal, 1 tablespoon chopped walnuts, and 1 sliced banana
- Two handfuls of almonds (about 50 total) and a cup of fruit juice or coffee

Replenish with Dinner for a Productive Night's Sleep

When you sit down to dinner within an hour or two after training, it's important to make sure you're eating foods that will speed your recovery and provide the energy necessary for overnight growth. You see, you don't become more fit when you're training but, rather, when you're resting and sleeping. Exercise merely provides the stimulus for your body to respond to.

Human growth hormone (HGH) is one of the major hormones that control muscle development, fat mobilization (burning or moving fat from your belly to areas where it's used to repair and build cell walls), and even positive changes in bone and connective tissue. Your body secretes HGH from the pituitary gland in several distinct pulses each day, the largest of which occurs about an hour after you reach a state of deep sleep. Exercise also increases the total daily amount of HGH your body produces. When you exercise in the evening, it's important to make sure your dinner provides the best fuels to take full advantage of that positive double-whammy effect. To maximize recovery, take advantage of elevated HGH production, and replenish energy stores for tomorrow, follow these dinnertime guidelines.

- Eat dinner within 60 minutes of exercising or as soon after that as possible, when your muscles are the most willing to accept carbohydrate and protein. These nutrients have to file through specific gates to get into muscle cells, and immediately after exercise, there are simply more gates open. When you wait to eat, the doors gradually close, which means it takes longer for you to recover and increases the chances your body may resort to storing excess energy as fat.
- Eat more protein. Most of the adaptations that occur while you're sleeping, including the building and maintaining of muscles, tendons, ligaments, and blood vessels, involve protein. Focus on high-quality, complete protein sources, including salmon, tuna, white-meat chicken and turkey, lean cuts of red meat (sirloin, eye of round steak), tofu, and low-fat dairy products.
- Choose complex carbs over simple sugars. Purely for energy replenishment, simple and complex carbohydrates work equally well. But for maximizing the impact of HGH, you want to lean toward complex carbohydrates from whole grains, brown rice, buckwheat, barley, sweet potatoes, and squash. Eating simple sugars, like those in cookies and soda, during this time frame will put a serious dent in the amount of HGH secreted and thwart your body's efforts to adapt to your training.

Lest you think you'll be at some kind of disadvantage if you work out in the morning instead of after work, let me reiterate that exercise is most effective when it fits seamlessly into your lifestyle. If you're stressed out because trying to work out in the evening disrupts your family or work schedule, you're not going to stick with the program long enough for any difference between morning and evening training to emerge. Likewise, sleep quality plays a larger role in recovery and muscle building overnight than when you worked out. If working out in the morning means your evening progresses more smoothly and you go to bed relaxed, you'll benefit more than if you're keyed up and toss and turn.

TAKING THE CARMICHAEL PERFORMANCE PROGRAM ON THE ROAD: FITNESS

I spend more time in airports than I want to, and there was a time when all that travel worked against me. It started soon after I founded Carmichael Training Systems in 1999. All of a sudden, the number of trips increased and completely disrupted my exercise and nutrition habits. After just 2 months, my weight shot up by 7 pounds and my fitness level declined dramatically.

The problem I had is the same one many busy professionals encounter: When you leave home, you shift into a separate set of routines that you developed specifically for successful business travel, and these routines rarely include time for exercise or any consideration for nutrition. You schedule every minute from sunup to sundown with meetings, phone calls, and sometimes corporate entertainment events. You eat on the run, in hotel rooms, or with clients, and convenience and corporate expectations to maximize your productivity on the road govern your choices more than sound nutrition does.

This is why it's so important to incorporate exercise into your itinerary. The most successful business travelers keep their daily schedules as consistent as possible, whether at home or in a foreign country. This means waking up and going to bed at similar times, exercising at a similar intensity and time of day (if possible), and maintaining similar eating habits. And increased strength helps you shoulder heavy bags from the faraway parking space to the ticket counter. There have been times when my fitness meant the difference between getting to a flight on time and spending the night in the airport.

Most people I encounter are willing to exercise away from home; they just aren't sure how to do it. Both the fitness and nutrition portions of the Carmichael Performance Program easily accommodate travel. Use the following guidelines to stick with the program during your next trip, but please understand that there is no reason to obsess about your daily exercises or nutrition. Changes in your body happen gradually and gather momentum. If you have to skip a day or even a few days of exercise or your eating habits are less than perfect, you'll be fine. You won't lose the positive adaptations your body has made over the past several weeks.

Fitness Momentum

IT TAKES A LOT OF ENERGY TO get a heavy SUV to move, but once it's rolling, it's just as difficult to stop. Fitness operates in much the same way.

The changes that occur in your body as a result of exercise take place gradually. Once you have put the wheels of health and fitness into motion with consistent exercise, you can coast through a day or a few days of complete rest before you begin to lose any of the gains you've made. I refer to this as fitness momentum, and moderately fit people can be sedentary for about 7 days before lab testing shows any decline in physical markers of fitness. More fit individuals may have up to 10 days of momentum, whereas beginners tend to have about 4 or 5 days before they start to feel any impact from not training.

Don't stress about a missed day; just try to get back on the program as rapidly as possible. The same goes for nutrition. Don't starve yourself the day after overindulging at a party in some misguided effort to make up for your dietary transgression.

Schedule Exercise Time

It is all too easy to let time get away from you during business trips. For many of us, the goal is to pack in as many meetings and calls as possible. I've worked with many executives who fill every minute of their days on the road because somewhere inside they believe everyone back home thinks they are goofing off. To prove them wrong, these guys work to justify every minute away from the office. When they're not traveling, they consistently set aside a small portion of the day for exercise and experience the positive impact that has on productivity and energy levels.

There's no reason an exercise routine should be put on hold during a business trip. Put exercise time into your travel schedule—and I mean literally write it into your travel itinerary—by utilizing the strategies below.

- Take an earlier flight so you get to your destination with enough time to get to the hotel and complete a 30- to 45-minute workout. If you arrive too late in the evening, you'll be too tired to work out or too concerned about the following day's meeting.
- Schedule a later return flight so you can finish your meeting, go back to the hotel, and get a good workout in before you have to catch your plane.
- Allow 1 to 2 hours between your last meeting and dinner so you can work out, shower, dress, and get to the restaurant. And don't be shy about your intentions. Remember, top managers perceive a commitment to activities outside of work as a sign that you lead a successful, balanced, and stable life. Let that perception work in your favor.

Work Fitness into Your Business Meetings

Successful business meetings have as much to do with the personal relationships between company representatives as they do with the numbers or contracts. You're probably not the only one who sometimes struggles to fit physical activity into your workday; if the person you're meeting also exercises, use that common ground as a way of enhancing your business relationship.

- **Schedule a postmeeting run with the client.** This provides a benefit besides exercise: It gives the client another reason to remember you and your proposal because there was something significantly different about the interaction.
- **Use fitness to break the ice.** Ask about using their company's fitness facilities or for directions to a nearby park where their people like to run. Besides giving you practical information for your own exercise plan, this builds additional context in your business relationship; you're not just another talking suit.

Pack Some Gear

This program was designed to be portable, which is why there are no large pieces of fitness equipment required. Throwing a few extra items of clothing into your bag is quick and easy and increases your options.

- **A pair of running shoes:** Replace your shoes every 4 months or 400 miles, whichever comes first. When the cushioning wears down, you are at increased risk for injuries.
- **Loose-fitting clothing:** Choose moisture-wicking fabrics like Coolmax. Cotton is not a good choice because it holds on to moisture instead of helping it evaporate to regulate your body temperature. At the very least, you'll want a T-shirt, running shorts, and Coolmax athletic socks. If it's cold where you're going, pack thin gloves, a warm beanie cap, and a long-sleeved shirt and running pants.
- **A swimsuit:** Though the fitness program doesn't include specific swimming workouts, a swimsuit takes up no space in your bag and provides you with one more option. Plus, you'll be able to use the hotel's hot tub to relax after a hard day.
- **A rain jacket:** A lightweight wind- and water-resistant jacket virtually guarantees that you can at least get outdoors for a run or walk.

The Hotel Room Workout

Every hotel says it has a fitness center, but that's the same as saying that every hotel has beds. A hotel might throw a treadmill and a weight-lifting machine into an oversize broom closet, hang a few mirrors on the wall, and call it a fitness center. Whether your hotel is well equipped or not, your room alone is enough to accomplish a thorough workout.

The Hotel Room Workout takes just 15 to 20 minutes from start to finish, and you can do it in your underwear. It's best done as a circuit, so start with the first exercise and proceed through the last, taking 45 seconds of rest between each exercise. Then take 2 minutes of rest and repeat the circuit. If you have the time and fitness to complete a third circuit, that's great, but start out with two and work up to completing three.

Bed pushups: Place your feet on the bed and your hands shoulder-width apart on the floor. Complete 10 to 12 pushups from this position.

Runway broad jumps: Find the longest clear stretch in the room–typically, from the door to the opposite wall. Start at one end and leap your way to the other side. Turn around and continue until you have completed 10 jumps. Remember to leap forward, not up, so you don't hit the ceiling.

Chair dips: Place your hands behind you on the edge of a chair (or the bed if there's no chair). Lower your body until your elbows are at about 90-degree angles (your upper arms will be about parallel to the ground). Press back up until your arms are nearly straight, but don't lock your elbows. Repeat 10 to 12 times.

Combination lunges: Using the runway area of the room, start at one end and cross the room with forward lunges. When you get to the other wall, turn 90 degrees and do side lunges, leading with your right leg, back to where you started. Cross the room a third time with forward lunges, and then turn 90 degrees and do side lunges back again, leading with your left leg.

Windshield wipers: Lie down between the two double beds with your waist aligned with the ends of the beds (so your legs can be lowered to the right and left, all the way to the floor). Point your legs up to the ceiling, with your arms straight out to your sides, palms down (and hope you don't find anything nasty under the beds). Lower your legs to the right, stopping within 1 to 2 inches of the floor. Raise them back to center and down to the left. Lower to each side 10 to 15 times.

Plyometric wall pushes: Stand about a foot more than arm's length away from a wall. Then, with your arms outstretched in front of you, fall forward and catch yourself on the wall. Bend your arms until your nose comes within 2 inches of the wall, pause, and then push explosively with your arms and chest to return to a standing position. Repeat 10 to 12 times.

Phone book crunches: Lie on your back with your knees bent and feet flat on the floor. Extend your arms straight along the floor above your head, grasping the sides of a phone book with your hands. Keep your arms straight and raise your shoulders off the ground as you lift the phone book off the ground. Be sure to use your abdominal muscles for the crunch; don't just use your shoulders to lift the phone book. Repeat 12 to 15 times.

Travel with Resistance

Rubber exercise bands won't take up much space in your bag, and they're a great way to add resistance exercises to the body-weight exercises in the Hotel Room Workout.

Overhead presses: Stand on the band with your feet shoulder-width apart and your hands at your sides, holding on to the band's handles. Curl your arms up so your hands are level with your shoulders, then turn your palms so they face forward and the band is behind your elbows. Keeping your torso tight, lift both arms straight up toward the ceiling; pause, then lower to shoulder height. Repeat 10 to 12 times, recover for 45 seconds, and repeat.

Kneeling crunches: Anchor the band to the top of a closed door. Kneel with your back to the door with your butt on your heels, grasping the handles of the band just above your head. In a smooth motion, crunch forward with your abdominal muscles, pulling your head and the band toward the floor. Pause and return to the starting position. Repeat 10 to 12 times, recover for 45 seconds, and repeat.

Abdominal twists: Anchor the band at shoulder level in a closed door. Stand perpendicular to the door, holding the handles close to your body at chest level. Keeping your feet planted and knees slightly bent, twist your upper body away from the door, using your abdominal muscles. Return to the starting position. Repeat 10 to 12 times, recover for 45 seconds, and repeat. Switch sides so you're facing the other direction, then repeat the sequence.

TAKING THE CARMICHAEL PERFORMANCE PROGRAM ON THE ROAD: NUTRITION

A few years ago, I called my wife from my hotel room in New York City following a business dinner with a few of my board members. She asked about the restaurant, and as

Navigating through Restaurant Menus

WHEN YOU'RE ABLE TO MAKE choices beyond the drive-thrus, you have more beneficial options available to you—but you still have to make smart choices.

Asian: Good Asian restaurants use a wide variety of great ingredients, including chicken, broccoli, beef, peppers, and rice. But if the restaurant has "buffet" in its name, move on. When you find a better place, request brown rice (if they have it), and skip the egg rolls and the battered and fried dishes. A stir-fry can be a good thing; deep-fried wontons can't. Sushi is an excellent option, as are noodle bowls at Thai and Vietnamese restaurants. They are typically made with rice noodles, a light broth, and plenty of vegetables.

Italian: Olives, both whole and as oil, are good for you. So is pasta and even pizza, because these dishes are packed with clean-burning carbohydrate and additional vegetables and lean meats. Skip cream sauces, cheese-stuffed manicotti, sausage, and pepperoni. Watch portions, too; many Italian restaurants bring you a plate that should feed three people.

Mexican: Find a place that doesn't cook beans and tortillas in lard, and try not to fill up on chips—but if you do eat them, at least have the salsa, too. Tomatoes are a great source of lycopene, an antioxidant that may help prevent cancer and preserve eyesight. Pile on the vegetables, skip the deep-fried options, and go light on the sour cream.

I told her about the meal, I realized I'd eaten an enormous amount of food. After talking with her and saying good night to our kids, I hung up the phone and made some quick calculations. Sure enough, I'd had about twice the number of calories I typically eat for dinner, and quite a bit more fat, as well.

Eating on the road can be a challenge, but there are some simple ways to focus on whole foods and keep your calories under control.

Tips for Business Dinners

A lot of critical business deals have been sealed over tables laden with rich food and expensive wine, and that's not going to change. But by making some simple choices, you can have an energizing and healthy meal without being that strange guy having a dinner salad and water. These guidelines will help you make lower-calorie and lower-fat choices without taking all the fun out of eating out on the company account.

CHOOSE THESE	PASS ON THESE	REASON
Red wine	Beer	Though wine has more calories than beer, it is served in smaller glasses. A 4 oz glass of wine has 85–95 calories, whereas a pint of beer contains 150–200 calories.
Spinach salad with vinaigrette on the side	Iceberg lettuce wedge with blue cheese dressing	Spinach is more nutrient dense, vinaigrette contains heart-healthy unsaturated fat from olive oil, and "on the side" means you control how much you use.
Roasted, broiled, or grilled salmon	Breaded and fried fish	Both may be rich in heart-healthy omega-3 and omega-6 fatty acids, but breading and frying add a ton of bad fat calories.
Sirloin, tenderloin, or round steak	Filet mignon or bacon-wrapped porterhouse	Steaks with "loin" or "round" in the name are lean choices. Filet mignon is packed with saturated fat.
Baked potato with 1–2 pats butter	Mashed potatoes, french fries, or "loaded" baked potato	Restaurants make mashed potatoes with a lot of cream and butter. Fries and loaded baked potatoes are also packed with fat calories.
Espresso	Cappuccino	If you're ending the meal with coffee, cappuccino is a higher-calorie option than espresso.

If you're not with a wine-drinking crowd and beer is the drink of choice, consider having it with your meal instead of before. The same is true for soft drinks. If one is sitting in front of you as you're waiting for your food, you're likely to drink a full 16- to 20-ounce glass before your meal and then get another. This adds up to 200 empty calories to your meal.

Above all, don't hesitate to leave food on the plate. Steak houses often serve excessively large cuts of meat (12- to 20-ounce steaks), although you'd feel full after half that size. Restaurant portions have grown out of control over the past decade—you're served at least twice the amount of food you would normally eat at home. Eat according to your hunger and habits, not according to the amount of food placed in front of you.

Eating on the Road

Whether you are literally driving or traveling by some other means, there's a slew of smart options for eating well on the road. It would be easy to recommend swearing off fast food altogether, but there are times in small towns and airports and late at night when that's the only option. So which fast-food joint do you pull into, and what do you order?

You can count on Subway and Wendy's for some decent choices that are rich in nutrients and low in fat and calories. (McDonald's is getting there, with more health-conscious options—and no more supersizing of meals.) The following tables list good choices at Wendy's and Subway, as well as one example of a bad choice—to put your good choices in perspective.

GOOD CHOICES AT WENDY'S

FOOD	CALORIES	FAT (G)	PERCENT CALORIES FROM FAT	SATURATED FAT (G)
Baked Potato (plain)	270	0	0	0
Sour Cream and Chives Potato	320	4	11	2.5
Mandarin Oranges Cup	80	0	0	0
Mandarin Chicken Salad (no noodles, almonds, or dressing)	170	2	9	0.5
Chili (small)	220	6	27	2.5
Ultimate Chicken Grill Sandwich	360	7	17	1.5
Frosty (Junior)	160	4	22	
How Bad Can You Get at Wendy's?				
Big Bacon Classic	580	29	45	12

GOOD CHOICES AT SUBWAY

FOOD	CALORIES	FAT (G)	PERCENT CALORIES FROM FAT	SATURATED FAT (G)
Grilled Chicken and Baby Spinach Salad with fat-free Italian dressing	175	3	15	1
Oven Roasted Chicken Breast on Wheat (6 in)	330	5	15	1.5
Roast Beef (6 in)	290	5	15	2
Turkey Breast (6 in)	280	4.5	14	1.5
Veggie Delite (6 in)	230	3		1
Subway Club (6 in)	320	6	17	2
How Bad Can You Get at Subway?				
Meatball Marinara (6 in)	560	24	39	11

There are decent choices at other fast-food restaurants as well. In the tables below, I've listed gold, silver, and bronze choices for each restaurant, along with a lead choice to put your better choices in perspective.

BURGER KING		CALORIES	TOTAL FAT (G)	PERCENT CALORIES FROM FAT	SATURATED FAT (G)
Gold	BK Veggie Burger (no mayo)	340	8	21	1
Silver	TenderGrill Chicken Sandwich with Honey Mustard	450	10	20	2
Bronze	TenderGrill Garden Salad with ½ packet Ken's Border Ranch dressing	285	12	38	4
Lead	Burger King Quad Stacker	1,000	68	61	30

MCDONALD'S		CALORIES	TOTAL FAT (G)	PERCENT CALORIES FROM FAT	SATURATED FAT (G)
Gold	Premium Grilled Chicken Classic	420	9	19	2
Silver	Caesar Salad with Grilled Chicken (with low-fat balsamic dressing)	260	9	31	3
Bronze	Hamburger	260	9	31	3.5
Lead	Double Quarter Pounder with Cheese	730	40	49	12

TACO BELL		CALORIES	TOTAL FAT (G)	PERCENT CALORIES FROM FAT	SATURATED FAT (G)
Gold	Fresco Style Ranchero Chicken Soft Taco	170	4	21	1
Silver	Fresco Style Burrito Supreme—Chicken	350	8	20	2
Bronze	Bean Burrito	370	10	24	3.5
Lead	Fiesta Taco Salad	860	46	48	14

Just as with the fitness program, it's important to maintain perspective. There will be days dominated by fast food, airplane snacks, and buffalo wings. You will consume 3 days' worth of calories in one sitting sometime in the next 6 months, and I absolutely guarantee you'll eat an entire bag of something (potato chips, tortilla chips, pretzels, cookies, etc.) while watching television or a movie. These things happen, and the important thing is not to let occasional missteps derail you.

Forget the guilt over an overindulgent business dinner or a 2-day fast-food-laden road trip, and don't double up on exercise in an attempt to reverse the impact those calories may have on your system. You'll just prolong the period that you're completely off your routine, which makes it less likely that you'll ever get back to it. Reestablish your healthy eating routine as rapidly as possible, and move forward. Minor transgressions are no reason to cut calories as some demented means of penitence. You need the energy to stick with the fitness program so you can maintain a high energy level to meet the demands of your job and family life.

CHAPTER 5

Fortify Your Relationships

THE PEOPLE AROUND US PROVIDE CONTEXT FOR OUR LIVES, AND WE ALL HAVE VALUABLE personal relationships that influence the decisions we make. Similarly, the people around you will play a critical role in your success with the Carmichael Performance Program, and that success will in turn enhance your relationships. When you're more fit and eating foods that deliver cleaner energy without all the waste, you'll have more energy to be focused and engaged at home instead of lethargic and cranky. During the program, you will make more progress more quickly if your spouse or partner is involved, as well. In a sense, this person is on the program, too, even if that simply means being supportive of the changes in your nutrition choices and allocation of time. The reality is that you won't stick with a long-term change that moves you farther away from the person you care about most, so I'm going to show you how this program can bring you and your partner closer.

As your body and energy levels change over the 9 weeks of this program, the people around you are going to notice. They can't miss the fact that you're losing a significant amount of weight and probably wearing some new clothes. They're certainly going to see a more energetic change in your demeanor, too.

Exercise and good nutrition lift your mood, so your sense of humor will reemerge. This program's carbohydrate-rich eating plan keeps serotonin levels high enough to preserve your good mood, whereas too little carbohydrate can suppress it.

GET PEOPLE INVOLVED

The changes you're making in your life will positively affect the important relationships in your life. But in the beginning, you may disrupt some long-established patterns. To help smooth the transition, it's important to involve these people in the changes you are making so they understand the rationale behind your new choices.

Create Training Triads

A twosome may be nice, but a threesome is always better. Even a highly motivated professional benefits from training partners because they make sure you show up when you say you will. Having someone waiting for you at the park or gym will make you shut down the computer or drag your butt out of bed.

Optimal performance often depends on involving the perfect number of people. In business, a team that's too big struggles to make decisions, and a team that's too small doesn't have the brainpower to cover all the angles. Likewise, having too many people in a training group makes it too complicated to coordinate schedules and preferences.

I've found that three is the perfect number for a reliable training group. A triad ensures that if one person can't make it, there's still one person depending on you to show up. The importance of a third person is evident even in an environment as pro-exercise as the Carmichael Training Systems office. We have a company policy that encourages people to add an hour to their lunch break up to three times each week for workouts. Even with that kind of flexibility, I noticed that several employees were struggling to stick with their fitness programs, so I encouraged them to establish training triads.

Jim Rutberg, Brian Delong, and Jason Koop are an example of one such triad. Jim is director of publishing, Brian is director of IT, and Jason is director of external coaches (coaches who work outside of our Colorado Springs office). Jim kept signing up for endurance events, like the Leadville 100 mountain-bike race, and then completing a fraction of the necessary training. When just he and Jason were training partners, Jim had only a little more success sticking with his training. When Jason had to miss a session, Jim missed it, too. Adding Brian to the team created a training triad, and the chances that at least two people were available for a session increased by 100 percent. In the winter and spring of 2006, Jim recorded more workout time than he had over the previous 2 years, and it showed in the faster paces he was able to maintain during training and in competitions.

Involve Your Family

You're more likely to make lasting changes to your dietary habits if your partner and family make similar changes. Since you live with and share a kitchen with these people, trying to maintain a nutrition program completely independent of theirs will doom your best intentions. It's not like you're asking your loved ones to sacrifice with this program. They don't have to suffer through months of cabbage soup or a prohibition on carbohydrates. This program is not about restriction and deprivation—it's about good nutrition and performance, and the foods and recipes that are helping you feel better and more energetic will have the same impact on them.

What's more, your children learn their eating habits from you. Whereas some children raid the cabinets for cookies, I have to stop my son from taking too many pieces of fruit from the bowl he sees his mother and me snacking from. There's no doubt that children enjoy sweets, but you can teach them to associate fruit with their cravings instead of candy.

The same is true with leisure activity. Children raised with active parents perceive exercise and outdoor activities as natural parts of the day. When they grow older and begin to look for activities to master, they gravitate to sports and outdoor hobbies. Improved health, fitness, coordination, balance, and physical development are just by-products of what they enjoy. You can also turn exercise into play. To children, many of the agility and plyometric workouts in the Carmichael Performance Program look like playground games. Go with that. Your workout may take a little longer, but who cares? You're spending meaningful time with your son or daughter, and you're getting the work done.

Getting the Kids Into It

ONE OF THE LEADING CONCERNS people have is that starting a new fitness program will just further reduce their time with their children. Some face additional pressure from spouses who see exercise as a luxury that shifts too much of the responsibility of watching the kids to them. These are legitimate concerns, but there are ways you can get your children, depending on their ages, involved in what you're doing.

UNCLUTTER YOUR LIFE

Clutter stifles performance, and many of the clients I work with come to me with highly cluttered lives full of people who serve no good purpose. I don't mean to be callous, but you have a finite number of hours in the day and a limited amount of energy to divide among them, and people who cost you energy and add nothing positive in return are simply dead weight. It's difficult and sometimes uncomfortable to realize that the time you're spending on a person is hurting you more than helping you, but it's a necessary part of reclaiming your time and energy.

Your partner and children are the most important people in your life. These relationships provide the most direct support; when they are strong, you can devote time and energy to being productive at work and in an exercise program. When they are strained, however, they become a source of additional stress. Instead of enhancing your ability to focus at work, your mind is occupied by strained relations at home. You get even less done during the day, which adds more stress and increases the likelihood that it will spill over into your home life.

Many people are afraid to clear away the clutter in their personal lives because they worry about confrontation and bad feelings, but you can simplify without publicly announcing that you're downsizing your circle of friends. You're not handing out pink

Boost Your Emotional Energy

EMOTIONAL ENERGY IS THE mental fuel that enables you to be enthusiastic about life. A common complaint among executives I work with is a disconnect between the obvious reasons they *should* be enjoying their lives and the reality of their exhaustion and indifference. Exhaustion is real, not imagined, and you cannot think your way out of it. When you're giving every bit of your brainpower to your business or constantly doing things for other people, you're burning emotional energy and failing to take time to replenish it.

In my work, I've found that there are three key steps to alleviating emotional exhaustion and boosting the emotional energy you need to rediscover your enthusiasm for life.

The first is to identify and distance yourself from those who suck energy out of every room they enter.

The second step is to carve out quiet time. Before you scoff and say you barely have time to blow your nose, I'm not talking about finding 4 hours a day to meditate. Quiet time can be the drive to work, a 15-minute walk with the dog, your workout, or sitting on your back porch with a glass of iced tea. It's not the amount of time but what you're doing—or not doing—that counts.

When you first start taking short breaks for yourself, they'll seem like a waste of time, but stick with it. After a few weeks, you'll be amazed by how refreshed you feel after consciously stopping the flood of ideas and obligations for just a few minutes. The most successful executives I know carve out at least 30 minutes for themselves each day.

The third step is to realize that energy spent worrying about circumstances beyond your control is energy you can't put toward enhancing your life and performance. If there's a chance your job might be outsourced or fall victim to downsizing, griping and wringing your hands won't help. The best thing you can do is put your energy toward doing your job well, maintaining contacts you might need later on, and saving money to help you get through the transition.

slips; you're simply evaluating the value of your time by asking, What value am I receiving in exchange for spending time on this person?

This is part of the way good athletes get ensnared by doping. When I was racing and throughout my career as a coach, there have been athletes who started their careers completely opposed to performance-enhancing drugs only to have their careers ended by drug use. In many cases, they got trapped because they continued relationships with athletes around them who were doping. Dopers are needy people; they need help getting their drugs and keeping their secrets. Clean athletes who help them end up spending more time and effort supporting unhealthy relationships and less time with the people who are committed to competing clean.

At the elite level, athletes are under tremendous pressure to succeed, and it's not really any different at high levels of corporate management. In either environment, the people surrounding you help guide your decisions, whether they're right or wrong. Sure, everyone encounters the occasional crisis of confidence, and setbacks are an inevitable part of progress in any career, but that's when your decisions about relationships can save or destroy you. If you spent time building relationships with supportive, optimistic, and resilient people, they will see you through your crisis. On the other hand, if you have distanced yourself from those people because you chose to support relationships with unscrupulous people who cheat and seek shortcuts, the cheaters are the only ones left to guide you. Ethical teams, both corporate and athletic, stay clean by surrounding themselves with supportive, honest people and refusing to support any team member who is making unethical decisions.

You need to be selective with your time so you can devote more of it to the people and efforts that enhance your life. Some people—usually the ones dragging you down—look at this as selfishness, and they're right. But they see selfishness as a bad thing; I view it as a virtue. Selfishness is simply the decision to act in your own self-interest, and if you don't, who will?

You control only a portion of the components that lead to your success or failure. You can't control the economy or the whims of your boss, and you can't orchestrate every aspect of your partner's and children's lives, but you can make sure your time is allocated to the people and tasks that return the greatest reward.

THE BEST SEX YOU'VE EVER HAD—AND MORE OF IT

To a young man, sex is performance, and that is an association we retain throughout our lives. When you were a teenager, losing your virginity was a sign of success. Maybe you reached that goal before some of the other guys and maybe you didn't, but you reached it. When you were single, you had to be successful in order to have sex. You used your skills and charm to meet a woman you desired, seduce her, and get her to desire you in return. There may have been a time when you did this purely for pleasure, and perhaps you still do, but it's also the process a man uses to find and fall in love with the woman who sets his world on fire.

Sex is success, and it always has been for both men and women. Yet even though sex helps us feel successful, many men and women in long-term, committed relationships have less sex than they used to, and the sex they do have is less passionate.

Some people assume this is the nature of the game. You're not kids anymore, so what does it matter that you're not pawing at each other all the time? You know you love each other, right? You know she still wants you—or do you? You can answer yes to these questions, but I'm going to tell you that without a healthy sex life, you're not living a high-performance life. Reawakening the passion is an important part of restoring your high-performance life. It's also a whole lot of fun.

How the Carmichael Performance Program Will Improve Your Sex Life

Stronger Abs Increase Stamina

A washboard stomach won't make your wife or girlfriend love you more, but stronger abs may very well make her enjoy having sex with you more. Most of the thrusting motion originates in your core muscles, and better conditioning leads to increased stamina, as well as greater opportunity for more imaginative positions. Specific exercises in the program that help in this department include reverse crunches, back extensions, and core bridges.

A Strong Body Increases Your Options

Remember the acrobatic sex of your youth? Well, during this 9-week program, you're gaining strength in your legs, arms, shoulders, chest, abs, and back and even working on balance. Think you can put all that to good use in the bedroom? Give it a try, but don't hurt yourself.

Lose Fat and Gain Inches

All right, you might not gain inches, but losing fat weight will effectively add some length to your manhood. Think of it this way: There's a portion of your manhood, near the base, that's hidden by a layer of fat. During the course of this program, that fat pad will get thinner, which means that while you're losing weight, you'll appear to be gaining a whole lot of something else.

Good Food Yields Great Erections

Maybe the heart-disease experts would have more success convincing men to cut back on saturated fat and cholesterol if they focused less on the heart and more on the penis.

Exercise and Weight Loss Boost Testosterone Levels

UNLESS YOU DO SOMETHING about it, testosterone levels begin to fall once you reach your midthirties. Testosterone is a muscle-building hormone that's also connected to your virility, but if you're not giving your body any reason to make more muscle or maintain what you have, there's no stimulus to keep your testosterone production from falling.

While there are blood tests to tell if you're running low on testosterone, a simple indication can be a lack of spontaneous morning erections. Testosterone levels are highest in the morning, so if you're never hard or amorous in the morning anymore, you may want to have your levels checked.

HOW THIS PROGRAM BOOSTS TESTOSTERONE LEVELS:

» **It contains enough fat.** Testosterone is produced from cholesterol, which your body naturally produces and you can get from animal foods. To optimize production, you need a reasonable amount of dietary fat and all the essential fatty acids your body can't produce. With roughly 20 percent of your calories coming from fat—including salmon, nuts, and seeds rich in omega-3 and omega-6 fatty acids—this program optimally supports your ability to produce testosterone.

» **It promotes moderate weight loss.** Crash dieting and drastic calorie restriction trick your body into believing that it's starving. Since reproduction is testosterone's primary job, and it's a waste of time and energy to reproduce when you're starving, testosterone levels fall. By focusing on the energy and nutrients you need to support your activity level, this program keeps your calorie level well above the starvation threshold while still promoting steady weight loss.

» **It provides enough protein.** Consuming sufficient protein to support muscle growth and repair is an important precursor to increasing testosterone production and release. If protein intake is too low, and your body has to burn it for energy instead of using it for repair and building, there's no reason to produce and release the anabolic (muscle building) hormone.

» **It includes resistance training.** Studies show that multijoint strength movements—like the squats, lunges, and plyometrics in this program—increase testosterone production more than isolated-muscle movements (biceps curls).

» **It gives you enough rest.** Insufficient rest can cause testosterone levels to plummet because your body can't keep up with the stress you're placing on it.

Fat and cholesterol have the same clogging effect on cardiac arteries and the blood vessels that give you a hard-on. If men know that more whole grains and less saturated fat can help them get hard and stay hard, you'll see some real changes in the way they eat.

Revive Your Sex Life

Now, to get down and dirty, here's what you need to do.

Look Beyond Your Own Hard-On

While you may feel your sex drive increase as you move through the Carmichael Performance Program, don't forget that there's another person involved. This is one of the areas where clients of mine have sometimes experienced difficulties. They regained their desire to have sex and met with unexpected resistance when they tried to act on that desire with a woman they had been virtually neglecting for years.

The problem was relatively simple: The men wanted to have sex, and their partners wanted to connect (and then have sex). If your sex life stalled months or even years ago, your most important task is to reconnect with your partner and restore or enhance her desire to make love with you. When you're disconnected and just going through the motions, your partner is likely to shift her focus to other relationships that offer the meaningful exchange of attention, affection, and communication you're not providing. If you're focused on the act or sensation of having sex but neglecting a deep interpersonal connection with your partner, you're not doing enough to stimulate her desire.

To have better sex more often, you need to look beyond what you want in the bedroom and make sure you're providing what your partner wants, both in and out of the sack. In other words, if you make the effort, your rewards will be heartfelt and plentiful.

Touch Her for No Reason

A mezuzah is a small ornament Jewish families place on their doorposts. It holds a small scroll that contains prayers for good fortune, and by touching it every time you enter the home, you are in essence blessing the family and their home. During a gathering at my parents' home, the conversation turned to one of my father's deceased colleagues from the hospital. He had died about a year earlier at age 83, after 56 years of marriage. At one point in the conversation, his widow looked at me and said, "I was his mezuzah, you know," as if she truly thought I would.

Unfortunately, I was completely unfamiliar with the reference, so I asked her to explain. She told me that for more than 50 years, her husband didn't pass her without touching or kissing her. Sometimes it was just a simple touch on the small of her back or a squeeze of her shoulder, other times it was a peck on the cheek or neck, but he was constantly touching her, his mezuzah. She said that sometimes it was incredibly annoying, but it also kept them connected through some rough periods of their lives, and she joked that it was probably the reason they had four children.

Touch is a critical part of maintaining and deepening your connection to your partner, and most times it has nothing to do with sex. You're simply keeping the lines of communication open and reminding your partner that he or she is the person you desire and that you are thinking about. You can't expect to go from two disconnected people who have barely communicated all day to passionate lovers simply because you climb into the same bed. The more you just pass each other in the hallways of your home, the closer you come to being roommates instead of partners.

Learn to Read

As the saying goes, it takes two to tango, so you need to keep your partner interested. Experts in the field of human sexuality agree that women appreciate partners who pick up on their verbal and nonverbal cues before and during sex. Figure out how to decipher those noises she keeps making, and she'll be more than happy to keep making them for you.

Take Your Love Life Out for a Walk

Take your sex life out of the bedroom. This doesn't mean you have to make love on the kitchen floor or against the washing machine, but it doesn't mean you shouldn't, either. The point is, you don't spend that much time in your bedroom, so if your sex life is completely confined to that space, you're going to have a tough time having more sex.

Your ability to show affection in public can also have a big impact on your love life. Walk arm in arm or hold hands. Guide your partner through doorways or crowds. Kiss your wife in the middle of the sidewalk at rush hour. Don't give her a peck on the cheek—hold her close and kiss her like you two are the only people on the street.

Confidence is sexy, and your confidence to publicly display your affection for your partner will most likely turn her on. The fact that you identify her as desirable in front of other people can also increase her confidence. Remember, everyone wants to be successful, and being desired is a form of success.

The Best Foods for Great Sex

Sometimes side effects turn out to be a lot more fun than a food or drug's original purpose. Viagra was originally developed to treat cardiovascular disease, until Pfizer started receiving reports that healthy test subjects were experiencing erections as a side effect. You can benefit from similar side effects from the foods you eat, but at a far lower price.

Erectile dysfunction is often a circulation problem. A hard erection results from heightened bloodflow into the penis. If your arteries are clogged with plaque from a diet high in saturated fat and cholesterol, your perpetual limpness may be due to the fact that you simply can't get enough blood into the vessels to stand at attention.

Replacing high-fat, high-sodium processed foods with whole foods, in conjunction with exercise, improves your cardiovascular health. Cleaning out the pipes, so to speak, not only reduces your chances of suffering a heart attack or stroke, but also increases the chances you'll be able to get, sustain, and use an erection whenever you feel like it instead of whenever you pop a pill.

The foods below are included in the Carmichael Performance Program because they provide nutrients that play critical roles in health, weight loss, muscle building, and brain function. As a bonus, some of the nutrients they carry help enhance circulation, which means they can help reduce your risks for erectile dysfunction.

- Whole grains: Fiber can help clean out plaque deposits.
- Blueberries, strawberries, raspberries, and blackberries: Studies show that these berries have an inhibitory effect on LDL cholesterol.
- Salmon, tuna, halibut, and mackerel: Omega-3 and omega-6 fatty acids naturally keep blood from coagulating and clotting. If your blood is flowing like sludge, it won't move very quickly through the small vessels in your penis.
- Flaxseeds and flaxseed oil: These are also rich in omega-3 and omega-6 fatty acids.
- Garlic and onions: Though the odor on your breath may scare your partner away, the chemicals responsible for the pungent smell may also help lower heart-disease risk.

Foods That Will Kill Your Sex Life

Greasy foods and a diet excessively high in sodium have been connected to a reduced libido; after eating them, you'd rather take a nap than frolic between the sheets. Stay away from foods like these when you want some action.

- Chicken-fried steak
- Fettuccine Alfredo
- Fast food—a double whammy from sodium and fat. Just watch *Super Size Me*, Morgan Spurlock's Oscar-nominated documentary about his 30-day fast-food-only diet.

CHAPTER 6

Supercharge Your Health

LANCE ARMSTRONG'S CAREER IS LARGELY REMEMBERED FOR HIS ACHIEVEMENTS AFTER cancer, but two of his most impressive achievements occurred at the 1996 Summer Olympics in Atlanta, where he finished 12th in the road race and sixth in the individual time trial. On the surface, those results seem to pale in comparison with winning the Tour de France seven times, but you have to remember, *Lance raced the Olympics with an advanced case of testicular cancer.* He beat more than a hundred of the best cyclists in the world while carrying tumors in his lungs, brain, abdomen, and testicle.

Prior to October 2, 1996, Lance didn't go to doctors very often, and, frankly, neither did I. We held the very typical male attitude that there's no reason to set foot in a doctor's office unless you're bleeding to death. All that changed for me with one phone call. Lance had cancer; a 25-year-old professional athlete with youth, good nutrition, and excellent fitness on his side had a disease that was most likely going to kill him. The incongruity of those facts made me suddenly feel extremely vulnerable. If Lance had been training so hard and performing so well *with* cancer, without knowing it was there, I wondered what might be wrong with me. What could be going on in my body without my knowledge?

Ever since 1996, I've been visiting the doctor's office at least once a year, not so much because I think I'm sick, but because if anything dangerous starts to develop, I want to know about it as soon as possible. Early detection reduces the severity and increases the odds of surviving almost any cancer. It also helps keep elevated blood pressure from developing into dangerous hypertension or minor blood sugar problems from blossoming into type 2 diabetes. Visiting your doctor more often and getting the right tests can save your life, but very few American men get even an ordinary physical on a regular basis.

Most people wait until things break before trying to fix them. We do it with our cars and appliances, sometimes even our marriages. However, with health, there seems to be a threshold that separates those who are generally healthy from those who are constantly ill. The higher above this threshold you stay through exercise and nutrition, meaningful relationships, constructive outlets for job stress, and medical screenings, the better off you'll be. When you're barely above the threshold, it takes only one serious illness or injury to start a cascade of events that lead to even greater health problems. Think of it in terms of debt: If you're barely able to pay your monthly bills, it takes just one little emergency to put you in debt for years. On the other hand, if you've been diligently putting money into savings, you can handle the occasional emergency and still stay in the black.

THE MEDICAL TESTS THAT CAN SAVE YOUR LIFE

According to an American Medical Association study, many men put off seeing a doctor because they are afraid, embarrassed, in denial about obvious health problems, or threatened by the idea that going to the doctor will be perceived as a sign of weakness. Yet men have 2.5 times as many heart attacks as women before the age of 65, and one in three strokes in the male population happens to someone under the age of 65. A heart attack or stroke is a terrible price to pay for being afraid or stubborn; do yourself a world of good and follow a schedule for preventive health screenings. While optimal nutrition and exercise plans like the Carmichael Performance Program can reduce your disease risks and add years to your life, they can't protect you from everything, especially diseases you're genetically predisposed to.

I compiled the following list of recommended medical tests from the published literature as well as interviews with physicians and researchers throughout the medical establishment. I recommend taking this list to your physician and discussing it with him or her. Your physician knows your medical history and is the most qualified person to put together a schedule that addresses your unique situation.

This list of health screenings is more extensive than some recommendations from the American College of Preventive Medicine (ACPM), the US Preventive Services Task Force (USPSTF), and the American Academy of Family Physicians (AAFP) because different tests may be appropriate for different people. I believe, however, that you should be familiar with all of these tests so you can have an educated conversation with your physician about your screening and treatment program.

It's also important to remember that reducing health-care costs is one of the primary driving forces behind the recommendations from organizations like the ACPM, USPSTF, and AAFP. While that's certainly a goal I support, I also believe that an accurate set of baseline health data is important for promoting optimal health and performance, both now and in the decades to come. Comprehensive screenings on a regular basis help define trends in your health status. Your total cholesterol may be below 240 right now, but it also may have increased by 10 percent each year for the past 2 years. That's an indication that changing your habits now may keep you from reaching the point where your cholesterol level becomes an issue that requires medication.

Don't be a slave to your insurance company. With health-care costs rising at a rapid and uncontrolled pace, medical insurance is an absolute necessity. However, it's important not to let the three-way tug-of-war between doctors, lawyers, and insurance companies shortchange the care you receive. Your insurance company may not be willing to pay for all the tests recommended in this book or at the frequency recommended here, and your doctor may initially be reluctant to perform uncovered tests. They're trying to save money at the wrong end of the system; the price of a test is minimal when compared with the cost of treating a patient with an advanced illness. A $200 test your insurance company won't cover could save you $10,000 in treatment and medication costs associated with a heart attack.

And if your doctor isn't interested in working with you to develop a comprehensive plan for preventing disease and keeping you healthy, look for a new doctor who will.

BLOOD PRESSURE TEST

TESTS FOR	Hypertension			
NORMAL VALUE	120/80 millimeters of mercury (mmHg)			
ABNORMAL VALUES	Prehypertension: 120–139/80–90 mmHg Stage 1 hypertension: 140–159/90–99 mmHg Stage 2 hypertension: 160+ mmHg/100+ mmHg			
WHERE TO GO	Primary care physician			
TYPE OF TEST	Part of regular physical exam			
FREQUENCY BY AGE GROUP	30–40	41–50	51–60	61+
	Annual	Annual	Annual	Annual

Hypertension not only increases your risk of a heart attack by making your heart work harder to pump blood through your body, it's also connected with erectile dysfunction. Studies have shown that roughly two-thirds of men with high blood pressure also suffer from some level of erectile dysfunction, and it was considered severe for about 45 percent of them. Hypertension can keep you from having an erection by preventing arteries that supply blood to the penis from expanding to allow enough blood to flow in. Pre- and stage 1 hypertension can often be brought back down to normal with a combination of exercise and nutrition like that recommended in the Carmichael Performance Program.

BONE DENSITY TEST

TESTS FOR	Osteoporosis risk			
NORMAL VALUE	T-score between 2.5 and -1; Z-score above -1.5			
ABNORMAL VALUES	T-score between -1 and -2.5: below-normal bone density and increased risk of osteoporosis; T-score below -2.5: osteoporosis; Z-score below -1.5: abnormally low bone mass for your peer group			
WHERE TO GO	Primary care physician, who will refer you to a radiologist			
TYPE OF TEST	Specific procedure			
FREQUENCY BY AGE GROUP	30–40	41–50	51–60	61+
	Once to establish baseline	Once for comparison to baseline	Every 5 years	Every 5 years

The health of your bones is directly connected to how long you live and the quality of life you enjoy. This test uses x-rays to compare the density of your bones with that of others. The T-score compares your bones to those of a healthy 30-year-old; a negative score means your bones are less dense than the standard, and the farther below zero the score, the worse it is. The Z-score compares your bone density to that expected of a person of your age and gender, and a very low Z-score can indicate that something other than age is causing you to lose bone mass.

DIGITAL RECTAL EXAM (DRE)

TESTS FOR	Abnormalities of the prostate, growths (cancer) in the rectum, hemorrhoids			
NORMAL VALUE	No abnormalities felt			
ABNORMAL VALUES	Enlarged or inflamed prostate gland, hardened area within prostate or rectum, abnormal growths			
WHERE TO GO	Primary care physician			
TYPE OF TEST	Can be part of regular office visit			
FREQUENCY BY AGE GROUP	30–40	41–50	51–60	61+
	Every 5 years	Every 2 years	Annual	Annual

A DRE may not be a pleasant experience, but it's certainly worth the alternative of possibly not finding prostate or colorectal cancer until it's advanced. How important is this test? Some reports suggest that the death rate from colon cancer could be cut by up to 50 percent if everyone over age 50 participated in regular screenings.

HIGH-SENSITIVITY C-REACTIVE PROTEIN TEST (HS-CRP)

TESTS FOR	Risk of sudden heart attack			
NORMAL VALUE	Levels below 1 mg/L associated with least risk; between 1 and 3 mg/L, average risk			
ABNORMAL VALUES	Above 3 mg/L			
WHERE TO GO	Primary care physician, who will refer you to a cardiologist			
TYPE OF TEST	Blood test; can be part of comprehensive blood screen			
FREQUENCY BY AGE GROUP	30–40	41–50	51–60	61+
	Once; twice if family history of heart attack or stroke	Every 2 years	Annual	Annual

C-reactive protein (CRP) is released by the liver in response to inflammation within the body, and recent studies show that high levels of CRP are a good indicator of increased risk of heart disease, as well as of the chance of sudden heart attack or stroke. An HS-CRP test can detect even small amounts of the substance in your blood, which gives your doctor a clearer picture of your heart-disease risk.

CHOLESTEROL AND TRIGLYCERIDES TEST

TESTS FOR	Risk of developing coronary artery disease, risk of suffering heart attack or stroke			
NORMAL AND ABNORMAL VALUES		Desirable (mg/dL)	Borderline (mg/dL)	Undesirable (mg/dL)
	Total cholesterol	< 200	200–239	240+
	HDL cholesterol	> 60	40–60	< 40
	LDL cholesterol	< 100	130–159	> 160
	Triglycerides	< 150	150–199	200–499+
WHERE TO GO	Primary care physician			
TYPE OF TEST	Blood test; can be part of comprehensive blood screen			
FREQUENCY BY AGE GROUP	30–40	41–50	51–60	61+
	Once; twice if family history of heart attack or stroke	Every 2 years	Annual	Annual

There's extensive information available about the good and evil sides of cholesterol, far too much to cover comprehensively here. The short story is that LDL cholesterol is bad for your health, and higher levels of this blockage-causing substance increase your risk for a heart attack or stroke. The good type of cholesterol, HDL, scours arteries and carries LDL cholesterol back to the liver to be broken down and reused for making hormones, including testosterone, and a variety of other beneficial purposes.

Exercise and nutrition significantly affect cholesterol levels, and the foods and workouts in this program meet medical experts' recommendations for increasing HDL levels and reducing LDL. Recent research shows that dietary changes have less impact on the amount of LDL cholesterol in the blood but can have more impact on HDL. Unsaturated fat from fish, avocados, nuts, and peanut butter can raise HDL without adding more LDL. Avoiding trans fatty acids is a good idea, as they can reduce HDL. Adding more soluble fiber, like the kind found in oatmeal, oats, fruits, vegetables, and legumes, is also good because it both lowers LDL and raises HDL.

COLONOSCOPY

TESTS FOR	Colorectal cancer, polyps, diverticulitis			
NORMAL VALUE	No growths, lesions, or pouches in colon walls			
ABNORMAL VALUES	Polyps, tumors, ulcers, pouches in colon walls (diverticulitis)			
WHERE TO GO	Primary care physician, who will refer you to a gastroenterologist			
TYPE OF TEST	Specific procedure in an outpatient facility			
FREQUENCY BY AGE GROUP	30–40	41–50	51–60	61+
	Not appli-cable	Once	Every 5–10 years; 3–5 years if increased risk factors and family history	Every 5–10 years; 3–5 years if increased risk factors and family history

This is a more comprehensive test than the DRE, but it's also much more complex, time-consuming, and expensive. Prepping for a colonoscopy typically involves a liquid diet for a day and powerful laxatives to empty the colon. A flexible instrument equipped with a camera is inserted into the rectum so the doctor can view the length of the colon, looking for abnormalities. The colonoscope also takes samples of suspicious tissue. Since you'll be given a sedative prior to the test, you'll need someone to take you home afterward. Your doctor may choose a less invasive screening for colorectal cancer if you are not at a particularly high risk. Sigmoidoscopy uses a flexible instrument to inspect the rectum and about a third of the colon but doesn't require extensive prep or sedation. A fecal occult blood test (FOBT) is recommended annually for men older than 50, as there is a correlation between gastrointestinal bleeding and colorectal cancer.

ELECTROCARDIOGRAM (ECG OR EKG)

TESTS FOR	Abnormal electrical activity in the heart			
NORMAL VALUE	Regular heartbeat; normal readings on all parts of signal tracing			
ABNORMAL VALUES	Irregular heartbeat or abnormalities on signal tracing			
WHERE TO GO	Primary care physician			
TYPE OF TEST	Specific procedure during office visit			
FREQUENCY BY AGE GROUP	30–40	41–50	51–60	61+
	Prior to beginning exercise program if family history of sudden heart attack	Prior to beginning exercise program if family history of sudden heart attack	Recom-mended prior to beginning exercise program	Recommended prior to beginning exercise program

An electric current keeps your heart beating from the time you're in the womb until the day you die, and an ECG lets your doctor determine whether your heart is operating normally or if an electrical problem is causing an irregular heartbeat. This test is often skipped for sedentary individuals because other tests, including cholesterol and blood pressure screenings, provide an indication of heart-disease risk. However, some irregularities show up only at higher exertion levels, so strenuous exercisers may benefit from a stress test that monitors the electrical activity at increasing exercise intensities. Abnormalities that affect heart function can occur across the full spectrum of fitness, weight, and health, so this test is just as important for fit and active individuals as it is for those who are unfit and looking to become more physically active.

SKIN CANCER EXAM

TESTS FOR	Early signs of skin cancer			
NORMAL VALUE	No new moles or skin lesions; no changes in diameter, shape, color, or thickness of existing moles			
ABNORMAL VALUES	Asymmetry between the two halves, irregularities in the borders, uneven pigmentation, or growth of a mole; any mole bigger than 0.2 in. (6 mm) in diameter.			
WHERE TO GO	Dermatologist			
TYPE OF TEST	Specific procedure during office visit			
FREQUENCY BY AGE GROUP	30–40	41–50	51–60	61+
	Monthly self-exam	Every 5 years	Every 2 years	Annually

See "Skin Cancer Kills One American Every Hour."

TESTICULAR SELF-EXAM

TESTS FOR	Testicular cancer, varicocele (varicose vein in the scrotum)			
NORMAL VALUE	Firm testicles, smooth surfaces			
ABNORMAL VALUES	Small, hard lump on testicle's surface; soft mass of thin tubes (often described as a "bag of worms" or "spaghetti")			
WHERE TO GO	Self-exam; if you find anything suspicious, see your primary care physician or urologist immediately			
TYPE OF TEST	Self-test			
FREQUENCY BY AGE GROUP	30–40	41–50	51–60	61+
	Monthly	Monthly	Monthly	Monthly

There are a lot of jokes about testicular self-exams, but there's more to this test than fondling yourself. Testicular cancer is the most common cancer for men between ages 20 and 35, but, when caught early, it is largely curable. In fact, the survival rate is 96 percent, but if you wait until you have a case as advanced as Lance Armstrong's was, you'll be given the same slim chances of survival he received. Lance beat cancer, but thousands of men who fight just as hard don't. And with the exception of skin cancer, it may be one of the most easily detected types of cancer. Simply roll each testicle between your thumb and fingers, feeling for lumps. It is normal to find a small, free-floating mass in the scrotum, not connected to either testicle. However, see a doctor immediately if either testicle significantly changes in size or you have pain in the scrotum or lower abdomen.

Skin Cancer Kills One American Every Hour

WHEN I RECENTLY SPOKE AT A conference at the Canyon Ranch resort in Tucson, I decided to take advantage of their excellent medical facilities and have a complete physical workup. One stop was with dermatologist Robert Friedman, MD. Statistics from the American Academy of Dermatology and the Skin Cancer Foundation state that one in five Americans will be diagnosed with skin cancer at some point, and more than one million new cases are diagnosed each year. Nationally, the majority of people with melanoma are men over age 50. Considering the countless hours I spent in the sun without sunscreen as a younger man, skin cancer is one of my primary health concerns. In fact, I've already had a handful of suspicious growths removed; fortunately, none turned out to be cancerous.

Dr. Friedman had some interesting new information about skin cancer prevention, including the fact that most people fail to apply enough sunscreen. It takes about 1 ounce (about a full shot glass) of sunscreen to adequately cover your exposed skin when you're wearing a T-shirt and shorts. Areas most commonly forgotten are the back of the neck, tops of ears, backs of hands, and tops of feet. Other recommendations include:

» Use sunscreen with a sun protection factor (SPF) of 30.

» Look for zinc oxide in the ingredients. For a product that dries clear (leaves no white residue), look for "micronized" or "microfine" zinc oxide on the label.

» Schedule outdoor activity for before 10 a.m. and after 2 p.m. to minimize exposure to the sun's most intense rays. However, you should still wear sunscreen during morning and afternoon outings and even if the sky is overcast.

» Protect yourself while skiing and boating. Highly reflective surfaces like snow and water increase the risk of sunburn. Your risks are even greater at high altitudes.

» Use artificial tanning products instead of tanning parlors if you want a bronzed look; the bulbs in booths emit the same potentially harmful rays as natural sunlight.

One other piece of skin care information I found very useful concerns moisturizers. Most of us get out of the shower and rub ourselves dry, but Dr. Friedman recommends patting skin partially dry and then applying moisturizer so it has more impact on the health and elasticity of your skin. Applying moisturizer to bone-dry skin is like pouring water on a sealed hardwood deck or picnic table; it doesn't penetrate the surface enough to make a difference.

Throw a tube of Brave Soldier Solar Shield sunscreen into your gym bag or golf bag, and take 30 seconds to apply moisturizer after a shower.

SUPPLEMENTATION FOR A LIFETIME OF PROTECTION

One of the reasons I've been so successful as a coach is that I believe in the additive effect of combining strategies that work. Good nutrition, strenuous exercise, meaningful relationships, and a fulfilling job all enhance your life individually, but their combined impact can elevate your performance and quality of life more than any one of them can alone. Some people find it antithetical to advocate a nutrient-dense nutrition program rich in whole foods in one breath and then promote vitamin and mineral supplementation in the next, but I believe those people like the idea of sitting on a high horse instead of pursuing high performance.

While they can be used to overcome deficiencies, supplements, including calcium and antioxidants, can also enhance performance or provide more protection than your diet normally would. However, you need to remember that the bottles of pills and powders cannot make up for poor nutrition. Think of supplementation as the Quikrete you use to patch your driveway; it works best for relatively small holes. You can reinforce your nutrition program with supplements, but it's not a good idea to make them the core of the plan.

Calcium

Why take it: To preserve bone density and prevent fractures

How to take it: 500-milligram doses twice a day for optimal absorption

Daily recommendation (including from food): 1,000 to 1,500 milligrams

Daily upper limit (including from food): 2,000 milligrams

Best nonfood source: Chelated calcium carbonate (with food) and calcium citrate (anytime)

Best taken with: Vitamin D

Nonfood sources to avoid: Coral calcium

Avoid taking with: Iron (calcium can reduce iron absorption)

From a weight-loss perspective, calcium from low-fat dairy products is the most effective form of the mineral, but few of us consume enough dairy (or green leafy vegetables) to meet the recommended 1,000 to 1,500 milligrams a day to best protect bone density.

Let's face it—the older you get, the less you want to break any bones. When you snapped your wrist as a young man, it healed quickly and ended up as good as new. But once you ease past about age 35, bones gradually take longer to heal and are less likely to regain their former strength. And it's not just your big bones, like your femurs and hips, that you have to worry about; the small bones in your spine lose calcium, too. Supplements may lessen or prevent the pain that comes with degenerating bones in your spine.

Yet the true long-term benefit of calcium is that it can keep you from breaking a hip when you're over 65. People who shatter a hip later in life face a long recovery process and a permanent reduction in mobility because of unsteadiness, lack of confidence, or limited strength and range of motion. Their activity levels fall dramatically, accelerating the progression of chronic diseases, reducing social interactions, and hastening decline. If you want to add years to your life—and, more important, quality years—bone up on calcium right now.

Vitamin D

Why take it: To preserve bone density, prevent fractures, and preserve muscle strength

How to take it: In a multivitamin formula that contains 400 IU of vitamin D per dose

Daily recommendation (including from food): 200 to 400 IU a day up to age 50, 400 to 600 IU a day from 50 to 70, and 600 IU a day after age 70

Daily upper limit (including from food): 2,000 IU

Best taken with: Calcium

Behind the Headlines

EARLY IN 2006, FINDINGS FROM the Women's Health Initiative (WHI) attracted national attention by casting doubt on long-standing recommendations for supplementing with calcium and vitamin D. As the media seized upon the news that researchers found lower-than-expected benefits from calcium and vitamin D supplementation, a lot of important information was lost in translation.

A closer look at the studies in question, as well as comments from the researchers themselves, indicates there were several problems that led to unexpected results. One example was that fewer than half the participants took the supplements as they were directed to; but among the participants who took at least 80 percent of their supplements, there was a 29 percent decrease in the risk of suffering a bone fracture.

The media fervor was heightened by the release of another round of studies that seemed to conflict with established recommendations about low-fat diets for cancer prevention and heart health and, to some extent, glucosamine and chondroitin supplementation for joint pain.

Ultimately, when the data from all of these studies were considered in context with the accumulated research over the past few decades, it was not significant enough to cause the medical establishment to change existing recommendations.

Vitamin D is largely unnoticed and ignored because calcium gets all the attention for preserving bone density. However, new research suggests that vitamin D plays a big role in bone health and preserving muscle strength as we get older. Some studies even suggest that 1,000 IU a day may reduce colon cancer risk by 50 percent and breast cancer risk by 30 percent.

Because vitamin D increases calcium absorption, it's best taken with dairy products (most of which are fortified with D) or other calcium-rich foods, such as fortified orange juice. Other than dairy, fish like salmon, mackerel, and tuna are about the only natural food sources that will get you anywhere close to meeting your daily requirement.

For a long time, vitamin D wasn't an issue because sunlight triggers our bodies to make all we need. However, with sun exposure linked to increased risk for skin cancer, most of us have wisely chosen to use more sunscreen and/or cover up more often. We also spend more time indoors now, often leaving for work early in the morning and returning after sunset.

Fish Oil

Why take it: To reduce heart attack and stroke risk, protect against Alzheimer's disease, and protect against inflammation

How to take it: Twice a day (half the daily dosage in the morning, half in the evening)

Daily recommendation (including from food): 750 to 1,500 milligrams

Daily upper limit (including from food): None (but don't get carried away)

Best nonfood source: EPA and DHA forms of omega-3

Nonfood sources to avoid: Cod liver oil (high calorie, too much vitamin A, fishy taste)

Eating 8 to 12 ounces of oily fish like salmon and tuna each week is a great way to reduce your heart-disease risk and protect the integrity of brain cells, but recent studies suggest that a daily intake of 750 to 1,500 mg of fish oil, whether from fish or capsules, can reduce sudden cardiac deaths by up to 45 percent and heart-disease deaths from all causes by up to 20 percent.

Research has been focusing on inflammation as a contributing cause of heart disease and sudden cardiac death. Current research suggests that inflammation increases the potential danger of plaques on artery walls by making them more likely to rupture, which can lead directly to a heart attack or stroke. The omega-3 and omega-6 fatty acids in fish oil have been shown to reduce inflammation, whether it's from a workout or a clogged artery.

Reduced heart-disease risk isn't the only reason to consume fish oil. Omega-3 and omega-6 fatty acids, the unsaturated fatty acids that help your heart and arteries so much, also preserve the integrity of cell membranes in brain cells, and healthier brain cells mean better short-term memory and mental performance. As an added long-term benefit, improving brain cell health and cranial bloodflow can help keep dementia at bay and delay the onset of memory loss.

Since it's impractical to eat fish every day and doing so could expose you to excessive amounts of mercury and other heavy metals, fish oil capsules can be a good source of this health-protecting fat. Be sure to purchase capsules that have been purified of mercury and other contaminants.

B-Complex Vitamin (including B_6, B_{12}, and folic acid)

Why take it: To reduce risks of heart attack, stroke, and colon cancer

How to take it: Typically 1 tablet per day, often dissolved under the tongue

Daily recommendation (including from food): See table on page 98

Daily upper limit (including from food): See table on page 98

B-complex vitamins are essential for optimizing the way your body breaks food down into energy, especially because they play roles in manufacturing more than 200 enzymes involved in the process of burning carbohydrate, protein, and fat. Three of the components of a B-complex supplement have even more impressive benefits for your health—they may reduce your chances of suffering a heart attack or stroke.

For men and women of all ages, folic acid provides protection against heart attack and stroke by reducing the amount of a particular amino acid, homocysteine, in the blood. Elevated levels of homocysteine can damage artery walls and make it easier for clots and fatty plaques to form. Like folic acid, vitamins B_6 and B_{12} have been shown to reduce homocysteine levels, and many supplements contain all three nutrients because they appear to act synergistically. Several studies have also associated a consistent intake of folic acid with a reduced risk for developing colon cancer in men and women. Women also see a reduction in breast cancer risk.

Folate and the other B vitamins are found in green vegetables (spinach, broccoli, turnip greens, and asparagus), citrus fruits, beans, and peas. Folic acid supplementation is especially important for people who don't regularly eat breakfast cereal, which (like breads, flour, and rice) is fortified with folic acid, the synthetic form of folate. Just one ¾-cup serving of most cereals provides the complete daily requirement (400 micrograms).

If you're already taking a daily multivitamin, look at the label before adding a B-complex supplement. While there's no danger associated with moderately exceeding the Recommended Dietary Allowance (RDA) for B vitamins, extraordinarily high amounts can lead to nerve damage, especially in the arms and legs. The following table shows the upper limits you should be aware of.

VITAMIN	RDA	AMOUNT TYPICALLY IN SUPPLEMENTS	UPPER LIMIT (INCLUDING FROM FOOD)
B_6	1.3–1.7 mg	50 mg	100 mg
B_{12}	2.4 mg	50 mg	None
Folic acid	400 mcg	400 mcg	1,000 mcg

Glucosamine and Chondroitin

Why take it: To protect joints from degenerating and reduce joint stiffness and pain

How to take it: Typically, three capsules a day

Daily recommendation: 1,500 milligrams of glucosamine sulfate and 1,200 milligrams of chondroitin sulfate

Best nonfood source: Glucosamine sulfate and chondroitin sulfate

Nonfood sources to avoid: Shark cartilage

Avoid taking with: Anticlotting medications (consult your physician)

As an active man in my midforties, I feel a big difference from taking glucosamine and chondroitin. I broke my femur right above the knee in a cross-country skiing accident in 1987 and endured four knee surgeries on my way back to professional cycling. About 10 years later, I started to be bothered by knee pain when walking and running. Taking glucosamine and chondroitin helped reduce the pain and allowed me to keep exercising. I take it to this day, especially after the pain returned following a period a few years ago when I stopped taking it. My physician has looked at my knees several times over the past decade and has been pleased to see little to no degradation in the cartilage.

Joint pain is often caused by worn or damaged cartilage, and glucosamine sulfate and chondroitin sulfate appear to provide an important building block that allows your body to better support the cartilage you still have. The research on whether this supplement, which has a very low risk of side effects, can reverse joint damage is inconclusive, and it's likely that it can't actually repair joints. Some studies have shown, however, that supplements can relieve pain to a degree similar to that of over-the-counter pain medications, especially for people with moderate to severe pain. People with minor joint pain may see little or no improvement from supplementation. There also appears to be a lot of personal variation; it works better for some people than others.

Low-Dose Aspirin

Why take it: To reduce risk of suffering a first heart attack or stroke

How to take it: One tablet, taken in the morning

Daily recommendation (including from food): 75 to 325 milligrams

Daily upper limit (including from food): No more than 4 grams a day or 900 milligrams in a 4-hour period

Best taken with: Food to avoid upset stomach

Avoid taking with: Alcohol

Salicylic acid, the active ingredient in aspirin, is one of the truly miraculous substances scientists have discovered to date. It is found naturally in berries like blueberries, raspberries, black currants, and strawberries, and a steady low-dosage supply of salicylic acid has been shown to act as a mild anticoagulant and reduce the chance of suffering a heart attack or stroke. These events occur when blockages, including blood clots, prevent oxygen-carrying blood from reaching heart and brain tissues, so keeping blood inside your arteries from clotting is important for keeping you alive.

Low-dose aspirin is available in most grocery stores and pharmacies and is a good preventive measure for men and women over age 40. People with a family history of heart disease may want to start taking it earlier. Consult your physician before taking aspirin on a long-term basis, however, because it might not be recommended if you have uncontrolled hypertension, stomach ulcers, or some other disorders. Be aware that one regular-strength tablet meant to relieve pain or fight fever contains 325 milligrams of salicylic acid—the upper limit recommended for a supplemental dose. Taking that dose long-term can have some side effects, including stomach problems, although most people experience few side effects from taking a low dose. Your physician can suggest the most appropriate dosage for you.

FITNESS AND NUTRITION CAN REDUCE DEPENDENCE ON MEDICATION

Gary's problems began when he stopped walking. Though the 56-year-old CPA and father of two grown children enjoyed hiking in the mountains outside of his home in Phoenix, it had been a long time since he hit the trails. His weight had ballooned to

245 pounds, and when he visited the doctor, complaining of fatigue, inability to sleep, and impaired vision, he was informed that he had atrial fibrillation, congestive heart failure, and type 2 diabetes.

A quick examination of Gary's diet and lifestyle revealed plenty of reasons for the diagnosis. He was overweight, inactive, and eating primarily takeout. His cholesterol level was 240, and his blood pressure was elevated but had not yet reached full-blown hypertension. Faced with the prospect of taking drugs to lower his cholesterol and blood pressure, as well as others to control diabetes, Gary did some calculations. As a CPA, he was curious about how much he was going to be paying for drugs and was shocked to determine that his annual cost would be $2,400!

He followed his doctor's recommendations and started taking medications, but he also took to heart the doctor's advice to change his exercise and eating habits. He threw himself back into hiking and set a goal of completing the 23.9-mile rim-to-rim hike through the Grand Canyon the following summer. At the same time, he cut back on the cholesterol in his diet and replaced it with high-fiber fruits and vegetables, unsaturated fats, fish, and whole grains.

Four months before his hike through the Grand Canyon, Gary's doctors took him off all the cholesterol and blood pressure drugs because he didn't need them anymore. All the symptoms of diabetes were gone, as well. After successfully completing the hike, he has maintained his healthy eating and exercise habits, and his hospital and clinic expenses declined from $1,100 in 2004 to just $85 in 2005; he estimates that over the past 2 years, he's saved close to $5,000 in total medical expenses.

Exercise and good nutrition can't keep you from ever having a medical problem, but they can minimize the severity of disease, enhance the healing process, minimize complications, and give you a better chance of making a complete recovery. A comprehensive fitness and nutrition program like the one in this book can reduce the chances you'll need to take or pay for drugs that lower cholesterol, control hypertension, or alleviate erectile dysfunction.

USE IT OR LOSE IT: PUTTING THE BRAKES ON ALZHEIMER'S

Alzheimer's disease and other causes of dementia were long seen as unfortunate but inevitable consequences of aging, but scientists now know that several factors, including nutrition and fitness, influence your risk of losing your memory. This is significant because delaying the onset of Alzheimer's for people particularly vulnerable to the disease can significantly increase the quality of life in a person's later years.

With the life expectancy of Americans rising, the risk of Alzheimer's is increasing. According to the Alzheimer's Association, the number of patients suffering from the disease has more than doubled since 1980, affecting one in 10 people over age 65 and nearly half of Americans over 85. The lifetime cost of caring for an individual with the disease is $174,000 and projected to rise.

Alzheimer's currently has no cure, nor is there a vaccine. Yet, there is compelling evidence that preserving the health of your heart and brain can delay the onset of memory loss and keep you mentally sharp well into your twilight years. Research compiled by medical experts and the Alzheimer's Association supports the following strategies for keeping your brain healthy for a lifetime.

Stay mentally active. Like other parts of your body, your brain responds to the level of stimulation you provide. A steady dose of challenging mental exercises over the course of a lifetime maintains the connections between brain cells and improves cognitive function. Research suggests that people who fall into cognitive ruts and stop learning because their careers and habits are no longer mentally stimulating face an increased risk of Alzheimer's or develop it earlier in life. However, a challenging career isn't always enough; intellectual pursuits outside of work, like taking adult education courses, playing a musical instrument, writing, and doing carpentry, provide mental stimulation and establish the groundwork for activities you can pursue into retirement.

Stay socially engaged. People who maintain a strong network of social connections enjoy a lower risk for developing dementia. Of course, it's even better if your social activities are also intellectually stimulating, which actually supports the idea of a weekly poker night! Poker, bridge, and other games that involve strategy and social interaction are great for keeping the brain in top shape. It remains to be seen whether multiplayer video games, the modern equivalent of bridge for seniors, have a protective influence on the brain, but they have been shown to have a positive impact on some areas of cognitive function, including reflexes, reaction time, and the ability to make quick decisions.

Stay fit. What's good for your heart is good for your brain. Increased bloodflow to the brain delivers more oxygen and nutrients that are necessary for keeping cells healthy. If the arteries in your brain are clogged, you not only increase your risk of suffering a stroke but accelerate the decline in cognitive function. New research from Thomas Jefferson University in Philadelphia found that patients with elevated heart disease risk factors also had elevated amounts of beta-amyloid, a sticky protein that collects in the brains of Alzheimer's patients and is thought to play a major role in the progression of the disease. These deposits can begin to develop decades before the onset of memory loss, suggesting that your fitness habits now can significantly affect your chances of developing Alzheimer's later.

Support your brain nutritionally. Maintaining brain health provides one more good reason to center your nutrition program on nutrient-dense whole foods. Beyond the impact on cardiovascular health, there is evidence that antioxidants from colorful fruits and vegetables may help protect brain cells from damage. Likewise, omega-3 fatty acids from fish like salmon and tuna have been shown to help preserve the long-term integrity of brain cells.

Protect your head. Head injuries increase your chances of developing Alzheimer's, so wear a helmet when you ride a bike, inline skate, rev up the motorcycle, or hit the slopes.

MALE DEPRESSION: DENIAL CAN KILL YOU

Mental health experts cite growing evidence that male depression affects millions of American men who are unwilling to seek treatment and that their reluctance to deal with psychological issues contributes to the onset of several diseases, including heart disease, diabetes, cancer, and Alzheimer's.

Men generally agree that there might be a problem but that it's someone else's problem, not theirs. In my experience, high-performance individuals are more vulnerable to male depression than anyone else. You know what it is to perform at a high level, and in a way, that means you can fall from a higher height. Optimism and resilience, attributes common to high-performance individuals, provide a buffer against depression, and so can fitness and nutrition.

Symptoms of male depression vary somewhat from those seen in women. Men are far less likely to break into sudden and uncontrollable crying fits but more likely to get frustrated or angry over trivial matters. Experts also list the following depression symptoms specific to men.

- Increase in risky behaviors—from driving recklessly to extramarital affairs
- Violent behavior—picking fights with strangers, road rage, flying into spontaneous rages
- Withdrawal from friends and family—finding excuses to avoid taking part in social gatherings
- Feelings of burnout—loss of interest in work, feeling empty and disengaged, lack of enthusiasm for activities you previously enjoyed, inability to rise to mounting challenges

I have seen firsthand the positive impact fitness and nutrition can have on mental performance, feelings of stress, and symptoms of depression in both executives and athletes. And let's face it; most of us aren't going to sit down with a therapist, no matter how much evidence there is to support the benefits. Mental health experts encourage exercise as part of the treatment for depression, as well as a way to keep life stresses from leading to depression in the first place. Physically, strenuous exercise leads to the release of endorphins and other mood-lifting hormones, but recent research indicates that this may play a relatively minor role in the link between exercise and depression. Neurotransmitters—special chemical messengers that pass information between nerve cells throughout the body and brain—may be more important. Exercise increases the production of many neurotransmitters and the sensitivity of the receptors they attach to, mimicking some of the effects of selective serotonin reuptake inhibitor (SSRI) antidepressant drugs.

Perhaps the most important impact of regular exercise on depression, at least for men, is the feeling of mastery and control it provides. Experts cite lack of control over decisions and responsibilities as a leading cause of depression in men, as well as unrelenting demands for performance coupled with underdeveloped coping strategies for relieving work- and family-related stress. Exercise, however, is something men can control. It's a productive and healthy way to relieve stress and burn off steam, and it provides opportunities for accomplishment and achievement. Improved physical performance and greater control over body weight have also been associated with increased feelings of self-worth and self-esteem. Beyond exercise, a balanced lifestyle can prevent or mitigate male depression in the following ways.

- Strengthening relationships: The people closest to you can provide the support you need to better handle the stresses of work and daily life. However, they can be supportive only if you spend time nurturing your relationships.
- Challenging yourself at work: When you're stuck in a rut, you can't utilize achievements to reinforce your sense of value. Keep challenging yourself, and if there's no more challenge to be had at your current workplace, look for a new job.

TO YOUR HEALTH, NOW AND IN THE DECADES TO COME

Your diet, the exercise you do, the level of challenge in your career, and the sincerity of your relationships have a big impact on how long you live and the quality of your years. During the 9 weeks you're on this program, you'll see some important changes in your body, and those changes will be reflected in better results in cholesterol and blood pressure screenings, as well as a lower body mass index (BMI) and a lower body fat percentage. However, 9 weeks is only enough to get you started in the long-term process of reducing your risks for heart disease, diabetes, cancer, and osteoporosis. Protecting your long-term health is a matter of making the habits and techniques you learn during this program part of your everyday lifestyle and continuing to make your health a top priority for life.

Workouts, Meal Plans, and Recipes

The 5 Essentials Challenge Team Story

HONDA HAS A TRADITION OF PUSHING THE ENVELOPE OF TECHNOLOGY IN SEARCH OF FASTER Formula 1 racecars and then incorporating those technological advancements into their family cars, like the Civic. Lance Armstrong and the other world-class athletes my coaches and I work with are our Formula 1 division, and what we learned about making them champions formed the blueprint for the 5 Essentials.

Even though I've successfully used the Carmichael Performance Program with athletes and nonathletes for years, I decided to prove its worth with concrete data before publishing this book. I asked for volunteers for a 9-week nutrition and fitness program, and our office was flooded with responses. My staff and I randomly selected 25 respondents to form the 5 Essentials Challenge Team and started them on their 9-week journey.

I wanted to show that the program in this book would produce positive results for everyday adults, so I purposely limited the interaction the Challenge Team had with my staff. We brought the participants into our office for initial testing (weight, blood pressure, skin-fold thickness, etc.), asked them to fill out a survey, and handed them a copy of the program and a bag of equipment that included a stability ball, resistance cords, a medicine ball, and six cones. They were instructed to read the program and follow it closely, then come back to the office after the 3rd and 6th weeks for testing and to fill out more surveys. Except for the testing and surveys, the Challenge Team put themselves through the program the same way any other reader would.

After 9 weeks, we ran the participants through a final set of tests and surveys and took their "after" photos. The results were outstanding. The men lost an average of 11 pounds, and one lost 27 pounds. The women in the group lost an average of 9 pounds, and some lost up to 23. We saw decreases of 5 to 6 inches in waist circumference, and plenty of people were shopping for new clothes.

Yet, even though participants lost weight, I was more impressed by the improvements we observed in their health profiles and physical performances. In the pursuit of a winning life, weight loss is only one component, so I looked further into the Challenge Team's results to find evidence that the program improved their long-term health and capacity for daily activities.

LOWER BLOOD PRESSURE

Average before: 136/91 mmHg (men) and 121/96 mmHg (women)

Average after: 127/86 (men) and 118/80 (women)

All-star performance: Lynn J. went from 150/108 down to 124/84!

At the beginning of the program, the average blood pressure for the men was 136/91 mmHg, which a cardiologist would classify as prehypertension, bordering on hypertension (120/80 is normal, 121–139/80–89 is considered prehypertension, and hypertension is 140–159/90–99). After 9 weeks, the average blood pressure for men had dropped to 127/86. Lynn J. started with a blood pressure of 150/108 and ended with 124/84—a blood pressure that led his doctor to say, "I don't know what you're doing, but don't stop!"

LOWER WAIST-TO-HIP RATIO (WHR) FROM REDUCED BELLY FAT

Average before: 0.96 (men) and 0.88 (women)

Average after: 0.94 (men) and 0.84 (women)

All-star performance: Mark P. started at 246 pounds with a WHR of 1.0 and dropped 27 pounds to 219 with a WHR of 0.93!

BEFORE&AFTER: Anita

The ratio between the distance around a person's hips and waist has proven to be an important marker for disease risk. Reducing belly fat brings this ratio down, ideally to 0.90 for men and 0.85 for women. The higher your WHR, the worse your risk, so even though Mark P. didn't reach 0.90, he brought it down a long way from 1.0 and significantly reduced his disease risk by dropping 5¼ inches from his belly.

"The knowledge I've gained will help me obtain my long-term goals of increasing my strength and leading a healthier lifestyle." –ANITA

OTHER HEALTH BENEFITS: IMPROVED BODY COMPOSITION, LOWERED CHOLESTEROL

Body composition provides a body fat percentage, or how much fat a person is carrying. Our before-and-after skinfold measurements indeed showed that participants lowered their body fat percentages during the 9-week program. John B. dropped his body fat percentage from a whopping 44 percent to 36 percent. Thirty-six percent fat is still high, but he's headed in the right direction, especially since he lost 17 pounds and his WHR dropped from 0.95 to 0.91.

Though we didn't draw blood samples from Challenge Team participants, many participants followed the medical testing advice in the Supercharge Your Health chapter and had physicals and routine bloodwork. On his end-of-program survey, Mark P. revealed that he stopped taking his cholesterol-lowering drug Vytorin. Mark later told me, "I thought my doctor was going to yell at me for going off my meds, but once he saw my blood tests, he didn't. In fact, he was very supportive once I told him about the program."

WHAT ABOUT PERFORMANCE?

You rarely hear people saying, "That guy over there—he's got awesome blood pressure." But people will comment on performance, and the 5 Essentials Challenge Team gave people plenty to talk about. In just 9 weeks, participants achieved the following improvements in physical performance:

175 percent more upper-body strength

100 percent more lower-body strength

22 percent greater endurance

26 percent greater flexibility

9 percent improved agility

BEFORE&AFTER: Gene

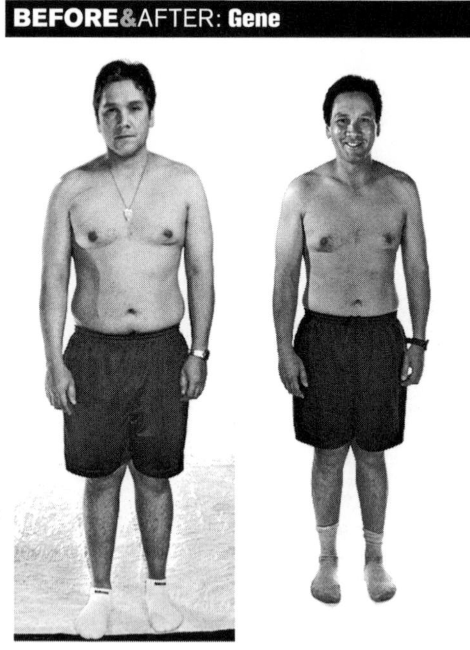

"My two sons noticed the changes in me. It's nice to hear them say, 'Dad, you're more fun now.'" –GENE S.

When I work with elite athletes, improvement of 1 to 2 percent in any aspect of performance is cause for celebration; 1 percent is the difference between riding away from your competition and watching them leave you behind. At the elite level, if you can get 1 percent better, you win championships, and when you take methods proven at the elite level and apply them to everyday adults, you get tremendous results.

IN THEIR OWN WORDS

Of course, as a coach, I know you can't measure everything by the numbers. People are capable of more than the sum of their statistics, so the final word on whether the program was a success had to come from the 5 Essentials Challenge Team themselves.

"In terms of mood, I feel better about myself. And in terms of my weight, I can see the difference, and so can others."
–JOHN B.

"This program was amazing! After four kids, it was hard to motivate myself to get back on track. With this program, it was easy! Now my kids even want to work out with me."
–JILL C.

"In the very first week my attitude changed. I had more energy, and I was happier, and my sex life is better, too!"
–CAROLINE T.

"I find it amazing to realize just how careless we had become with our day-to-day eating habits."
–ERIN E.

BEFORE&AFTER: Kevin

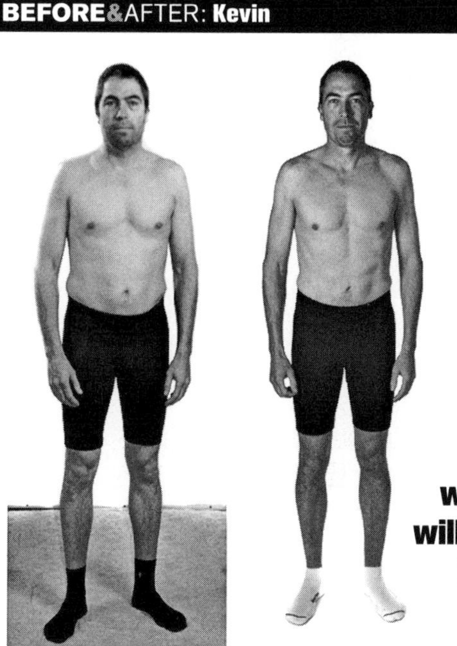

"I'm stunned by how well it worked after only 9 weeks, and it will have a permanent impact on my life, my wife's life, and the meals we feed our children." –KEVIN M.

"I was impressed with how easy it was to complete, compared with other programs I have done."

–MARK P.

"At 60 I had accepted a lower energy level and loss of mobility. The program has changed my outlook, and I no longer accept any restriction on activities or endurance."

–RICK S.

"Carmichael's program has been a lifesaver for me. I feel healthy for the first time in years."

–ANGELO C.

BEFORE&AFTER: Jesse

"I don't have afternoon slumps anymore, and I definitely feel more confident now that I've lost weight." –JESSE K.

Getting Started

NAVIGATING THROUGH PART II

IN THIS PART OF THE BOOK, YOU'LL FIND THE DAILY MEAL PLANS AND WORKOUTS THAT will transform your body, boost your energy level, and elevate your performance. To make the program easier to follow, I've arranged the fitness and nutrition programs in the following way.

The Programs

After the "Getting Started" sections, I've laid out the fitness program and meal plans by period. The workouts, meal plans, and recipes are grouped together so you can easily find your daily training and meal plan. For instance, for the Commit Period, you'll see:

"Week One Workouts" (page 126)

"Week One Shopping List" (page 128)

"Week One Meal Plan" (page 129)

Weeks Two and Three follow in the same format, followed by:

"Commit Period Recipes" (page 147)

The Workout Instructions

Step-by-step instructions for each exercise featured in the Carmichael Performance Program begin on page 267. I recommend reading these instructions before starting your workouts because properly completed exercises are more effective, and you'll be less likely to experience soreness or injury.

GETTING STARTED: FITNESS PROGRAM

The fitness portion of the Carmichael Performance Program is easy to begin, but before you jump in and start working out, I want you to take a few simple tests. We have to know how fit you are right now and use that information to guide your training. You'll retake these tests at the end of the program so you can measure exactly how far you have progressed.

The test is divided into four parts: walking, strength, agility, and flexibility, and you can do them all in about an hour. In addition to proper running shoes and clothes, you'll need a stopwatch and a 12-inch ruler. If you have a heart-rate monitor, I recommend using it for the walking portion of the test so you can calculate heart-rate training ranges for the aerobic portion of the program that follows. Record the results of each part of the test in the table in "Evaluating Your Carmichael Fitness Test Results" on page 115. You can revisit it at the end of the program to evaluate your progress.

Before you start the test, warm up by walking at a brisk pace for 10 to 15 minutes. By the time you're done, your heart and breathing rates should both be elevated, and you should be sweating lightly. If you choose to perform all three portions of the test back-to-back, use the following progression.

10- to 15-minute warmup

1-Mile Walk Test

5-Minute Easy Recovery

Reach Test

Agility Test

3- to 5-Minute Rest

Upper-Body Strength Test

3- to 5-Minute Rest

Lower-Body Strength Test

Carmichael Fitness Tests

Part 1: 1-Mile Walk Test

To test your aerobic endurance, I've chosen a 1-mile walk because it provides a very good measure of the exercise level you can sustain for a prolonged period of time. A running test wouldn't work as well because a lot of people simply cannot run for a full mile, and a shorter distance wouldn't provide good enough information about your *sustainable* intensity level. Using a scale of 1 to 10, where 1 is standing still and 10 is walking as fast as your legs will carry you without breaking into a run, I want you to walk at an effort level of 9 or 10. You'll be breathing hard, but you'll be able to sustain your pace for the full distance.

Complete the walking test at a standard high school or college running track, on a length of road or trail you know to be a mile, or on a treadmill. Record the time it takes to complete each quarter mile (or one lap of a track), the total time it takes to complete 1 mile, and your heart rate immediately following the end of the test. To measure your heart rate, find a pulse on the inside of the wrist or just under your jaw on the side of your neck. Count your pulse for 10 seconds and multiply that number by 6. Record your time and heart rate in the table on page 115. If you use a heart-rate monitor, record your average heart rate for the test.

Part 2: Flexibility—Reach Test

To measure flexibility, we are going to use a sit-and-reach test. Sit on the ground with your legs straight and your feet pressed flat against a wall. Hold a 12-inch ruler between your hands so that at least 6 inches of it extend beyond your fingertips. Keeping your knees straight but not locked, bend forward from your hips, reaching toward the wall. Allow the ruler to make contact with the wall and slide backward between your palms. Once you have stretched as far as you can without pain, read the measurement on the ruler closest to the tip of your middle finger. If you can touch the wall, note if you can touch it with your fingers, knuckles, or palms. Repeat the stretch two more times and record each measurement, then record the average number in the table.

Part 3: Agility Test

To measure agility, we are going to use a square drill to test your ability to quickly move forward, sideways, and backward. The exercise utilizes four cones (cans, shirts, Frisbees, or cups will work, too) positioned in a 5-by-5-foot square on a court or field. Assign each cone a number (1, 2, 3, and 4) in a counterclockwise order. Run around the outside of the square of cones three times without stopping, all while facing forward. Start on the outside of the square, to the right of cone 1, facing cone 2 (see page 305). Run to cone 2, immediately shuffle sideways to cone 3, then run backward to cone 4, and shuffle sideways back to cone 1. In the table, record the time it takes to complete three laps around the square, and also record your heart rate immediately upon completion of the test.

Part 4: Strength Test

UPPER-BODY STRENGTH

For this test, we're going to use the classic pushup. The goal is to complete as many as you can with good form and without stopping. Lie on your stomach with your palms on the ground a few inches more than shoulder-width apart and aligned with your chest. Flex your toes under your foot and push your body off the floor until your arms are fully extended, but don't lock your elbows. Lower your body while keeping your elbows close to your torso, until your chest almost touches the floor (see figures on pages 286–87). Throughout the exercise, your body should form a straight line from your head and shoulders through your hips and legs and all the way to your heels. Breathe in as you lower yourself, and exhale as you rise up. Repeat until you can't do any more, and record the number you completed in the table.

LOWER-BODY STRENGTH

To test lower-body strength, I want you to do as many squats as possible without stopping. See the examples on page 270 for help. Start from a standing position with your feet slightly more than shoulder-width apart, and extend your arms out in front of you to help with balance. Lower your hips, pushing your butt out as if you're going to sit down in a chair, while keeping your shoulders back and chest and head up. Stop when your thighs are parallel to the ground or your hips are at the same height as your knees, then rise back to standing by driving with your legs and hips. If you have trouble lowering your hips to knee height without shifting your weight onto the balls of your feet, just go as low as possible while keeping your weight centered through your heels. Record the total number you were able to complete in the table below.

Evaluating Your Carmichael Fitness Test Results

Now compare your test values to performance levels in the columns on the right side. You may find that you are good or excellent in some measures and poor in others, and that's okay. The goal of this program is to increase your performance in all of these measures, even the ones you are already excellent in. Though you'll make noticeable progress in these tests, you'll also register your improvement every day by feeling stronger, more powerful, more agile, lighter on your feet, and more stable.

TEST	YOUR RESULT BEFORE	YOUR RESULT AFTER	LEVEL OF PERFORMANCE		
			LOW	GOOD	EXCELLENT
1-Mile Walk (time/ heart rate)			24–30 min	17–20 min	14–15 min
Reach Test (inches)			> 3 inches	3 inches to fingertips	first knuckle to flat palm
Agility Test (time/ heart rate)			> 30 sec	20–30 sec	< 20 sec
Upper-body strength (number of reps)			0–10	Age: 30–39: 20–34	Age: 30–39: 40+
				Age: 40–49: 15–29	Age: 40–49: 35+
				Age: 50–59: 10–24	Age: 50–59: 30+
				Age: 60+: 8–19	Age: 60+: 25+
Lower-body strength (number of reps)			0–10	Age: 30–39: 35–50	Age: 30–39: 50+
				Age: 40–49: 30–40	Age: 40–49: 40+
				Age: 50–59: 10–25	Age: 50–59: 25+
				Age: 60+: 8–15	Age: 60+: 15+

Establishing Training Intensities

Determining Endurance Training Intensities

There are many ways to determine training intensities, ranging from simple descriptions of easy, medium, and hard to very sophisticated analyses of power output and blood lactate levels. For this program, I've streamlined the process to three intensities: range 1, recovery/comfortable—you can breathe comfortably; range 2, endurance/aerobic—breathing is labored but in control; and range 3, interval/strenuous—you're breathing rapidly and deeply.

Each of these ranges plays an important role in developing a stronger cardiovascular system. As you progress through the program, you will be spending more time in the endurance and interval ranges (2 and 3) because these intensities spark adaptation and growth. At the beginning, you may not be able to spend more than 5 minutes in the interval range, but by the end of the program, your body will have built more muscle and more furnaces to burn more energy to let you perform longer and stronger.

Over the years, I've found that people think about intensity in very different ways. The table on the next page features different options for determining how hard you're working out, so you can choose what works best for you. The walk/jog option is best for individuals who have been inactive for 6 months or more or have knee or hip issues that make running uncomfortable. The walk/run option is best for moderately to highly active people who can maintain a running pace for 2 to 5 minutes. You may start the program using the walk/jog option and progress to the walk/run option after the first few weeks.

The perceived exertion scale is a simple 1-to-10 scale where 1 is very easy and 10 is walking or running as fast as you can. You can also use a breathing scale, where you're breathing normally in range 1, your breathing is deep and labored but in control in range 2, and you're nearly panting in range 3. Similarly, the talking scale measures how easy or difficult it is to speak while exercising. In range 1, you can carry on a conversation; in range 2, you're breathing heavily enough that you have to use short sentences; and in range 3, you can say only a few words between breaths.

If you used a heart-rate monitor during the 1-Mile Walk Test, you can use the average heart rate from that effort to calculate heart-rate ranges (see table for the endurance exercise sessions in the Carmichael Performance Program). Your average heart rate from the mile walk provides us with your maximum sustainable heart rate. From there, we can pinpoint the heart-rate ranges as percentages of your maximum sustainable heart rate (which is your average heart rate from the mile walk) to put just the right amount of stress on your body to make it stronger.

SCALE	RANGE 1	RANGE 2	RANGE 3
Walk/jog option	Slow walking	Fast walking	Jogging
Walk/run option	Steady walking	Jogging	Running
Perceived exertion scale (1–10)	2–5	6–8	9–10
Breathing scale	Normal	Labored	Heavy, nearly panting
Talking scale	Speaking comfortably	Short sentences only	3 or 4 words at a time
Heart rate–based intensities	50–80%	81–95%	96–105%

Determining Resistance for Strength Workouts

Using the right amount of resistance or moving the right amount of weight is an important part of making progress in this program. If the resistance you use is too light, whether in the form of a medicine ball, elastic cords, or dumbbells, you won't apply enough stress to your muscles, and they won't have any reason to get stronger. If, on the other hand, the resistance is too high, you won't be able to complete the movements properly, and you'll increase the risk of an injury.

Still, it's wise to be conservative when you first start on the program, so start with what you know is a light amount of resistance. From there, find a level or weight where the last repetition of a set is strenuous but doable. If it's easy, increase the resistance for the next set. If you cannot complete the prescribed number of repetitions due to muscle fatigue or bad form, reduce the resistance on the next set.

The table on page 118 provides some guidelines for resistance, based on the results of your Carmichael Fitness Test. Use these as a starting point, and adjust accordingly as you move through the program.

TEST	NUMBER COMPLETED	MEDICINE BALL WEIGHT	RESISTANCE CORD COLOR	DUMBBELL WEIGHT
Lower-Body Strength Test	1–10	4 lb	Purple/Pink	Not applicable
	11–15	6 lb	Orange/Red	Not applicable
	20+	8 lb	Yellow/Green	Not applicable
Upper-Body Strength Test	1–10	8 lb	Orange/Red	20 lb
	11–15	8 lb	Red/Yellow	30 lb
	20+	>8 lb	Yellow/Green/ Blue	40–45 lb

Recommended Equipment List

All the workouts in the program can be completed with the equipment listed in the table below. Guidelines for selecting the right equipment for you follow.

FITNESS EQUIPMENT	ALTERNATIVE
Stability ball	Bench (for seated exercises) and broomstick (for overhead exercises)
Medicine balls (2)	Water-filled basketball or volleyball
Resistance cords	Dumbbells
Jump rope	None
Cones	Towels, T-shirts, cans
Masking tape	Chalk

The Right Size Stability Ball

Stability balls have gained popularity during the past 10 years because they add more intensity to core strength exercises while also supporting the body and reducing the chance for injury. In this program, I don't use the stability ball for plain abdominal crunches because I find that individuals unknowingly make crunches easier and less effective when they perform them on a ball. This program uses a stability ball for only two exercises: overhead squats and overhead lunges. If you don't have a stability ball or don't want to purchase one, you can use a medicine ball for these exercises instead.

Though any size stability ball will work for the overhead squats and lunges, it's important to get the right size for your body so you can use it for additional exercises, including knee tucks and hip lifts. Use the table below as a guideline. When you sit on the top of a fully inflated ball, you should be able to maintain a 90-degree bend in your knees and hips.

YOUR HEIGHT	RECOMMENDED STABILITY BALL SIZE
5 ft 4 in or shorter	45 cm (18 in)
Between 5 ft 5 in and 5 ft 7 in	55 cm (22 in)
Between 5 ft 8 in and 6 ft	65 cm (26 in)
Between 6 ft 1 in and 6 ft 4 in	75 cm (30 in)

The Right Medicine Balls

I have found that using two medicine balls allows you to complete this program most effectively. You'll want a relatively light ball (4 to 6 pounds) for the chest pass and overhead hand-to-hand pass and a heavier one (8 to 12 pounds) for the wall touch, reverse lunge, and solo twist. Using a heavier ball forces you to use your core, hips, and legs instead of relying on your arms and shoulders to move the weight. The lighter ball, however, allows for more control on overhead moves. You can increase intensity with a lighter ball by increasing the speed of the exercise. On the opposite page, there is also a recommendation for medicine ball selection based on your fitness test results.

The Right Resistance Cords

Resistance cords provide an alternative to a bunch of dumbbells piled in the corner of a room. The cords (also available as bands) are color coded for different resistance levels, and the resistance you feel increases the more you stretch any band or cord. Most people start out with purple, pink, and orange. I recommend getting cords with handles at both ends and an adapter that allows you to anchor the cord to a door or wall. Use the table on page 120 as a buyer's guide. On the opposite page, there is also a recommendation for cord selection based on your fitness test results. There are variations between colors and corresponding resistances among the various brands, but resistance generally increases in the following manner.

CORD COLOR	RELATIVE RESISTANCE (IN APPROX. LB) AT 24"
Purple	Very light (15)
Pink	Light (20)
Orange	Medium (30)
Red	Medium heavy (40)
Yellow	Heavy (45)
Green	Heavy (50)
Blue	Very heavy (55)
Black	Heaviest (60)

GETTING STARTED: NUTRITION PROGRAM

Getting started on the nutrition portion of the Carmichael Performance Program will probably require a look through your refrigerator and cabinets, followed by a trip to the grocery store. You should look at the "Week One Shopping List" so you can make sure to pick up all the foods and ingredients you'll need to follow the meal plan. You'll note that the weekly shopping lists feature irregular amounts of food. For instance, you might see "2 slices whole grain bread" or "¾ avocado," even though there's no way to purchase that exact amount in the grocery store. I've listed items this way so you can easily determine if you already have enough at home.

Adjusting the Meal Plans

The meal plans in the Carmichael Performance Program assume you're going to be exercising 3 to 5 hours per week. I understand that some people may choose to try the nutrition program without participating in the exercise program. Though I encourage you to utilize both programs simultaneously for maximum benefits, the nutrition plan alone can improve your health and help you drop pounds—but your weight loss will be slower and may plateau sooner than if you follow the exercise plan, too.

I also understand that some people may follow this nutrition program along with exercise programs they're already comfortable with. If you're regularly doing both aerobic and strength training and seeing progress, you're welcome to stick with it. However, people who go this route sometimes need to adjust the amount of food called for in this program due to differences between the energy demands of their exercise program and the Carmichael Performance Program. I suggest consulting "How Much Is

Enough?" on page 122 as a guide to consuming the right amount of food to fuel your workouts.

Finally, I realize there may be foods in the meal plan that you don't like. You're welcome to make substitutions, but I encourage you to choose something comparable in portion size and character. The meal plan is designed to provide you with the energy and variety of nutrients necessary for optimal health and performance. It would be best, for example, to swap out a meal that's heavy in vegetables with another meal that also contains vegetables to ensure that you get a similar amount of energy, vitamins, minerals, and other beneficial compounds.

I've successfully utilized meal plans like the one in this book with people of many different sizes and shapes. As you begin the program, it's important to realize that the amount of food is a starting point, and you may need to adjust portions up or down slightly to meet your personal needs. "How Much Is Enough?" can help you determine if the meal plan is providing too much or too little energy for you.

Using the "Quick Cuts" Boxes

Each day of the meal plans contains a "Quick Cuts" box that shows you how to quickly and easily slash that day's caloric intake by 200 to 300 calories. This reduction is sometimes necessary for people, particularly men and women under 160 pounds, to lose weight at a consistent and safe rate. You should use the "Quick Cuts" if:

- Weight loss is your primary goal, and you're losing less than 1 pound per week after following the standard plan for 1 to 2 weeks. If you are struggling to lose weight, please consult "How Much Is Enough?" for tips on determining when you're eating more than you need.
- You're not participating in the exercise portion of the program and only following the meal plans.
- Your starting weight is 160 pounds or less (applies to men and women).

Don't use the "Quick Cuts" if:

- You're losing 2 or more pounds a week on the standard meal plans. If you are losing more than 3 pounds a week, please consult "How Much Is Enough?" to determine if you should actually increase your intake.
- Fitness performance and strength gains are your primary goals for participating in the program.
- You're exercising more than is prescribed in the fitness program.
- Your starting weight is greater than 160 pounds.

How Much Is Enough?

In every discussion I have about this program, this is the point where the person across the desk or on the other end of the phone says, "Okay, I see what I'm supposed to eat and I understand why, but how much should I be eating?" Choosing nutrient-dense foods is only one part of an effective nutrition program. The amount you eat is the other critical component, and pinpointing your optimal caloric intake involves equal parts art and science.

Years ago, I focused heavily on the science side of the question, but after many long and drawn-out talks, several of which included drawings and equations and a lot of arrows, I realized that the numbers were really important only to me. People don't normally think about food in terms of numbers; it's a plate of lasagna or a piece of fruit. The decisions you make in the grocery store or restaurant aren't mathematical; they're based on color, taste, texture, smell, and what you like and don't like. So I stopped talking so much about numbers and focused instead on helping people make the best choices.

Portion Sizes

PORTION SIZES IN THE UNITED States are out of control and sometimes border on the ridiculous. In the meal plans, foods are listed in ounces, cups, tablespoons, etc. The trouble is, very few people know what 4 ounces of fish, a cup of rice, or 1 tablespoon of peanut butter looks like. Fortunately, there are several visual cues you can use to help guide your portion sizes. In the table opposite, you'll find a list of USDA serving sizes and the normal portions for active adults (that's you). Because you're consistently following an exercise program, your portions should be a little bigger than the normal sedentary American's.

QUICK GUIDE TO PORTION SIZES

» One teaspoon is about the same size as the end of your thumb.

» There are 3 teaspoons in 1 tablespoon, or three thumb-size portions.

» One cup of lettuce is about four large leaves.

» A 1-pint take-out Chinese food container holds 2 cups.

» A medium-size baked potato is about the size of a computer mouse.

» One ounce of cheese is about the size of your entire thumb.

» A standard pancake is about the size of a CD.

Counting calories is not a pathway to making a significant and lasting change in your life. It's too difficult, time-consuming, and discouraging. Most of all, counting calories forces you to remain an amateur and keeps you from mastering your eating habits. Think about the things you have mastered in your life. It took time to learn how to create complex marketing campaigns, analyze stock reports, or operate heavy machinery with expert precision, but now it's second nature. You don't need to carry an instruction manual with you to drive your car, and you shouldn't need an instruction manual at the dinner table, either.

Besides being a bad idea, calorie counting usually becomes a moot point as you make the shift to consuming a wider variety of whole foods. As natural foods replace sugary, fat-laden processed ones, your caloric intake typically drops. Whole foods, especially fruits, vegetables, and grains, are nutrient dense but generally not calorie dense. Their higher fiber and water content allows them to be filling and satisfying, as does the protein in low-fat dairy products, nuts, and lean meats and fish.

FOOD	USDA SERVING SIZE	LOOKS LIKE	ACTIVE ADULT'S PORTION	LOOKS LIKE
Cooked oatmeal, rice, pasta	½ c	An ice cream scoop	1 c	A man's fist
Dry cereal	1 c	1 large handful	1 c	2 medium handfuls
Breads	½ bagel 1 slice bread ½ pita pocket	Not applicable	1 bagel, 2 slices bread, or 1 pita pocket	Not applicable
Beans and legumes, including peas and lentils	½ c	An ice cream scoop	1 c	A man's fist
Nuts	⅓ c	1 handful	½ c	2 medium handfuls
Meats	3 oz	A deck of cards or palm of your hand	4 oz	A checkbook or your palm plus first knuckle of your fingers
Fruit	One medium 1 c cut up	A baseball or clenched fist	1 large, 2 medium fruits, or 1 c cut up	A hand clasped around a baseball
Peanut butter and similar foods	2 Tbsp	A golf or Ping-Pong ball	2–3 Tbsp	A racquetball

Since matching your caloric intake to your activity level is a main premise of this program, it's important to understand how you can tell, without having to count, if you're eating just enough, too few, or too many calories to meet your goals. The meal plan in this book is designed to produce weight loss of 1 to 2 pounds per week for a 170-pound man. For every 15 pounds above that, you may need to add about 300 calories per day. Likewise, you may need to reduce your intake by about 300 calories for every 15 pounds below 170.

Signs that you're eating the right amount of food:

- » You sit down for meals hungry but not so famished that you have trouble making decisions.
- » You begin workouts feeling mildly hungry, like you'd be ready for a snack if you weren't starting a training session.
- » You have the energy to complete high-quality training sessions. You may feel some fatigue in your muscles, but not in your entire body and soul.
- » When you're done eating, you feel like you could eat more but don't need to. You're satisfied, but you don't need to loosen your belt or take a nap.
- » Your mind is sharp and clear between meals; you don't experience headaches or periods of diminished capacity due to hunger.
- » You're losing weight slowly, about 1 to 2 pounds per week. Later in the program, your weight loss may slow even further as you lose fat but gain lean muscle mass.

Signs that you're eating too few calories:

- » All you can think about is food in the hour leading up to a meal or snack.
- » You can't make it through workouts without a marked decline in performance.
- » You feel like taking a nap in the middle of your training session.
- » You have trouble getting to sleep and trouble waking up.
- » You're losing weight rapidly, at a rate greater than 2 pounds per week. I know this sounds like a good problem to have, but in the long run, it prevents you from making progress in the fitness program, which increases the chances that weight will come back.
- » You're irritable (or more so than usual), cranky, and unusually impatient.
- » Between meals, you experience headaches or periods when it's difficult to think clearly and make quick decisions.
- » You feel light-headed or nauseous in the hour leading up to your next meal.

Signs that you're eating too many calories:

- Increased activity does not lead to weight loss (you're still consuming more than you're expending).
- You sit down to meals because it's the normal time to eat, not because you feel like you need to eat.
- When you're done eating, you feel stuffed. (The more you learn to read the signals your body sends, the less likely you are to overeat.)
- You start training sessions feeling full and sometimes feel bloated during strenuous workouts.

WEEK ONE WORKOUTS

DAY 1

AEROBIC WORKOUT
20 MINUTES

- 5 min Range 1
- 5 min Range 2
- 5 min Range 1
- 5 min Range 2

STRENGTH WORKOUT
20 MINUTES

REST PERIODS: 45 SECONDS BETWEEN EACH EXERCISE

- 10 body-weight squats *(page 270)*
- 15 pushups *(pages 286–87)*
- 10 back extensions *(page 268)*
- 10 body-weight squats
- 15 pushups
- 10 back extensions
- 8 squats with cord *(page 291)*
- 10 medicine ball pick-ups *(per side)* *(page 277)*
- 10 reverse crunches *(page 285)*
- 8 squats with cord
- 10 medicine ball pick-ups *(per side)*
- 10 reverse crunches

DAY 2

AEROBIC WORKOUT
20 MINUTES

- 5 min Range 1
- 5 min Range 2
- 5 min Range 1
- 5 min Range 2

AGILITY WORKOUT
15 MINUTES

REST PERIODS: 60 SECONDS BETWEEN EACH EXERCISE

- 15 sec double-leg line jump *(page 300)*
- 15 sec double-leg line jump
- 15 sec double-leg line jump
- 4 × 10-foot shuttle run *(page 296)*
- 4 × 10-foot shuttle run
- 4 × 10-foot shuttle run

DAY 3

AEROBIC: REST

AGILITY/STRENGTH: REST

DAY 4

AEROBIC WORKOUT
20 MINUTES

- 5 min Range 1
- 2 min Range 2
- 5 min Range 1
- 2 min Range 2
- 5 min Range 1
- 1 min Range 2

STRENGTH WORKOUT
20 MINUTES

REST PERIODS: 45 SECONDS BETWEEN EACH EXERCISE

- 10 body-weight squats
- 15 pushups
- 10 back extensions
- 10 body-weight squats
- 15 pushups
- 10 back extensions
- 8 squats with cord
- 10 medicine ball pick-ups *(per side)*
- 10 reverse crunches
- 8 squats with cord
- 10 medicine ball pick-ups *(per side)*
- 10 reverse crunches

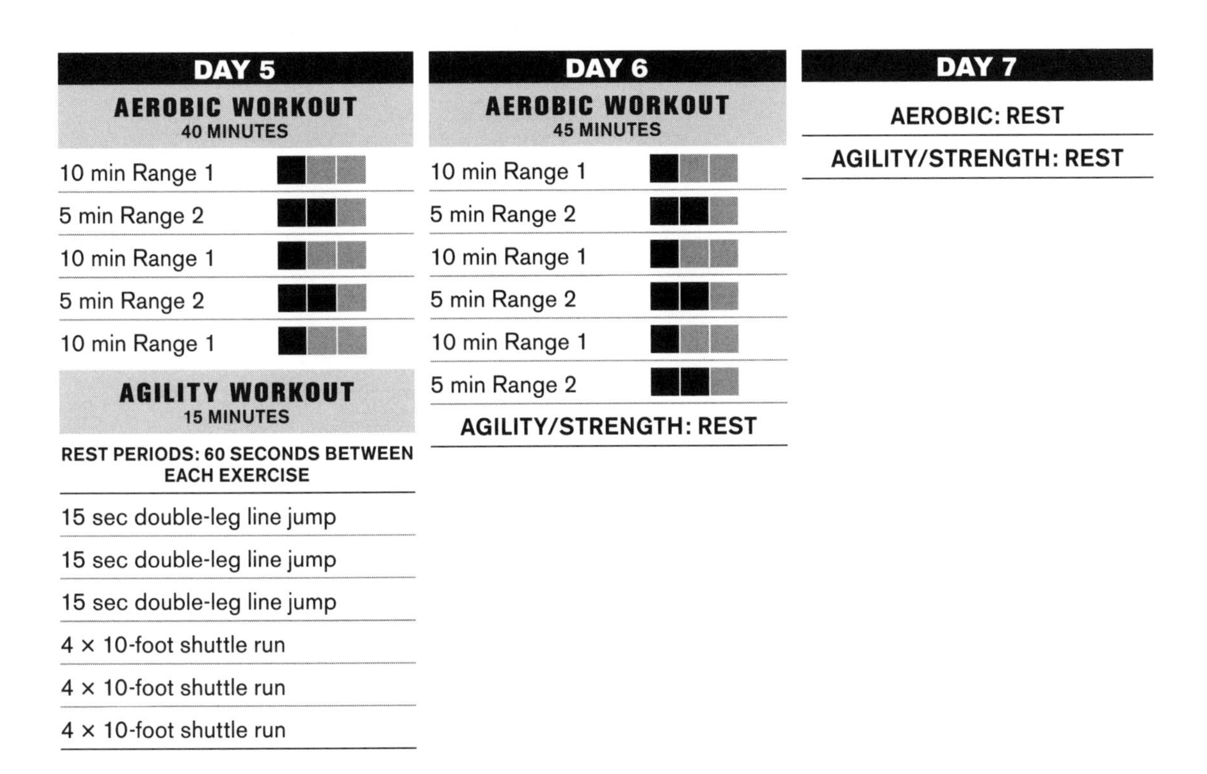

DAY 5

AEROBIC WORKOUT
40 MINUTES

10 min Range 1
5 min Range 2
10 min Range 1
5 min Range 2
10 min Range 1

AGILITY WORKOUT
15 MINUTES

REST PERIODS: 60 SECONDS BETWEEN EACH EXERCISE

15 sec double-leg line jump
15 sec double-leg line jump
15 sec double-leg line jump
4 × 10-foot shuttle run
4 × 10-foot shuttle run
4 × 10-foot shuttle run

DAY 6

AEROBIC WORKOUT
45 MINUTES

10 min Range 1
5 min Range 2
10 min Range 1
5 min Range 2
10 min Range 1
5 min Range 2

AGILITY/STRENGTH: REST

DAY 7

AEROBIC: REST

AGILITY/STRENGTH: REST

WEEK ONE SHOPPING LIST

BREAD/CEREALS/GRAINS

- ☐ 3 whole wheat English muffins
- ☐ 3 whole grain bagels
- ☐ 1 whole wheat pita
- ☐ 1 whole wheat hamburger roll
- ☐ 3 whole wheat tortillas (8" each)
- ☐ 2 whole wheat dinner rolls
- ☐ 2 slices whole grain bread

CONDIMENTS

- ☐ 1 tablespoon guacamole
- ☐ 6 tablespoons hummus
- ☐ 1" piece fresh ginger

FRUIT

- ☐ 1 Granny Smith apple
- ☐ 1 cup unsweetened applesauce
- ☐ 1 avocado
- ☐ 3 bananas
- ☐ 1 cup blackberries
- ☐ 1 grapefruit (or other citrus fruit)
- ☐ 3 oranges
- ☐ 1 peach
- ☐ 1 cup strawberries, sliced
- ☐ 2 cups fruit of choice
- ☐ 2 tablespoons raisins
- ☐ ½ cup dried papaya
- ☐ 1 clementine (or orange)
- ☐ 1 lime
- ☐ 1 can (15 ounces) pumpkin puree

VEGETABLES

- ☐ 8–10 asparagus spears
- ☐ 30 large baby carrots
- ☐ 5 medium carrots
- ☐ 3 bell peppers
- ☐ 6 large ribs celery
- ☐ 1 small head celeriac
- ☐ 5 black olives
- ☐ 1 cup broccoli
- ☐ 3¼ cups spinach
- ☐ 6½ cups greens of choice (mixed greens, romaine lettuce, etc.)
- ☐ 1 cup fresh green beans
- ☐ ¼ cup mushrooms
- ☐ 1 medium onion
- ☐ 2 red or new potatoes
- ☐ 1½ teaspoons chopped, dry-packed sun-dried tomatoes
- ☐ 3 medium tomatoes
- ☐ 1 sweet potato
- ☐ 1 cup veggies of choice (may not need to buy extra)
- ☐ 1 large parsnip
- ☐ ½ cup fresh basil

DAIRY/EGGS

- ☐ 3 eggs
- ☐ 1 container (6 ounces) fat-free yogurt (any flavor)
- ☐ 2¼ cups fat-free plain yogurt
- ☐ 2 ounces goat cheese
- ☐ 6 tablespoons light cream cheese
- ☐ ¼ cup low-fat shredded cheese of choice
- ☐ 2 slices low-fat cheese of choice
- ☐ 6¼ cups fat-free milk

MEAT/POULTRY/FISH

- ☐ 11 ounces chicken breast
- ☐ 4 ounces pork tenderloin
- ☐ 11 ounces cod
- ☐ 4 ounces ground turkey
- ☐ 2 ounces sliced turkey deli meat
- ☐ 11 ounces salmon

WEEK ONE MEAL PLAN

Day 1–1,712 Calories

BREAKFAST

¾ cup rolled oats (dry; prepare according to package directions)

¾ cup milk

½ cup halved strawberries

½ banana, sliced

SNACK

20 large baby carrots

LUNCH

Veggie/Hummus Pita

- 1 whole wheat pita bread
- 2 tablespoons hummus
- ½ cup veggies of choice (i.e., cucumber, spinach, red bell peppers, tomato)
- ½ avocado
- 1 slice low-fat cheese

1 orange

2 whole wheat fig cookies (like Fig Newmans)

SNACK

1 whole wheat English muffin

1 tablespoon natural peanut butter

½ banana

DINNER

4 ounces Cumin-Dusted Salmon over Mixed Greens with Clementines* (page 162)

1 whole wheat dinner roll

1 tablespoon olive oil spread, like Smart Balance Omega Plus with Flax spread

**Leftovers will be used in tomorrow's lunch. Just in case you need to make extra, check tomorrow's menu to see what is needed.*

Quick Cuts

How to Cut 200 to 300 Calories on This Day

- **Breakfast: Have ½ cup oats and ½ cup milk.**
- **Lunch: Have 1 fig cookie.**
- **Afternoon snack: Have ½ tablespoon peanut butter on the English muffin.**

Day 2–1,731 Calories

BREAKFAST

1 whole wheat bagel

2 tablespoons 100% fruit spread

1 banana

1 cup fat-free milk

SNACK

1 orange

LUNCH

Salmon Salad

- 2 cups spinach or greens of choice
- 3 ounces leftover salmon
- 3–6 black olives, chopped
- 3–6 cherry tomatoes, halved
- 2 tablespoons shredded Parmesan cheese
- 2 tablespoons low-fat dressing of choice

SNACK

1 whole wheat English muffin

1 tablespoon light cream cheese

DINNER

4 ounces grilled chicken breast

1 cup steamed broccoli

1 serving Root Vegetable and Apple Slaw* (page 158)

**Leftovers will be used in tomorrow's lunch. Just in case you need to make extra, check tomorrow's menu to see what is needed.*

Quick Cuts

How to Cut 200 to 300 calories on This Day

- **Breakfast: Have half a bagel and 1 tablespoon fruit spread.**
- **Dinner: Have 3 ounces chicken breast.**

Day 3—1,727 Calories

BREAKFAST

1½ cups whole grain cereal
1 cup fat-free milk
1 cup strawberries, sliced

SNACK

Fruit Smoothie (12 ounces)
- 2 cups fruit of choice
- 6 ounces fat-free yogurt (any flavor)
- ¼ cup fat-free milk
- 1 tablespoon wheat germ
- Ice

LUNCH

Turkey/Apple Pita
- 2 ounces deli turkey
- ¼ cup leftover slaw
- ¼ cup spinach

10 large baby carrots
2 whole wheat fig cookies (like Fig Newmans)

SNACK

8 whole grain crackers dipped in ¼ cup light cream cheese/salsa mixture

DINNER

1 serving Chili-Lime Baked Cod* (page 163)
1 cup quinoa
8–10 spears steamed asparagus

**Leftovers will be used in tomorrow's lunch. Just in case you need to make extra, check tomorrow's menu to see what is needed.*

Quick Cuts

How to Cut 200 to 300 Calories on This Day
- » **Breakfast: Have 1 cup cereal.**
- » **Morning snack: Have an 8-ounce smoothie.**
- » **Afternoon snack: Dip the crackers in salsa only.**
- » **Dinner: Have ½ cup quinoa.**

Day 4—1,739 Calories

BREAKFAST

1 cup rolled oats (dry)
1 cup fat-free milk
1 sliced peach

SNACK

Baked tortilla chips (1 baked whole wheat tortilla, broken)
¼ cup salsa

LUNCH

Fish Taco
- 3 ounces leftover cod
- 1 whole wheat tortilla
- ¼ avocado
- 2 tablespoons mango salsa
- ¼ cup romaine lettuce
- 2 tablespoons light cream cheese

1 apple

SNACK

1 red pepper, sliced
4 whole wheat crackers
¼ cup hummus

DINNER

Turkey Burger
- 1 whole wheat bun
- 4-ounce turkey burger
- 1 tablespoon guacamole
- 2 slices tomato
- 1 large romaine lettuce leaf

½ ear sweet corn*
1 serving Curried Carrot Salad (page 159)

**Leftovers will be used in tomorrow's lunch. Just in case you need to make extra, check tomorrow's menu to see what is needed.*

Quick Cuts

How to Cut 200 to 300 Calories on This Day
- » **Breakfast: Have ¾ cup oats and ¾ cup milk.**
- » **Lunch: Use 1 tablespoon cream cheese.**
- » **Dinner: Have a 3-ounce burger and no corn.**

WEEK ONE MEAL PLAN

Day 5–1,804 Calories

BREAKFAST

1 serving Yogurt with Papaya, Blackberries, and Seeds (page 149)

SNACK

1 orange

LUNCH

Southwestern Salad

- 2 cups mixed greens
- ¼ cup leftover corn
- ¼ cup canned black beans
- ¼ avocado
- ¼ cup low-fat cheese
- ¼ cup salsa
- 1 whole wheat tortilla, baked and crumbled on top

SNACK

1 whole grain bagel

2 tablespoons 100% fruit spread

DINNER

4 ounces grilled, baked, or broiled chicken*

1 sweet potato, sliced, brushed lightly with olive oil, cinnamon, and brown sugar, then grilled

1 cup brown rice

**Leftover chicken will be used in tomorrow's lunch. Just in case you need to make extra, check tomorrow's menu to see what is needed.*

Quick Cuts

How to Cut 200 to 300 Calories on This Day

- **Afternoon snack: Have half a bagel and 1 tablespoon fruit spread.**
- **Dinner: Have 3 ounces chicken.**

Day 6–1,753 Calories

BREAKFAST

1 whole grain bagel

2 tablespoons low-fat cream cheese

1 grapefruit (or other citrus fruit)

SNACK

1 cup unsweetened applesauce

LUNCH

Spinach Salad

- 2 cups spinach
- 3 ounces leftover chicken
- 2 tablespoons shredded Parmesan cheese
- ½ cup veggies of choice
- 2 tablespoons light dressing of choice

1 whole wheat roll

2 tablespoons butter or olive oil spread, like Smart Balance Omega Plus with Flax

SNACK

1 serving Celery Sticks Filled with Goat Cheese and Sun-Dried Tomatoes (page 168)

DINNER

4 ounces pork tenderloin, grilled, roasted, or baked

1 cup steamed green beans

2 baked small new potatoes

2 teaspoons Smart Balance spread (for the green beans and potatoes)

Quick Cuts

200 to 300 Calories on This Day

- **Breakfast: Have 1 tablespoon low-fat cream cheese and ½ grapefruit.**
- **Lunch: Skip the roll and spread.**
- **Dinner: Have 3 ounces pork.**

Day 7–1,815 Calories

BREAKFAST

Breakfast Sandwich

1 whole wheat English muffin

3 egg whites, scrambled with ¼–½ cup chopped bell peppers, onions, and mushrooms

1 slice low-fat cheese

1 banana

SNACK

2 whole wheat graham crackers

1 cup fat-free milk

LUNCH

1 serving Pumpkin and Ginger Soup* (page 151)

2 slices whole wheat toast

1 tablespoon butter or olive oil spread

SNACK

1 individual bag 94% fat-free popcorn

DINNER

Tomato and Basil Pasta

1½ cups whole wheat pasta, prepared according to package directions

2 tomatoes, cut up

½ cup fresh basil

2 tablespoons Parmesan cheese

2 teaspoons olive oil

1 tablespoon red wine vinegar

**Leftovers will be used in tomorrow's lunch. Just in case you need to make extra, check tomorrow's menu to see what is needed.*

Quick Cuts

How to Cut 200 to 300 Calories on This Day

- **Breakfast: Have 2 egg whites.**
- **Morning snack: Have 1 graham cracker.**
- **Lunch: Have 1 slice toast and ½ teaspoon spread.**
- **Afternoon snack: Have half of the popcorn.**

WEEK TWO WORKOUTS

DAY 8

AEROBIC WORKOUT
30 MINUTES

5 min Range 1
5 min Range 2
2 min Range 3
5 min Range 1
5 min Range 2
2 min Range 3
6 min Range 2

STRENGTH WORKOUT
20 MINUTES

REST PERIODS: 45 SECONDS BETWEEN EACH EXERCISE

10 medicine ball squats *(page 280)*
15 pushups *(pages 286–87)*
10 medicine ball wall touches *(per side) (page 281)*
10 medicine ball squats
15 pushups
10 medicine ball wall touches *(per side)*
10 reverse crunches *(page 285)*
8 overhead reverse lunge and presses *(per leg) (page 283)*
12 overhead medicine ball passes *(page 282)*
10 lateral arm raises *(page 274)*
10 reverse crunches
8 overhead reverse lunge and presses *(per leg)*
12 overhead medicine ball passes
10 lateral arm raises
10 reverse crunches

DAY 9

AEROBIC WORKOUT
30 MINUTES

5 min Range 1
5 min Range 2
2 min Range 3
5 min Range 1
5 min Range 2
2 min Range 3
2 min Range 2
2 min Range 1
2 min Range 3

AGILITY WORKOUT
15 MINUTES

REST PERIODS: 60 SECONDS BETWEEN EACH EXERCISE

15 sec double-leg cone jump *(page 299)*
15 sec double-leg cone jump
15 sec double-leg cone jump
3 × square drill *(page 305)*
3 × square drill
3 × square drill

DAY 10

AEROBIC: REST

AGILITY/STRENGTH: REST

DAY 11

AEROBIC WORKOUT
30 MINUTES

5 min Range 1
5 min Range 2
5 min Range 3
5 min Range 1
5 min Range 2
5 min Range 3

STRENGTH WORKOUT
20 MINUTES

REST PERIODS: 45 SECONDS BETWEEN EACH EXERCISE

10 medicine ball squats
15 pushups
10 medicine ball wall touches *(per side)*
10 medicine ball squats
15 pushups
10 medicine ball wall touches *(per side)*
10 reverse crunches
8 overhead reverse lunge and presses *(per leg)*
12 overhead medicine ball passes
10 lateral arm raises
10 reverse crunches
8 overhead reverse lunge and presses *(per leg)*
12 overhead medicine ball passes
10 lateral arm raises
10 reverse crunches

(continued)

WEEK TWO WORKOUTS

DAY 12

AEROBIC WORKOUT
40 MINUTES

5 min Range 1

5 min Range 2

5 min Range 3

5 min Range 1

5 min Range 2

5 min Range 3

5 min Range 2

5 min Range 1

AGILITY WORKOUT
15 MINUTES

REST PERIODS: 60 SECONDS BETWEEN EACH EXERCISE

15 sec double-leg cone jump

15 sec double-leg cone jump

15 sec double-leg cone jump

3 × square drill

3 × square drill

3 × square drill

DAY 13

AEROBIC WORKOUT
40 MINUTES

5 min Range 1

5 min Range 2

5 min Range 3

10 min Range 2

5 min Range 1

5 min Range 1

5 min Range 2

AGILITY/STRENGTH: REST

DAY 14

AEROBIC: REST

AGILITY/STRENGTH: REST

WEEK TWO SHOPPING LIST

BREAD/CEREALS/GRAINS

- ☐ 1 whole grain bagel
- ☐ 6 slices whole grain bread
- ☐ 3 medium whole wheat dinner rolls
- ☐ 5 whole wheat pitas
- ☐ 1 whole wheat tortilla (8")

NUTS/SEEDS/LEGUMES

- ☐ 8 ounces tempeh
- ☐ 1 tablespoon hummus

FRUIT

- ☐ 1 apple
- ☐ 1 avocado
- ☐ 3 medium bananas
- ☐ 1 cup blueberries or blackberries
- ☐ 3 cups fruit salad of choice
- ☐ 2 cups grapes
- ☐ 1 honeydew melon
- ☐ 1 medium pear
- ☐ 3 miniature boxes (0.5 ounce each) raisins
- ☐ ½ cup strawberries
- ☐ 2 tangerines
- ☐ 2 kiwifruits
- ☐ 1 lemon
- ☐ 2 oranges
- ☐ 1 peach

VEGETABLES

- ☐ 20 large baby carrots
- ☐ 3 bell peppers (1 red, 1 green, 1 of choice)
- ☐ 1 cup broccoli
- ☐ ½ cup shredded carrots
- ☐ 1 medium rib celery
- ☐ ½ cup mushrooms
- ☐ 2 medium onions
- ☐ 7 medium scallions
- ☐ 2 cups romaine lettuce
- ☐ 3½ cups spinach
- ☐ 1 small spaghetti squash
- ☐ 1 small cucumber
- ☐ 4 plum tomatoes
- ☐ 2 medium tomatoes
- ☐ 1 sweet potato
- ☐ ½ cup mung bean sprouts
- ☐ 5 cloves garlic
- ☐ 1 small head napa cabbage
- ☐ 2 tablespoons fresh cilantro
- ☐ 1 bulb fennel
- ☐ ½ jalapeño pepper
- ☐ 1 cup vegetable juice (such as V8)

DAIRY/EGGS

- ☐ 7 eggs
- ☐ 3 containers (6 ounces each) fat-free yogurt (any flavor)
- ☐ 1 container (6 ounces) fat-free plain yogurt
- ☐ 1 container (6 ounces) fat-free vanilla yogurt
- ☐ 2 tablespoons feta cheese (or goat or blue cheese)
- ☐ ¼ cup low-fat buttermilk
- ☐ ½ cup light cottage cheese
- ☐ 1 slice low-fat cheese of choice
- ☐ ½ cup low-fat shredded cheese of choice
- ☐ 5½ cups fat-free milk

MEAT/POULTRY/FISH

- ☐ 1 pound 14 ounces chicken breast
- ☐ 7 ounces salmon
- ☐ 1 pound trout (whole fish)
- ☐ 4 slices turkey bacon
- ☐ 4 ounces grilled tuna steak
- ☐ 8 slices turkey pepperoni

WEEK TWO MEAL PLAN

Day 8—1,767 Calories

BREAKFAST

¾ cup rolled oats (dry)

¾ cup fat-free milk

1 mini box raisins

SNACK

1 ounce (about 50 kernels) pistachios

LUNCH

Soup and Salad

1 cup leftover soup from Day 7

Spinach Salad

1 cup spinach

¼ cup chopped tomatoes

¼ avocado

1 pear, chopped

2 tablespoons sunflower seeds

1 tablespoon light salad dressing

SNACK

Pita Chips and Salsa

2 whole wheat pitas, baked, toasted, or grilled

½ cup salsa

DINNER

1 serving Grilled Citrus and Garlic Chicken* (page 160)

1 cup boiled spaghetti squash with 1 tablespoon honey or brown sugar

1 whole wheat roll with 1 tablespoon 100% fruit spread

** Leftovers will be used in tomorrow's lunch. Just in case you need to make extra, check tomorrow's menu to see what is needed.*

Quick Cuts

How to Cut 200 to 300 Calories on This Day

» **Breakfast: Have ½ cup oatmeal and ½ cup milk.**

» **Morning snack: Have ½ ounce (about 25) pistachios.**

» **Dinner: Skip the fruit spread on the roll.**

Day 9—1,720 Calories

BREAKFAST

1½ cups whole grain cereal

1 cup fat-free milk

1 banana

SNACK

1 cup grapes

LUNCH

1 serving Asian Chicken Salad Sandwich (page 152) (prepare fresh chicken or use leftovers)

Yogurt-Carrot-Raisin Salad

6 ounces fat-free vanilla yogurt

½ cup shredded carrots

1 mini box raisins

SNACK

2 stalks (5" each) celery

1 tablespoon natural peanut butter

DINNER

Breakfast Sandwich

2 slices whole grain toast

1 whole egg and 2 egg whites, scrambled

1 slice low-fat cheese

2 slices turkey bacon*

1 cup mixed fruit salad

**Leftovers will be used in tomorrow's lunch. Just in case you need to make extra, check tomorrow's menu to see what is needed.*

Quick Cuts

How to Cut 200 to 300 Calories on This Day

» **Breakfast: Have ¾ cup cereal and ⅔ cup milk.**

» **Dinner: Have 3 scrambled egg whites.**

WEEK TWO MEAL PLAN

Day 10—1,700 Calories

BREAKFAST

1 cup rolled oats (dry)

1 cup sliced strawberries

1 cup fat-free milk

SNACK

1 apple

LUNCH

Spinach Salad

- 2 cups spinach
- 2 slices leftover turkey bacon, crumbled
- ½ cup raw mushrooms
- 1 mini box raisins
- 2 tablespoons vinegar and oil

2 tangerines or clementines

SNACK

1 serving Yogurt with Melon, Honey, and Nuts (page 167)

DINNER

4 ounces grilled salmon*

1 sweet potato, baked, with 2 teaspoons olive oil spread, cinnamon, and 1–2 teaspoons brown sugar

1 cup bulgur, cooked

**Leftovers will be used in tomorrow's lunch. Just in case you need to make extra, check tomorrow's menu to see what is needed.*

Quick Cuts

How to Cut 200 to 300 Calories on This Day

- **Breakfast: Have ½ cup oats and ½ cup milk.**
- **Lunch: Have 1 tangerine or clementine.**
- **Dinner: Have 3 ounces salmon and ½ cup bulgur.**

Day 11—1,739 Calories

BREAKFAST

½ cup rolled oats (dry)

½ cup fat-free milk

½ cup sliced strawberries

1 tablespoon ground or milled flaxseed

SNACK

1 peach

LUNCH

Barbecued Salmon Sandwich

- 2 slices whole grain bread
- 2 tablespoons barbecue sauce
- 3 ounces leftover salmon

1 cup grapes

SNACK

Veggie/Hummus Pita

- 1 small whole wheat pita
- ½ cup spinach
- 1 tablespoon hummus
- ¼ cup chopped bell peppers
- ¼ avocado

DINNER

1 serving Gingery Tempeh Stir-Fry* (page 164)

1 cup wild rice, cooked

**Leftovers will be used in tomorrow's lunch. Just in case you need to make extra, check tomorrow's menu to see what is needed.*

Quick Cuts

How to Cut 200 to 300 Calories on This Day

- **Breakfast: Skip the oatmeal, but have 2 tablespoons flaxseed instead of 1.**
- **Lunch: Have 1 tablespoon barbecue sauce.**
- **Dinner: Have ½ cup wild rice.**

WEEK TWO MEAL PLAN

Day 12–1,756 Calories

BREAKFAST

1 whole grain bagel

2 tablespoons 100% fruit spread

SNACK

1 cup melon

½ cup light cottage cheese

LUNCH

Chicken wrap (leftover stir-fried chicken, veggies, and wild rice rolled in a whole wheat tortilla)

SNACK

6 ounces fat-free yogurt (any flavor)

1 banana

1 tablespoon ground or milled flaxseed

DINNER

1 serving Whole Trout Stuffed with Fennel and Lemon (page 161)

1 cup cooked quinoa

Quick Cuts

How to Cut 200 to 300 Calories on This Day

» **Breakfast: Substitute a whole wheat English muffin for the bagel and have 1 tablespoon fruit spread.**

» **Dinner: Have ½ cup quinoa.**

Day 13–1,800 Calories

BREAKFAST

1 serving Oatmeal Pancakes with Blueberries (page 148)

4 teaspoons butter or olive oil spread

¼ cup 100% maple syrup

SNACK

10 large baby carrots

LUNCH

Grilled Pizza Sandwich

- 2 slices whole grain bread
- 2–3 tablespoons marinara or pizza sauce
- 8 slices turkey pepperoni
- ⅓ cup low-fat mozzarella cheese
- 4 tomato slices and other veggies of choice

SNACK

Fruit smoothie (made with 2 cups fruit of choice, 6 ounces fat-free yogurt, ¼ cup fat-free milk, 1 tablespoon wheat germ, and ice)

DINNER

4 ounces grilled tuna steak

1 cup brown rice

1 cup steamed broccoli

Quick Cuts

How to Cut 200 to 300 Calories on This Day

» **Breakfast: Have 2 pancakes.**

» **Afternoon snack: Have half of a smoothie.**

» **Dinner: Have 3 ounces tuna steak.**

WEEK TWO MEAL PLAN

Day 14—1,738 Calories

BREAKFAST

1 cup rolled oats (dry)

1 cup fat-free milk

1 cup blueberries

SNACK

2 kiwifruits

LUNCH

1 serving Gazpacho (page 150)

1 whole wheat roll with 1 tablespoon butter or olive oil spread

20 large baby carrots

SNACK

2 whole wheat fig cookies (like Fig Newmans)

1 cup fat-free milk

DINNER

Cobb Salad

- 2 cups romaine lettuce
- 3 ounces grilled chicken*
- 3 large hard-cooked egg whites
- ¼ avocado
- 2 tablespoons crumbled low-fat blue, goat, or feta cheese
- 1 plum tomato, chopped
- 2 tablespoons light dressing

1 whole wheat roll with 1 tablespoon butter or olive oil spread

**Leftovers will be used in tomorrow's lunch. Just in case you need to make extra, check tomorrow's menu to see what is needed.*

Quick Cuts

How to Cut 200 to 300 Calories on This Day

- **Breakfast: Have ¾ cup oats and ¾ cup milk.**
- **Lunch: Skip the olive oil spread on the roll and have 10 baby carrots.**

WEEK THREE WORKOUTS

DAY 15

AEROBIC WORKOUT
20 MINUTES

5 min Range 1

5 min Range 2

5 min Range 3

5 min Range 2

STRENGTH WORKOUT
20 MINUTES

REST PERIODS: 45 SECONDS BETWEEN EACH EXERCISE

25 jump-rope jumps *(page 273)*

10 squats with cord *(page 291)*

20 sec prone core bridge *(page 271)*

25 jump-rope jumps

10 squats with cord

20 sec prone core bridge

10 reverse medicine ball lunges *(per leg) (page 288)*

12 overhead medicine ball passes *(page 282)*

20 sec side core bridge *(per side) (page 271)*

10 reverse medicine ball lunges *(per leg)*

12 overhead medicine ball passes

20 sec side core bridge *(per side)*

DAY 16

AEROBIC WORKOUT
40 MINUTES

2 min Range 1

2 min Range 3

5 min Range 2

5 min Range 3

6 min Range 2

5 min Range 1

10 min Range 2

5 min Range 3

AGILITY WORKOUT
15 MINUTES

REST PERIODS: 60 SECONDS BETWEEN EACH EXERCISE

2 × 10-foot shuttle run *(page 296)*

2 × 10-foot shuttle run

15 sec single-leg line jump *(page 301)*

15 sec single-leg line jump *(opposite leg)*

15 sec single-leg line jump

15 sec single-leg line jump *(opposite leg)*

3 × square drill *(page 305)*

3 × square drill

3 × square drill

DAY 17

AEROBIC: REST

AGILITY/STRENGTH: REST

DAY 18

AEROBIC WORKOUT
15 MINUTES

5 min Range 1

5 min Range 3

5 min Range 2

STRENGTH WORKOUT
20 MINUTES

REST PERIODS: 45 SECONDS BETWEEN EACH EXERCISE

10 squat and jumps *(page 289)*

20 sec side core bridge *(per side)*

10 squat and jumps

20 sec side core bridge *(per side)*

25 jump-rope jumps

10 reverse medicine ball lunges *(per leg)*

6 windshield wipers *(page 295)*

25 jump-rope jumps

10 × reverse medicine ball lunges *(per leg)*

6 windshield wipers

DAY 19

AEROBIC WORKOUT
40 MINUTES

5 min Range 1	
10 min Range 2	
5 min Range 3	
5 min Range 1	
10 min Range 2	
5 min Range 3	

AGILITY WORKOUT
15 MINUTES

REST PERIODS: 60 SECONDS BETWEEN EACH EXERCISE

- 2 × 10-foot shuttle run
- 2 × 10-foot shuttle run
- 15 sec single-leg line jump
- 15 sec single-leg line jump *(opposite leg)*
- 15 sec single-leg line jump
- 15 sec single-leg line jump *(opposite leg)*
- 3 × square drill
- 3 × square drill
- 3 × square drill

DAY 20

AEROBIC WORKOUT
50 MINUTES

10 min Range 1	
10 min Range 2	
5 min Range 3	
10 min Range 1	
10 min Range 2	
5 min Range 3	

STRENGTH WORKOUT
20 MINUTES

REST PERIODS: 45 SECONDS BETWEEN EACH EXERCISE

- 25 jump-rope jumps
- 10 squats with cord
- 20 sec prone core bridge
- 25 jump-rope jumps
- 10 squats with cord
- 20 sec prone core bridge
- 10 reverse med ball lunges *(per leg)*
- 20 sec side core bridge *(per side)*
- 10 reverse med ball lunges *(per leg)*
- 20 sec side core bridge *(per side)*

DAY 21

AEROBIC: REST

AGILITY/STRENGTH: REST

WEEK THREE SHOPPING LIST

BREAD/CEREALS/GRAINS

- ☐ 1 whole grain bagel
- ☐ 5 slices whole grain bread
- ☐ 1 medium whole wheat dinner roll
- ☐ 3 whole wheat pitas
- ☐ 3 whole wheat tortillas (8" each)
- ☐ 1 whole wheat English muffin

NUTS/SEEDS/LEGUMES

- ☐ 6 tablespoons hummus
- ☐ 14 ounces soft tofu

FRUIT

- ☐ ½ avocado
- ☐ 3 medium bananas
- ☐ 1 cup fruit salad of choice
- ☐ 1 grapefruit or other citrus fruit
- ☐ 1 cup grapes
- ☐ 1 melon of choice
- ☐ 1 medium peach
- ☐ 1 medium pear
- ☐ ½ cup pineapple
- ☐ 1 miniature box (0.5 ounce) raisins
- ☐ 3 small boxes (1.5 ounces each) raisins
- ☐ ½ cup strawberries
- ☐ 2 medium plums
- ☐ 1 apple

VEGETABLES

- ☐ 8–10 spears asparagus
- ☐ 5 baby carrots
- ☐ 5 large red bell peppers
- ☐ 1¼ cups broccoli
- ☐ ¼ cup shredded carrots
- ☐ 4 ribs celery
- ☐ 2 whole cucumbers
- ☐ 1 small eggplant
- ☐ 1 cup fresh green beans
- ☐ 5 cups mixed greens
- ☐ 2½ onions
- ☐ 1 large portabella mushroom (4 ounces)
- ☐ ½ cup sliced mushrooms
- ☐ ¼ cup romaine lettuce
- ☐ 6 scallions
- ☐ 10 cups spinach
- ☐ ½ cup squash
- ☐ 2 dry-packed sun-dried tomatoes
- ☐ 1 tomato
- ☐ 1 cup cherry tomatoes
- ☐ ½ cup vegetable of choice
- ☐ 3 zucchini (1 yellow, 1 green, 1 of choice)
- ☐ 1 clove garlic
- ☐ 1 can (6.5 ounces) artichokes
- ☐ ½ cup parsley
- ☐ 1 tablespoon capers (optional)

DAIRY/EGGS

- ☐ 6 eggs
- ☐ 5 containers (6 ounces each) fat-free yogurt (any flavor)
- ☐ ½ cup light cottage cheese
- ☐ ¼ cup part-skim ricotta cheese
- ☐ 2 tablespoons low-fat sour cream
- ☐ 4 cups fat-free milk
- ☐ 1 ounce part-skim string cheese
- ☐ 3 tablespoons light cream cheese
- ☐ 1½ cups shredded low-fat Cheddar cheese
- ☐ ½ stick butter

MEAT/POULTRY/FISH

- ☐ 11 ounces chicken breast
- ☐ 7 ounces salmon
- ☐ 4 ounces tilapia
- ☐ 4 ounces tuna steak
- ☐ ½ lb turkey sausage
- ☐ 2 cans (6 ounces each) water-packed tuna

WEEK THREE MEAL PLAN

Day 15—1,742 Calories

BREAKFAST

2 slices whole grain toast

2 tablespoons 100% fruit spread

½ honeydew or cantaloupe

SNACK

Baked pita chips (made with 1 large whole wheat pita)

2 tablespoons hummus

LUNCH

Grilled Chicken and Pecan Salad

- 2 cups greens of choice
- 3 ounces leftover grilled chicken
- 1 apple, sliced
- 1 tablespoon pecans
- 1 small box raisins
- 2 tablespoons light salad dressing

SNACK

6 ounces fat-free yogurt (any flavor)

¾ cup whole grain cereal

1 tablespoon chopped walnuts

1 banana, sliced

DINNER

4 ounces grilled tuna steak*

1 serving Ratatouille (page 156)

**Leftovers will be used in tomorrow's lunch. Just in case you need to make extra, check tomorrow's menu to see what is needed.*

Quick Cuts

How to Cut 200 to 300 Calories on This Day

- **Breakfast: Have a fourth of a melon.**
- **Lunch: Have 2 ounces chicken in the salad.**
- **Afternoon snack: Have ½ cup cereal.**
- **Dinner: Have 3 ounces tuna steak.**

Day 16—1,737 Calories

BREAKFAST

¾ cup rolled oats (dry)

2 teaspoons brown sugar

1 mini box raisins

¾ cup fat-free milk

SNACK

1 piece part-skim string cheese

LUNCH

1 serving Tuna Salad with Sun-Dried Tomatoes and Artichokes (page 153)

2 slices whole wheat bread

SNACK

Strawberry and Avocado Pita

- 1 whole wheat pita
- ½ cup sliced strawberries
- ¼ avocado

DINNER

Chicken Stir-Fry

- 4 ounces chicken*
- 1 cup veggies (bell peppers, mushrooms, onions, broccoli, etc.)
- ½ cup diced pineapple
- 3 tablespoons teriyaki sauce

1 cup brown rice

**Leftovers will be used in tomorrow's lunch. Just in case you need to make extra, check tomorrow's menu to see what is needed.*

Quick Cuts

How to Cut 200 to 300 Calories on This Day

- **Breakfast: Have ½ cup oats and ½ cup milk.**
- **Lunch: Have 1 slice bread.**
- **Dinner: Have 3 ounces chicken and ¾ cup rice.**

WEEK THREE MEAL PLAN

Day 17—1,730 Calories

BREAKFAST

1 whole grain bagel
3 tablespoons light cream cheese
1 grapefruit

SNACK

6 ounces fat-free yogurt (any flavor)
1 cup whole grain cereal

LUNCH

Chicken Pita
- 1 whole wheat pita
- 3 ounces leftover chicken
- 1 tablespoon light mayonnaise, if desired
- 2 slices tomato
- 1 large romaine leaf
- ¼ avocado

1 cup grapes

SNACK

3 Whole Grain Cheddar Coins (page 166)

DINNER

Grilled Veggies on Quinoa
- 1 large portabella mushroom (4 ounces), grilled
- 1 red bell pepper, sliced and grilled
- 1 cup sliced squash and zucchini, grilled
- 1 tablespoon olive oil (brush on veggies as you put them on the grill)
- 1 cup cooked quinoa

Quick Cuts

How to Cut 200 to 300 Calories on This Day

» **Breakfast: Have 1 tablespoon cream cheese.**
» **Morning snack: Have ½ cup cereal.**
» **Lunch: Have ½ cup grapes.**
» **Afternoon snack: Have 2 Cheddar Coins.**
» **Dinner: Use 2 teaspoons olive oil on the grilled veggies.**

Day 18—1,713 Calories

BREAKFAST

Homemade Fruit and Yogurt Parfait
- 6 ounces fat-free yogurt (any flavor)
- ¾ cup whole grain cereal
- 1 medium banana, sliced
- 1 tablespoon ground or milled flaxseed

SNACK

1 large red bell pepper, sliced
½ cup cucumber slices
½ cup hummus

LUNCH

1 serving Mixed Greens Salad with Pears and Pine Nuts (page 154)

SNACK

1 cup fresh fruit
½ cup light cottage cheese
2 graham crackers

DINNER

4 ounces grilled salmon*
1 cup steamed fresh green beans
1 cup bulgur

**Leftovers will be used in tomorrow's lunch. Just in case you need to make extra, check tomorrow's menu to see what is needed.*

Quick Cuts

How to Cut 200 to 300 Calories on This Day

» **Morning snack: Have ¼ cup hummus.**
» **Afternoon snack: Have 1 graham cracker.**
» **Dinner: Have 3 ounces salmon.**

WEEK THREE MEAL PLAN

Day 19—1,729 Calories

BREAKFAST

1 cup rolled oats (dry)
1 cup fat-free milk
1 small box raisins

SNACK

2 plums

LUNCH

Salmon Wrap
- 1 whole wheat tortilla
- 3 ounces leftover salmon
- 2 tablespoons chopped scallions
- ¼ cup chopped tomato
- ½ cup spinach or greens of choice
- 2 tablespoons low-fat sour cream

3 whole wheat fig cookies (like Fig Newmans)

SNACK

6 ounces fat-free yogurt (any flavor)
1 cup whole grain cereal
1 medium peach, sliced
1 tablespoon ground or milled flaxseed

DINNER

1 serving Grilled Turkey Sausage and Lentils with Spinach (page 165)
1 Veggie Salad
- 1 cup mixed greens
- ½ cup chopped veggies of choice
- 1 tablespoon light dressing of choice

1 whole wheat roll with 2 teaspoons olive oil spread

Quick Cuts

How to Cut 200 to 300 Calories on This Day

» **Breakfast: Have ¾ cup oats and ¾ cup milk.**
» **Lunch: Have 1 fig cookie.**
» **Dinner: Eat half of the roll with 1 teaspoon olive oil spread.**

Day 20—1,734 Calories

BREAKFAST

1½ cups whole grain cereal
1 cup fat-free milk
½ banana

SNACK

5 large baby carrots
3 ribs celery, halved
2 tablespoons low-fat ranch dressing

LUNCH

1 serving Tofu Scramble and Vegetable Wrap (page 155)

SNACK

Peanut Butter and Banana Sandwich
- 1 slice whole grain bread (fold or slice in half)
- 1 tablespoon natural peanut butter
- ½ banana

DINNER

Chicken Pasta
- 1½ cups whole wheat pasta, prepared according to package directions*
- 4 ounces grilled chicken
- 1½ cups sautéed spinach
- 2 teaspoons olive oil
- 1 cup marinara sauce

**Leftovers will be used in tomorrow's lunch. Just in case you need to make extra, check tomorrow's menu to see what is needed.*

Quick Cuts

How to Cut 200 to 300 Calories on This Day

» **Breakfast: Have 1 cup cereal and ⅔ cup milk.**
» **Dinner: Have 3 ounces chicken, 1 cup pasta, and ½ cup marinara sauce.**

WEEK THREE MEAL PLAN

Day 21–1,749 calories

BREAKFAST

1 serving Many Veggie Frittata (opposite)

1 whole wheat English muffin

1 tablespoon 100% fruit spread

SNACK

1 cup fat-free milk

3 whole wheat fig cookies
(like Fig Newmans)

LUNCH

Pasta Salad

- 1 cup whole wheat pasta, prepared according to package directions
- 1 cup broccoli, finely chopped
- 2 tablespoons fat-free Italian dressing

1 cup melon

SNACK

6 ounces fat-free yogurt (any flavor)

¼ cup shredded carrot

1 small box raisins

DINNER

4 ounces grilled tilapia

¼ cup mango salsa

1 cup wild rice*

8–10 spears asparagus

1 tablespoon olive oil

**Leftovers will be used in tomorrow's lunch. Just in case you need to make extra, check tomorrow's menu to see what is needed.*

Quick Cuts

How to Cut 200 to 300 Calories on This Day

» **Breakfast: Have 1 slice toast instead of the English muffin and 1–2 teaspoons fruit spread.**

» **Morning snack: Have 2 fig cookies.**

» **Dinner: Have 3 ounces tilapia and use 2 teaspoons olive oil.**

»Breakfasts

MANY VEGGIE FRITTATA

A frittata is basically an omelet that isn't folded, which is great for those of us who struggle to get an omelet to come out of the pan looking like anything other than scrambled eggs. This recipe can easily change with whatever vegetables are in season, including scallions, zucchini, summer squash, and tomatoes.

MAKES 2 SERVINGS

ACTIVE TIME: 30 MINUTES

TOTAL TIME: 30 MINUTES

1 teaspoon extra-virgin olive oil
1 onion, chopped
4 ounces button mushrooms (about 8), sliced
1 red bell pepper, sliced into ¼" strips
Salt
Freshly ground black pepper
1 packed cup chopped spinach
3 large eggs and 3 large egg whites, lightly beaten

1. Preheat the broiler.

2. In a small, ovenproof nonstick skillet, heat the oil over medium heat. Add the onion, mushrooms, and bell pepper. Season lightly with salt and black pepper to taste and stir gently to combine. Cover the skillet and cook the vegetables, stirring occasionally, for 7 minutes, or until softened. Uncover, add the spinach, and cook about 1 minute, until the liquid has evaporated.

3. Stir in the eggs, reduce the heat to medium-low, cover, and cook for 3 to 4 minutes, or until the frittata is almost set.

4. Transfer the skillet to the broiler and cook for 2 to 3 minutes, or until set and slightly browned on top. Slide the frittata out of the skillet, cut into wedges, and serve hot.

CALORIES/ SERVING	CARBS (G)	PROTEIN (G)	FAT (G)	SAT FAT (G)	SODIUM (MG)	FIBER (G)
210	12	18	10	3	244	3

»Breakfasts

OATMEAL PANCAKES WITH BLUEBERRIES

I recommend making a big batch of the dry ingredients in this recipe to cut down on the time and effort on subsequent mornings. One of the biggest differences between this recipe and typical pancake mix is the fact that it's sweetened with blueberries and banana instead of relying on added sugar in the dry ingredients. You can use regular milk if you don't have buttermilk on hand, and frozen, unsweetened blueberries enable you to prepare this recipe year-round.

MAKES 8 (4 PER SERVING)

ACTIVE TIME: 25 MINUTES

TOTAL TIME: 25 MINUTES

¾ cup rolled oats

1 cup low-fat buttermilk

1 egg

1 small banana, mashed with a fork (⅓ cup)

½ cup whole wheat flour

½ teaspoon baking soda

½ teaspoon baking powder

¼ teaspoon salt

½ cup blueberries

1. In a medium bowl, stir together the oats, buttermilk, egg, and banana until the oats are well coated. In another bowl, combine the flour, baking soda, baking powder, and salt. Whisk into the buttermilk mixture until combined. Add the blueberries and stir gently.

2. Lightly coat a nonstick skillet with cooking spray and heat over medium-high heat. When the skillet is hot, drop the batter by ¼ cupfuls and reduce the heat to medium. Cook each pancake for 3 minutes, or until golden brown and holding together well. Flip and cook for 2 minutes, or until the bottom is golden and the pancake is cooked through. Serve hot with maple syrup or a squeeze of lemon juice.

CALORIES/ SERVING	CARBS (G)	PROTEIN (G)	FAT (G)	SAT FAT (G)	SODIUM (MG)	FIBER (G)
337	60	13	5	2	986	7

»Breakfasts

YOGURT WITH PAPAYA, BLACKBERRIES, AND SEEDS

This may be the perfect power breakfast. It's packed full of so many nutrients, I could spend a chapter describing all the benefits. Nutritional highlights include: protein from yogurt and almonds, heart-healthy unsaturated fat and fiber from almonds and sunflower seeds, omega-3 fatty acids—good for both heart and brain—from flaxseeds, and salicylic acid (the active ingredient in aspirin) from blackberries. If fresh papaya is hard to find, use dried. The recipe is also good with mango.

MAKES 2 SERVINGS

ACTIVE TIME: 10 MINUTES

TOTAL TIME: 10 MINUTES

2 cups low-fat plain yogurt

1 cup chopped fresh papaya or ½ cup dried (2 strips chopped)

1 cup fresh blackberries

3 tablespoons sliced or whole almonds

1 tablespoon sunflower seeds

2 teaspoons flaxseeds

Divide each of the ingredients among two serving bowls and serve. Or make one big batch, eat half, and keep the remaining portion in an airtight container, refrigerated, for up to 2 days.

CALORIES/ SERVING	CARBS (G)	PROTEIN (G)	FAT (G)	SAT FAT (G)	SODIUM (MG)	FIBER (G)
325	34	18	13	3	176	8

»Lunches

GAZPACHO

I fell in love with gazpacho when I was racing in Spain, and I still believe there is nothing quite as refreshing as a big bowl of this chilled soup. Make a large batch that guarantees leftovers; this is one of those recipes that tastes even better when the flavors blend overnight. To adjust the kick, add more or less garlic, or add more jalapeño chile pepper, seeds and all.

MAKES 2 SERVINGS (3 CUPS TOTAL)

ACTIVE TIME: 25 MINUTES

TOTAL TIME: 2 HOURS 25 MINUTES (INCLUDING CHILLING)

1 slice whole wheat bread, torn into 2" pieces
1 cup lower sodium vegetable juice (such as V8)
4 plum tomatoes, roughly chopped
2 scallions, roughly chopped
1 small cucumber, peeled and roughly chopped
½ jalapeño chile pepper, seeded and minced (wear plastic gloves when handling)
1 small clove garlic
1 tablespoon extra-virgin olive oil
1 teaspoon red wine vinegar
¼ cup water (optional)
Salt
Freshly ground black pepper
2 tablespoons sliced almonds (optional)

1. Place the bread and vegetable juice in a blender or food processor and let sit for 2 minutes, or until the bread absorbs the juice.

2. Add the tomatoes, scallions, cucumber, and jalapeño chile pepper (with seeds, for a spicier gazpacho), garlic, oil, and vinegar. Blend or process until smooth. Add the water to thin the soup, if desired.

3. Season with the salt and black pepper to taste, and chill for at least 2 hours or overnight. Garnish with the almonds, if desired, and serve chilled.

CALORIES/ SERVING	CARBS (G)	PROTEIN (G)	FAT (G)	SAT FAT (G)	SODIUM (MG)	FIBER (G)
172	21	4	8	1	342	5

»Lunches

PUMPKIN AND GINGER SOUP

While this soup doesn't take long to prepare, it's so rich and flavorful that people will think you spent hours on it. Just be sure to get pumpkin puree, not sweetened pie filling! Nutritionally, this soup delivers an enormous amount of beta-carotene, the antioxidant that your body converts into vitamin A.

MAKES 2 SERVINGS (4 CUPS)

ACTIVE TIME: 30 MINUTES

TOTAL TIME: 30 MINUTES

¼ cup raw pumpkin seeds
1 tablespoon extra-virgin olive oil
¼ cup chopped onion
1½ teaspoons ground ginger
¼ teaspoon cinnamon
1 can (15 ounces) pumpkin puree
2 cups low-sodium vegetable broth
1 cup fat-free milk
¾ teaspoon salt
1 tablespoon honey
1 tablespoon creamy natural peanut butter

1. Preheat the oven or toaster oven to 375°F. Spread the seeds on a baking pan and bake for 7 to 9 minutes, or until browned. Remove from the pan and set aside.

2. In a small saucepan, heat the oil over medium heat. Add the onion, cover, reduce heat to medium-low, and cook for 5 minutes, or until softened. Stir in the ginger and cinnamon and cook for about 30 seconds, or until fragrant.

3. Whisk in the puree, broth, and milk. Increase the heat to medium-high and bring to a simmer. Whisk in the salt, honey, and peanut butter and simmer for 5 minutes. Sprinkle with the reserved pumpkin seeds and serve hot.

CALORIES/ SERVING	CARBS (G)	PROTEIN (G)	FAT (G)	SAT FAT (G)	SODIUM (MG)	FIBER (G)
408	43	24	20	4	961	9

ASIAN CHICKEN SALAD SANDWICH

This is the perfect recipe for leftover grilled chicken; it's quick and easy to prepare, and it has a refreshing, light, and nutty flavor. I'm definitely a fan of grilling extra chicken breasts or making more than a recipe calls for. They keep well in the refrigerator and make it very easy to add quality protein (without a lot of added fat) to a variety of meals and snacks. If you don't have sesame oil, olive oil or peanut oil will work well instead. You can also substitute spinach or romaine lettuce for the cabbage.

MAKES 2 SERVINGS

ACTIVE TIME: 15 MINUTES

TOTAL TIME: 25 MINUTES

4 cups thinly sliced cabbage
2 grilled boneless, skinless chicken breasts (4–6 ounces each), diced
1 seedless orange or 2 clementines, peeled and chopped
¼ cup chopped unsalted peanuts
2 tablespoons chopped cilantro
1 scallion, chopped (green part only)
1 tablespoon lime juice
½ teaspoon sesame oil
½ teaspoon honey
¼ teaspoon salt
Salt
Freshly ground black pepper
2 whole wheat pitas

1. In a medium bowl, combine the cabbage, chicken, orange, peanuts, cilantro, scallion, lime juice, oil, and honey. Toss to combine. Let sit for 10 minutes, or until the cabbage wilts and the flavors blend. Season with the salt and pepper to taste.

2. Slice the pitas in half and pack with the salad.

CALORIES/ SERVING	CARBS (G)	PROTEIN (G)	FAT (G)	SAT FAT (G)	SODIUM (MG)	FIBER (G)
569	48	56	17	3	348	10

TUNA SALAD WITH SUN-DRIED TOMATOES AND ARTICHOKES

Here's a grown-up tuna salad that can be served over salad greens, in a whole wheat pita, or on whole wheat bread or crackers. I really enjoy this version of tuna salad because it skips the mayonnaise and has a much lighter, more refreshing flavor. You can also use leftover cooked tuna instead of canned tuna.

MAKES 2 SERVINGS

ACTIVE TIME: 20 MINUTES

TOTAL TIME: 20 MINUTES

2 cans (6 ounces each) chunk albacore tuna packed in water, drained

1 can (6.5 ounces) marinated artichokes, drained

1 cup halved grape tomatoes

½ cup roughly chopped parsley

2 tablespoons extra-virgin olive oil

2 sun-dried tomatoes, chopped

1 tablespoon lemon juice

1 tablespoon capers, rinsed and drained (optional)

Salt

Freshly ground black pepper

In a medium bowl, combine the tuna, artichokes, grape tomatoes, parsley, oil, sun-dried tomatoes, lemon juice, and capers, if using. Mix well and season to taste with the salt and pepper.

CALORIES/ SERVING	CARBS (G)	PROTEIN (G)	FAT (G)	SAT FAT (G)	SODIUM (MG)	FIBER (G)
371	13	46	15	2	406	5

»Lunches

MIXED GREENS SALAD WITH PEARS AND PINE NUTS

This recipe proves that even a reasonably basic salad can be a joy to eat. This one is also incredibly easy to make, especially if you buy prewashed greens. To pick the best pears, go for those that are firm but responsive to a good squeeze—neither mushy or hard as a rock. To hasten ripening, place pears together in a closed brown paper bag.

MAKES 2 SERVINGS

ACTIVE TIME: 15 MINUTES

TOTAL TIME: 15 MINUTES

2 tablespoons pine nuts
2 cups baby spinach
2 cups mixed baby greens
2 ribs celery, thinly sliced
1 small cucumber, quartered lengthwise and thinly sliced
1 pear, cored and thinly sliced
2 tablespoons extra-virgin olive oil
2 teaspoons cider vinegar
Salt
Freshly ground black pepper
¼ cup part-skim ricotta cheese
2 Wasa Crispbreads

1. Place the pine nuts in a small skillet and toast over medium heat, gently shaking the skillet back and forth, for 3 minutes, or until the nuts are fragrant and light brown.

2. In a large bowl, combine the spinach, baby greens, celery, cucumber, pear, oil, and vinegar. Toss to combine and season to taste with the salt and pepper.

3. Spread the cheese on the crackers and serve with the salad.

CALORIES/ SERVING	CARBS (G)	PROTEIN (G)	FAT (G)	SAT FAT (G)	SODIUM (MG)	FIBER (G)
343	33	10	19	4	850	10

»Lunches

TOFU SCRAMBLE AND VEGETABLE WRAP

For a long time I wasn't a big fan of tofu, but recipes like this one and the significant nutritional benefits of soybeans changed my mind. Soy is one of the only vegetable sources of complete protein, and it also supplies isoflavones that may help prevent heart disease. Since a brick of tofu is packed in water, place a few paper towels under and on top of it, and then place a book or cutting board on top of that. This will squeeze extra water out, making the tofu easier to prepare.

MAKES 2 SERVINGS

ACTIVE TIME: 15 MINUTES

TOTAL TIME: 15 MINUTES

1 tablespoon extra-virgin olive oil
2 scallions, thinly sliced, whites and greens separated
2 cups spinach, roughly chopped
14 ounces (½ package) soft tofu, drained and crumbled
½ cup grated low-fat Cheddar cheese
Salt
Freshly ground black pepper
2 whole wheat tortillas (8" each)
2 tablespoons medium or hot salsa

1. Heat the oil in a medium skillet over medium heat. Add the scallion whites and cook for 1 minute, or until beginning to soften. Add the spinach and cook for 1 minute, until wilted.

2. Add the tofu and cheese and cook, stirring, for 1 to 2 minutes, or until the cheese melts. Remove from the heat, add the scallion greens, and season to taste with the salt and pepper.

3. Heat the tortillas in a microwave for 15 seconds, or until malleable, or in a dry skillet over medium heat for 1 minute, turning every 15 seconds.

4. Place half of the scramble in the center of a warmed tortilla, top with 1 tablespoon of the salsa, and wrap burrito-style. Repeat with the remaining tortilla.

CALORIES/ SERVING	CARBS (G)	PROTEIN (G)	FAT (G)	SAT FAT (G)	SODIUM (MG)	FIBER (G)
477	41	31	21	4	760	8

»Sides

RATATOUILLE

I frequently ate ratatouille when I was racing and living in France. It's a very tasty side dish for grilled chicken, steak, or fish, and it's a lot more interesting than steamed vegetables. Eggplant is primarily associated with ratatouille, but you can add seasonal vegetables to make different varieties of this flavorful and nutrient-packed side dish.

MAKES 4 SERVINGS (3 CUPS)

ACTIVE TIME: 45 MINUTES

TOTAL TIME: 45 MINUTES

1 small eggplant, cut into ½" cubes
½ teaspoon salt + more to taste
4 tablespoons extra-virgin olive oil
1 medium onion, chopped
1 red bell pepper, sliced into ½"-thick strips
1 clove garlic, sliced
1 small yellow zucchini, sliced lengthwise and cut into half-moons
1 small green zucchini, sliced lengthwise and cut into half-moons
1 tablespoon tomato paste
1 teaspoon dried herbes de Provence or mix of dried thyme, rosemary, basil, and marjoram
Freshly ground black pepper

1. Place the eggplant in a colander and toss with the ½ teaspoon salt. Let rest in sink.

2. Heat 1 tablespoon of the oil in a medium skillet over medium heat. Add the onion, cover the skillet, and cook for 3 minutes, or until softened. Add the bell pepper and salt to taste. Partially cover and cook, stirring occasionally, for 5 minutes, or until pepper slices are softened. Transfer the vegetables to a medium mixing bowl and set aside.

3. Heat 2 tablespoons of the oil in the skillet over medium heat. Add the garlic and cook for 30 seconds, or until fragrant. Add the yellow and green zucchini and salt to taste. Partially cover and cook, stirring occasionally, for 5 minutes, or until softened. Transfer to the bowl with the peppers and set aside.

4. Heat the remaining 1 tablespoon oil in the skillet over medium heat and add the tomato paste and herbs. Cook, stirring occasionally, for 2 to 3 minutes, or until the paste begins to darken. Squeeze and discard the liquid from the eggplant and add the eggplant to the skillet. Cook covered, stirring occasionally, for 7 to 8 minutes, or until the eggplant is softened. If the mixture appears dry, add up to ¼ cup water and stir the browning bits to create a sauce.

5. Return the reserved vegetables to the skillet and cook, stirring occasionally, for 5 minutes, or until heated through and flavors are incorporated. Season to taste with the salt and black pepper. Serve hot, warm, or at room temperature.

CALORIES/ SERVING	CARBS (G)	PROTEIN (G)	FAT (G)	SAT FAT (G)	SODIUM (MG)	FIBER (G)
167	14	3	11	1	53	6

»Sides

ROOT VEGETABLE AND APPLE SLAW

One of the major advantages of adding root vegetables to your nutrition program is that they are very filling yet very low in calories. To speed this recipe's preparation, throw everything in a food processor instead of using a grater. This is a perfect side dish for grilled or sautéed meats and fish, and you can also toss it with greens to make a larger salad. If you can't find celeriac, use 1½ cups grated carrots, jicama, or beets or 1 cup chopped celery or endive.

MAKES 2 SERVINGS (4 CUPS; 3 CUPS AFTER WILTING FOR 20 MINUTES)

ACTIVE TIME: 20 MINUTES

TOTAL TIME: 20 MINUTES

1 Granny Smith apple
1 small head celeriac, peeled (or alternatives listed above)
1 large parsnip, peeled
1 tablespoon freshly squeezed lemon juice
1 tablespoon extra-virgin olive oil
¼ teaspoon salt
¼ teaspoon freshly ground black pepper

Grate the apple, celeriac, and parsnip with a hand grater, food processor, or mandoline. Combine in a medium bowl and toss with the lemon juice, oil, salt, and pepper. Serve at once, or refrigerate until ready to serve.

CALORIES/ SERVING	CARBS (G)	PROTEIN (G)	FAT (G)	SAT FAT (G)	SODIUM (MG)	FIBER (G)
159	23	1	7	1	305	5

»Sides

CURRIED CARROT SALAD

This is a great side dish to serve with fish, such as oven-roasted or grilled salmon. The carrots provide a lot of beta-carotene, which becomes antioxidant vitamin A in your body. This recipe is also extremely low in fat and can be completely fat free if you use fat-free yogurt.

MAKES 2 SERVINGS (2½ CUPS TOTAL)

ACTIVE TIME: 15 MINUTES

TOTAL TIME: 15 MINUTES

2 cups water
5 medium carrots, peeled and sliced ¼" thick (2 cups)
2 tablespoons raisins
¼ cup low-fat plain yogurt
½ teaspoon curry powder
½ teaspoon coarse salt
⅛ teaspoon red pepper flakes (optional)
1 cup packed roughly chopped spinach leaves

1. Bring water to a boil in a small saucepan. Add the carrots and raisins. Boil 2 to 3 minutes, or until bright orange but still crispy and firm. Drain and cool.

2. In a medium bowl, stir together the yogurt, curry powder, salt, and red pepper flakes, if using. Add the carrots and raisins and stir to coat. Add the spinach and toss gently. Refrigerate until ready to serve.

CALORIES/ SERVING	CARBS (G)	PROTEIN (G)	FAT (G)	SAT FAT (G)	SODIUM (MG)	FIBER (G)
125	25	4	1	0	721	5

»Dinners

GRILLED CITRUS AND GARLIC CHICKEN

It's not often that you'll come across a recipe that combines soy sauce and orange juice, but trust me, you'll love what this marinade does for chicken. You can also throw the marinated chicken on the grill, and substitute olive oil if you don't have sesame oil.

MAKES 2 SERVINGS

ACTIVE TIME: 25 MINUTES

TOTAL TIME: 40 MINUTES

Juice of 1 orange (¼ cup)
3 tablespoons low-sodium soy sauce
2 scallions, chopped
2 cloves garlic, peeled and smashed
1 tablespoon honey
2 teaspoons sesame oil
2 boneless, skinless chicken breasts (6 ounces each)

1. In a medium bowl, whisk together the orange juice, soy sauce, scallions, garlic, honey, and oil. Add the chicken and marinate for 15 minutes at room temperature, turning occasionally to coat.

2. Heat a grill pan over high heat and lightly coat with cooking spray. Remove the chicken from the marinade and cook, turning often, for 10 minutes, or until a thermometer inserted in the thickest portion registers 160°F and the juices run clear.

3. Meanwhile, bring the marinade to a rapid boil in a small skillet over high heat. Pour the sauce through a strainer and discard the scallions and garlic. Drizzle each piece of chicken with a tablespoon of the sauce.

CALORIES/ SERVING	CARBS (G)	PROTEIN (G)	FAT (G)	SAT FAT (G)	SODIUM (MG)	FIBER (G)
254	18	41	2	1	1,000	1

»Dinners

WHOLE TROUT STUFFED WITH FENNEL AND LEMON

Unfamiliar with fennel? It's a white bulb you'll find in the produce section, and it sometimes has green stalks coming out the top. It has a mild licorice flavor similar to anise, and it's a great vegetable for weight loss because it's filling but contains very few calories. You can also use leftover trout in place of tuna in Tuna Salad with Sun-Dried Tomatoes and Artichokes (page 153).

MAKES 2 SERVINGS

ACTIVE TIME: 20 MINUTES

TOTAL TIME: 30 MINUTES

1 tablespoon extra-virgin olive oil

1 small bulb fennel, cored and cut into ¼"-thick wedges

1 small onion, cut into ¼" wedges

1 small lemon, thinly sliced widthwise, seeds discarded

Salt

Freshly ground black pepper

1 whole trout (1 pound), cleaned

1. Preheat the broiler.

2. Heat the oil in a medium skillet over medium-high heat. Add the fennel and onion and stir to coat. Cook, covered, stirring occasionally, for 5 to 7 minutes, or until the vegetables begin to soften.

3. Uncover, add the lemon, and continue cooking, stirring gently, for 3 to 5 minutes, or until the vegetables start to brown on the edges. Remove from the heat and transfer to a small bowl, reserving the skillet. Season the vegetables with the salt and pepper and toss in a few of the fennel fronds if you want as well.

4. Season the trout on the outside and inside with the salt and pepper. Stuff with some of the vegetables and mound the remaining vegetables in the center of the skillet. Lay the trout on top. Broil for 8 to 10 minutes, or until the trout is cooked through.

CALORIES/ SERVING	CARBS (G)	PROTEIN (G)	FAT (G)	SAT FAT (G)	SODIUM (MG)	FIBER (G)
355	15	40	15	3	272	5

»Dinners

CUMIN-DUSTED SALMON OVER MIXED GREENS WITH CLEMENTINES

Bored with plain old roasted salmon? This flavorful variation will wake up your taste-buds while you reap the benefits of quality protein and omega-3 and omega-6 fatty acids—and it's a wonderful recovery food. Substitute any kind of orange when you can't find clementines, which are typically available only in the winter. Toasting some of the cumin brings out more of the spice's flavor and gives the dish a nice kick.

MAKES 2 SERVINGS

ACTIVE TIME: 18 MINUTES

TOTAL TIME: 30 MINUTES

½ teaspoon ground cumin, divided
¼ teaspoon salt + more to taste
2 salmon fillets (4 ounces each), about 1" thick, skin removed
4½ teaspoons low-fat mayonnaise
1 teaspoon lemon juice
Salt
Freshly ground black pepper
2 cups mixed baby lettuce greens, packed
1 clementine, peeled and divided into sections
1 tablespoon sunflower seeds

1. Preheat the oven to 350°F.

2. In a small bowl, combine ¼ teaspoon of the cumin and ¼ teaspoon salt. Place the salmon in an ovenproof baking dish or skillet and coat with the cumin mixture. Bake for 12 minutes, or until cooked through.

3. Heat the remaining ¼ teaspoon cumin in a small skillet over medium heat and toast, gently moving the pan back and forth, for 30 seconds, or until fragrant. Remove from the heat, stir in the mayonnaise and lemon juice, and season with the salt and pepper to taste.

4. In a medium bowl, combine the greens, clementine, and sunflower seeds. Add the cumin-mayonnaise dressing and toss to coat. Serve the salmon with the greens.

CALORIES/ SERVING	CARBS (G)	PROTEIN (G)	FAT (G)	SAT FAT (G)	SODIUM (MG)	FIBER (G)
250	8	24	10	1	242	2

CHILI-LIME BAKED COD

Cod is great for those who like a milder, less "fishy"-tasting fish, yet it still packs the omega-3 and omega-6 fatty acid punch of other cold-water fish like salmon, tuna, and halibut. This incredibly easy recipe goes well with shredded cabbage or lettuce and warm corn tortillas or served over a bed of brown rice or buckwheat.

MAKES 2 SERVINGS

ACTIVE TIME: 15 MINUTES

TOTAL TIME: 15 MINUTES

¾ teaspoon chili powder
¼ teaspoon coarse salt
1 lime
1 tablespoon grapeseed or canola oil
½ pound skinless cod, cut into 2 portions

1. Preheat the oven to 375°F.

2. In a small bowl, combine the chili powder and salt. Zest the lime (you should have about 1 teaspoon zest) and add the zest to the chili powder mixture. Cut the lime in half.

3. Heat the oil in a small nonstick skillet over medium-high heat. Add the cod, flesh-side down, and cook 4 to 5 minutes, or until browned.

4. Turn the fillets and sprinkle the tops with the chili mixture. Place in the oven and bake 5 minutes, or until cooked through. Squeeze lime juice over the top of each fillet.

CALORIES/ SERVING	CARBS (G)	PROTEIN (G)	FAT (G)	SAT FAT (G)	SODIUM (MG)	FIBER (G)
168	4	20	8	1	149	1

»Dinners

GINGERY TEMPEH STIR-FRY

Tempeh is a soybean product that can be used in a wide variety of recipes, especially as a more nutrient-dense substitute for mushrooms. To save some time, consider buying minced garlic in a jar in the grocery store.

MAKES 2 SERVINGS

ACTIVE TIME: 30 MINUTES

TOTAL TIME: 30 MINUTES

4 tablespoons canola oil, divided
1 package tempeh (8 ounces), sliced into ¼"-thick strips
1 medium onion, cut into ¼" wedges
1 red bell pepper, seeded and cut into ¼" strips
1 green bell pepper, seeded and cut into ¼" strips
2 scallions, sliced, whites and greens separated
1 piece (1") fresh ginger, peeled and finely chopped
2 cloves garlic, minced
½ cup mung bean sprouts
3 tablespoons low-sodium soy sauce
1–2 teaspoons lime juice

1. Heat 1 tablespoon of the oil in a large nonstick skillet or wok. Add the tempeh and cook, turning once until golden, 3 to 4 minutes per side. Remove from the pan.

2. Increase the heat to high and add 1½ tablespoons oil. Add the onion and bell peppers and cook, stirring occasionally, for 3 to 4 minutes, or until the vegetables begin to brown.

3. Push the vegetables to the edge of the skillet and add the remaining 1½ tablespoons oil to the center of the skillet. Add the scallion whites, ginger, and garlic. Cook, stirring constantly, for 30 seconds, or until fragrant. Return the tempeh to the pan, stir together with the vegetables, and cook for 1 minute, or until warmed through.

4. Remove from the heat and add the scallion greens, mung bean sprouts, soy sauce, and lime juice. Stir to combine and serve hot.

CALORIES/ SERVING	CARBS (G)	PROTEIN (G)	FAT (G)	SAT FAT (G)	SODIUM (MG)	FIBER (G)
387	29	25	19	3	920	4

»Dinners

GRILLED TURKEY SAUSAGE AND LENTILS WITH SPINACH

With lentils and spinach, this recipe yields a dish that is rich in iron and folate, as well as quality protein from both the lentils and turkey sausage. For a more peppery taste, mix in some arugula, and for a bigger dose of vitamins and minerals, including vitamins A, C, and K and muscle-building manganese, substitute kale for the spinach. Serve this hearty dish with a green salad.

MAKES 2 SERVINGS

ACTIVE TIME: 15 MINUTES

TOTAL TIME: 45 MINUTES

2 cups low-sodium chicken broth

¼ teaspoon salt

¾ cup green lentils

3 cups packed spinach, roughly chopped

Canola oil

½ pound turkey sausage

1. In a small saucepan, bring the chicken broth and salt to a boil. Add the lentils, return to a boil, reduce the heat to low, cover, and cook 25 to 30 minutes, or until lentils are just soft. Remove from the heat, stir in the spinach, and cover for 1 minute, or until the spinach wilts.

2. While the lentils are cooking, heat a grill pan over medium heat and lightly brush with the oil. Grill the sausages, turning every 2 minutes, for 8 to 10 minutes, or until cooked through. Serve hot with the lentils.

CALORIES/ SERVING	CARBS (G)	PROTEIN (G)	FAT (G)	SAT FAT (G)	SODIUM (MG)	FIBER (G)
267	24	18	11	2	1,090	2

WHOLE GRAIN CHEDDAR COINS

These cookies aren't sweet like Maple, Oat, and Fig Cookies (page 209). They're more like a hearty, cheesy cracker. They make a great nutrient-dense snack and are good at parties. Make a big batch of the dough, form it into a log, and freeze it. Cut off slices and bake when you have guests—but increase the baking time to 25 to 30 minutes when using frozen dough.

MAKES 5 SERVINGS (20 COINS TOTAL)

ACTIVE TIME: 15 MINUTES

TOTAL TIME: 1 HOUR 55 MINUTES (INCLUDES FREEZING TIME)

½ cup walnuts
½ cup all-purpose flour
4 tablespoons cold unsalted butter, cut into small pieces
1 cup shredded low-fat Cheddar cheese
1 teaspoon flaxseeds
½ teaspoon dried thyme
½ teaspoon salt
¼ teaspoon black pepper
¼ cup fat-free milk

1. Preheat the oven to 275°F. Toast the walnuts on a baking sheet for 10 minutes, or until fragrant. Transfer to a food processor and cool, about 5 minutes.

2. Add the flour and pulse until finely ground. Add the butter and pulse for 20 seconds, or until the butter is the size of peas. Add the cheese, flaxseeds, thyme, salt, and pepper and pulse to combine, about 15 seconds. Add the milk in a slow, steady stream and pulse until the mixture forms a ball.

3. Turn the dough onto a sheet of plastic wrap and form into a 10" log. Wrap tightly and freeze until firm, about 1 hour.

4. Preheat the oven to 350°F. Coat a baking sheet with cooking spray. Remove the dough from the freezer and slice into ½"-thick coins. Place on a baking sheet and bake for 18 minutes, or until edges begin to brown. Transfer to a wire rack to cool.

CALORIES/ SERVING	CARBS (G)	PROTEIN (G)	FAT (G)	SAT FAT (G)	SODIUM (MG)	FIBER (G)
65	3	2	5	2	83	1

»Snacks

YOGURT WITH MELON, HONEY, AND NUTS

This is a very flexible recipe; you can use cantaloupe instead of honeydew melon, pecans or other nuts in place of walnuts, and vanilla yogurt instead of plain. To tell if a melon is ripe, hold it close to your ear and knock on the side. If it sounds hollow, it's ready and will be naturally sweet. If it's still very hard and sounds like you're knocking on wood, give it a couple of days (on the counter, not in the fridge) to ripen.

MAKES 2 SERVINGS

ACTIVE TIME: 10 MINUTES

TOTAL TIME: 20 MINUTES

⅓ cup walnut pieces
½ ripe honeydew melon, seeded and cut into chunks (about 2 cups)
1 cup fat-free plain yogurt
1½ teaspoons honey

1. Preheat the oven to 275°F. Place the walnuts on a baking sheet and bake for 10 minutes, or until fragrant and toasted. Let cool.

2. Meanwhile, place half of the melon in a bowl, top with ½ cup of the yogurt, and drizzle with ¾ teaspoon of the honey. Sprinkle with the cooled nuts and repeat for a second serving.

CALORIES/ SERVING	CARBS (G)	PROTEIN (G)	FAT (G)	SAT FAT (G)	SODIUM (MG)	FIBER (G)
294	30	12	14	2	117	3

»Snacks

CELERY STICKS FILLED WITH GOAT CHEESE AND SUN-DRIED TOMATOES

Here's a gourmet twist on a favorite childhood snack (celery and peanut butter). It's relatively low in calories but really fills you up because of the fiber in the celery and the fat and protein in the goat cheese. You can also double or triple the recipe to make an impressive contribution to a party.

MAKES 2 SERVINGS

ACTIVE TIME: 10 MINUTES

TOTAL TIME: 10 MINUTES

2 teaspoons sesame seeds
2 ounces low-fat goat cheese
1½ teaspoons chopped dry-packed sun-dried tomato
2 tablespoons fat-free milk
6 ribs celery, trimmed and cut in half widthwise

1. Place the sesame seeds in a small dry skillet over medium heat. Toast, stirring, for 3 minutes, or until light brown and fragrant. Transfer to a small bowl to cool.

2. Place the cheese in a medium bowl. Add the sun-dried tomato and milk and stir until light and creamy. Fill the crevice of each celery rib with about 1½ teaspoons of the cheese mixture. Sprinkle with the sesame seeds.

CALORIES/ SERVING	CARBS (G)	PROTEIN (G)	FAT (G)	SAT FAT (G)	SODIUM (MG)	FIBER (G)
124	6	7	8	4	230	2

WEEK FOUR WORKOUTS

DAY 22

AEROBIC WORKOUT
15 MINUTES

5 min Range 1	■□□
10 min Range 2	■■□

STRENGTH WORKOUT
20 MINUTES

REST PERIODS: 45 SECONDS BETWEEN EACH EXERCISE

- 25 jump-rope jumps *(page 273)*
- 10 overhead squats *(page 284)*
- 12 medicine ball situps *(page 278)*
- 25 jump-rope jumps
- 10 overhead squats
- 12 medicine ball situps
- 10 up-downs *(page 292)*
- 10 reverse medicine ball lunges *(per leg) (page 288)*
- 15 pushups *(pages 286–87)*
- 10 up-downs
- 10 × reverse medicine ball lunges *(per leg)*
- 15 pushups

DAY 23

AEROBIC WORKOUT
40 MINUTES

5 min Range 1	■□□
10 min Range 2	■■□
5 min Range 3	■■■
5 min Range 1	■□□
10 min Range 2	■■□
5 min Range 3	■■■

AGILITY WORKOUT
20 MINUTES

REST PERIODS: 60 SECONDS BETWEEN EACH EXERCISE

- 4 × 10-foot shuttle run *(page 296)*
- 4 × 10-foot shuttle run
- 20 sec single-leg line jump *(page 301)*
- 20 sec single-leg line jump *(opposite leg)*
- 20 sec single-leg line jump
- 20 sec single-leg line jump *(opposite leg)*
- 3 × 4-count zigzag line jumps *(page 306)*
- 3 × 4-count zigzag line jumps
- 3 × 4-count zigzag line jumps

DAY 24

AEROBIC: REST

AGILITY/STRENGTH: REST

DAY 25

AEROBIC WORKOUT
15 MINUTES

5 min Range 1	■□□
10 min Range 2	■■□

STRENGTH WORKOUT
20 MINUTES

REST PERIODS: 45 SECONDS BETWEEN EACH EXERCISE

- 15 squat and presses *(page 290)*
- 8 curl and presses *(page 271)*
- 8 medicine ball solo twists *(page 279)*
- 15 squat and presses
- 8 curl and presses
- 8 medicine ball solo twists
- 25 jump-rope jumps
- 15 bench dips *(page 269)*
- 10 medicine ball situps
- 25 jump-rope jumps
- 15 bench dips
- 10 medicine ball situps

(continued)

WEEK FOUR WORKOUTS

DAY 26

AEROBIC WORKOUT
40 MINUTES

5 min Range 1

10 min Range 2

5 min Range 3

5 min Range 1

10 min Range 2

5 min Range 3

AGILITY WORKOUT
15 MINUTES

REST PERIODS: 60 SECONDS BETWEEN EACH EXERCISE

4 × 10-foot shuttle run

4 × 10-foot shuttle run

20 sec single-leg line jump

20 sec single-leg line jump *(opposite leg)*

20 sec single-leg line jump

20 sec single-leg line jump *(opposite leg)*

3 × 4-count zigzag line jump

3 × 4-count zigzag line jump

3 × 4-count zigzag line jump

DAY 27

AEROBIC WORKOUT
25 MINUTES

5 min Range 1

10 min Range 2

5 min Range 3

5 min Range 2

STRENGTH WORKOUT
20 MINUTES

REST PERIODS: 45 SECONDS BETWEEN EACH EXERCISE

25 jump-rope jumps

10 overhead squats

12 medicine ball situps

25 jump-rope jumps

10 overhead squats

12 medicine ball situps

10 up-downs

10 reverse medicine ball lunges *(per leg)*

15 pushups

10 up-downs

10 reverse medicine ball lunges *(per leg)*

15 pushups

DAY 28

AEROBIC: REST

AGILITY/STRENGTH: REST

WEEK FOUR SHOPPING LIST

BREAD/CEREALS/GRAINS

- ☐ 2 whole wheat English muffins
- ☐ 1 whole grain bagel
- ☐ 8 whole wheat tortillas (8" each)
- ☐ 2 whole wheat tortillas (10" each)
- ☐ 2 small corn tortillas (6" each)
- ☐ 4 whole wheat dinner rolls
- ☐ 5 slices whole grain bread
- ☐ 3 ounces soba noodles, dry

CONDIMENTS

- ☐ 2 bay leaves
- ☐ 8 tablespoons hummus
- ☐ 1 tablespoon minced ginger
- ☐ 1" piece fresh ginger

FRUIT

- ☐ ¼ avocado
- ☐ 3 medium bananas
- ☐ ½ cup blueberries
- ☐ 2 peaches
- ☐ 1 plum
- ☐ ¾ cup strawberries, halved
- ☐ 5 cups fruit of choice

VEGETABLES

- ☐ 1 medium carrot
- ☐ 30 large baby carrots
- ☐ 1 spaghetti squash
- ☐ 4 bell peppers, variety of colors
- ☐ 3 large ribs celery
- ☐ 2 cups mixed greens
- ☐ 3½ ounces shiitake mushrooms
- ☐ 5 ounces cremini mushrooms
- ☐ 1 small red onion
- ☐ 2 medium onions
- ☐ 1½ cups romaine lettuce or greens of choice
- ☐ 6 cups spinach
- ☐ 2½ medium tomatoes
- ☐ 3 yams
- ☐ 2 cups veggies of choice
- ☐ 1 scallion
- ☐ 1 cup frozen baby peas
- ☐ 1 sheet nori (seaweed)
- ☐ 1 pound baby bok choy (leafy green)
- ☐ 1 pound parsnips
- ☐ 1 medium cucumber

DAIRY/EGGS

- ☐ 4 eggs
- ☐ 4 containers (6 ounces each) fat-free yogurt (any flavor)
- ☐ 1¾ cups low-fat shredded cheese
- ☐ 1 slice low-fat cheese of choice
- ☐ 3½ cups fat-free milk
- ☐ 2 ounces fresh mozzarella cheese
- ☐ 3 tablespoons low-fat cream cheese

MEAT/POULTRY/FISH

- ☐ 1 pound 6 ounces chicken breast
- ☐ 3 ounces canned water-packed tuna
- ☐ 7 ounces ground turkey
- ☐ 2 halibut fillets (4 ounces each)
- ☐ 4 ounces salmon
- ☐ 2 ounces deli turkey
- ☐ 7 ounces sirloin

WEEK FOUR MEAL PLAN

Day 22–1,793 Calories

BREAKFAST

6 ounces fat-free yogurt (any flavor)

½ cup whole grain cereal

½ cup blueberries

1 tablespoon ground or milled flaxseed

SNACK

5 whole wheat crackers

3 ounces tuna

LUNCH

Veggie Wrap

- 1 whole wheat tortilla
- 2 tablespoons hummus
- 1 cup veggies of choice (cucumber, spinach, red bell peppers, tomato, mushrooms, etc.)
- ¼ cup leftover wild rice
- 1 slice low-fat cheese

SNACK

1 whole grain bagel with 2 tablespoons 100% fruit spread

DINNER

1 serving Soba Noodle Soup with Chicken* (page 208)

1 whole wheat roll

**Leftovers will be used in tomorrow's lunch. Just in case you need to make extra, check tomorrow's menu to see what is needed.*

Quick Cuts

How to Cut 200 to 300 Calories on This Day

» **Morning snack: Eat 2 ounces of tuna.**

» **Afternoon snack: Have half a bagel and 1 tablespoon fruit spread.**

Day 23–1,758 Calories

BREAKFAST

1 whole wheat English muffin

1 tablespoon natural peanut butter

1½ cups fresh mixed fruit

1 cup fat-free milk

SNACK

1 individual bag 94% fat-free microwave popcorn

LUNCH

1½ cups leftover Soba Noodle Soup

Turkey Sandwich

- 2 slices whole grain bread
- 2 ounces deli turkey
- 2–4 slices tomato
- 2 teaspoons mustard
- ¼ cup spinach, romaine lettuce, or greens of choice

SNACK

15 large baby carrots

6 ounces fat-free yogurt (any flavor) with 1 tablespoon ground or milled flaxseed and 1 cup sliced strawberries

DINNER

1 serving Halibut with Sesame-Ginger Bok Choy* (page 202)

1 cup brown rice

**Leftovers will be used in tomorrow's lunch. Just in case you need to make extra, check tomorrow's menu to see what is needed.*

Quick Cuts

How to Cut 200 to 300 Calories on This Day

» **Lunch: Halve the sandwich by using 1 slice bread and 1 ounce turkey.**

» **Dinner: Have ½ cup rice.**

WEEK FOUR MEAL PLAN

Day 24—1,716 Calories

BREAKFAST

1½ cups whole grain cereal

1 cup fat-free milk

1 cup sliced strawberries

SNACK

½ large bell pepper, sliced

10 large baby carrots

3 tablespoons hummus

LUNCH

Leftover Halibut Salad

- 2 cups mixed greens
- 2 ounces leftover halibut
- 2 tablespoons sunflower seeds
- 2 tablespoons light dressing of choice

1 whole wheat roll

2 whole wheat fig cookies (like Fig Newmans)

SNACK

1 serving Cocoa–Peanut Butter Smoothie (page 212)

DINNER

Ground Turkey Tacos

- 2 small corn tortillas
- 4 ounces ground turkey*
- ½ cup shredded romaine
- ½ cup chopped tomato
- ½ cup low-fat cheese
- ¼ cup salsa

**Leftovers will be used in tomorrow's lunch. Just in case you need to make extra, check tomorrow's menu to see what is needed.*

Quick Cuts

How to Cut 200 to 300 Calories on This Day

- **Breakfast: Eat 1 cup cereal with ⅔ cup milk.**
- **Lunch: Have 1 tablespoon sunflower seeds and 1 fig cookie.**
- **Dinner: Have 3 ounces ground turkey.**

Day 25—1,774 Calories

BREAKFAST

¾ cup rolled oats (dry)

¾ cup fat-free milk

1 medium banana

2 tablespoons sliced almonds

SNACK

1 apple

LUNCH

Taco Salad

- 2 cups romaine lettuce
- 3 ounces leftover turkey
- ¼ cup chopped tomatoes
- ¼ avocado
- ¼ cup low-fat cheese
- ¼ cup salsa
- 1 whole wheat tortilla

SNACK

1 whole wheat English muffin

1 tablespoon 100% fruit spread

DINNER

4 ounces sirloin steak*

1 serving Spicy Parsnip Oven Fries (page 200)

1 grilled bell pepper

1 whole wheat roll with 2 teaspoons olive oil spread

**Leftovers will be used in tomorrow's lunch. Just in case you need to make extra, check tomorrow's menu to see what is needed.*

Quick Cuts

How to Cut 200 to 300 Calories on This Day

- **Breakfast: Eat ½ cup oats with ½ cup milk.**
- **Dinner: Have 3 ounces steak and half a dinner roll with 1 teaspoon olive oil spread.**

WEEK FOUR MEAL PLAN

Day 26–1,745 Calories

BREAKFAST

¾ cup rolled oats (dry)

1 tablespoon honey

1 sliced peach

¾ cup fat-free milk

SNACK

1 plum

LUNCH

Steak Quesadilla

2 whole wheat tortillas

2–3 ounces leftover steak

½ cup low-fat cheese

½ cup sliced red and green bell peppers

SNACK

1 cup sliced cucumbers, baby carrots, and celery

3 tablespoons hummus

DINNER

1 serving Spicy Black Bean Burritos (page 204)

Quick Cuts

How to Cut 200 to 300 Calories on This Day

- **Breakfast: Eat ½ cup oats with ½ cup milk.**
- **Lunch: Halve the ingredients for the quesadilla, and fold the tortilla in half.**

Day 27–1,728 Calories

BREAKFAST

2 eggs (prepared any style with cooking spray)

2 slices whole grain toast with 2 tablespoons 100% fruit spread

6 ounces fat-free yogurt (any flavor)

1 tablespoon ground or milled flaxseed

SNACK

1½ cups fresh mixed fruit

LUNCH

1 serving Hearty Vegetable and Barley Soup (page 196)

1 whole wheat roll

SNACK

1 tomato, sliced

2 ounces fresh mozzarella

DINNER

4 ounces baked salmon

1 cup boiled spaghetti squash with 1 tablespoon honey

1 cup quinoa

Quick Cuts

How to Cut 200 to 300 Calories on This Day

- **Breakfast: Eat 1 slice toast with 1 tablespoon 100% fruit spread.**
- **Afternoon snack: Have 1 ounce mozzarella.**
- **Dinner: Have 3 ounces salmon.**

WEEK FOUR
MEAL PLAN

Day 28—1,810 Calories

BREAKFAST

1 serving Sweet Potato Hash with Chicken and Poached Eggs (page 190)

SNACK

1 whole wheat tortilla, baked and cut into chips

½ cup salsa

LUNCH

Grilled PB and Banana Sandwich

- 2 slices whole grain bread
- 1 tablespoon natural peanut butter
- 1 medium banana, sliced

10 large baby carrots

SNACK

Fruit smoothie (made with 2 cups fruit of choice, 6 ounces fat-free yogurt, ¼ cup fat-free milk, 1 tablespoon wheat germ, and ice)

DINNER

Chicken Fajitas

- 2 whole wheat tortillas
- 4 ounces chicken*
- Veggies and seasoning of choice

**Leftovers will be used in tomorrow's lunch. Just in case you need to make extra, check tomorrow's menu to see what is needed.*

Quick Cuts

How to Cut 200 to 300 Calories on This Day

» **Lunch: Have 2 teaspoons peanut butter.**

» **Dinner: Have 1 tortilla with 3 ounces grilled chicken.**

WEEK FIVE WORKOUTS

DAY 29

AEROBIC WORKOUT
40 MINUTES

- 5 min Range 1
- 5 min Range 3
- 15 min Range 2
- 5 min Range 3
- 5 min Range 2
- 5 min Range 3

STRENGTH WORKOUT
20 MINUTES

REST PERIODS: 60 SECONDS BETWEEN EACH EXERCISE

- 12 squat and presses *(page 290)*
- 6 windshield wipers *(page 295)*
- 15 medicine ball chest passes *(page 276)*
- 12 squat and presses
- 6 windshield wipers
- 15 medicine ball chest passes
- 8 curl and presses *(page 272)*
- 20 sec side core bridge *(per side)* *(page 271)*
- 8 curl and presses
- 20 sec side core bridge *(per side)*

DAY 30

AEROBIC WORKOUT
40 MINUTES

- 5 min Range 1
- 5 min Range 2
- 5 min Range 3
- 5 min Range 1
- 5 min Range 2
- 5 min Range 3
- 5 min Range 1
- 5 min Range 2

NO AGILITY/STRENGTH WORKOUT

DAY 31

AEROBIC: REST

AGILITY/STRENGTH: REST

DAY 32

AEROBIC WORKOUT
20 MINUTES

- 10 min Range 2
- 5 min Range 3
- 5 min Range 2

STRENGTH WORKOUT
20 MINUTES

REST PERIODS: 45 SECONDS BETWEEN EACH EXERCISE

- 12 squat and presses
- 6 windshield wipers
- 15 medicine ball chest passes
- 12 squat and presses
- 6 windshield wipers
- 15 medicine ball chest passes
- 8 curl and presses
- 20 sec side core bridge *(per side)*
- 8 curl and presses
- 20 sec side core bridge *(per side)*

DAY 33

AEROBIC WORKOUT
20 MINUTES

5 min Range 1

10 min Range 2

5 min Range 3

AGILITY WORKOUT
20 MINUTES

REST PERIODS: 60 SECONDS BETWEEN EACH EXERCISE

4 × 10-foot shuttle run *(page 296)*

4 × 10-foot shuttle run

4 × 10-foot shuttle run

4 × 10-foot shuttle run

20 sec single-leg line jump *(page 301)*

20 sec single-leg line jump *(opposite leg)*

20 sec single-leg line jump

20 sec single-leg line jump *(opposite leg)*

20 sec single-leg line jump

20 sec single-leg line jump *(opposite leg)*

DAY 34

AEROBIC WORKOUT
60 MINUTES

5 min Range 2

5 min Range 3

15 min Range 2

5 min Range 3

15 min Range 2

5 min Range 3

5min Range 2

5 min Range 3

AGILITY WORKOUT
20 MINUTES

REST PERIODS: 60 SECONDS BETWEEN EACH EXERCISE

10 sec double-leg cone jump *(page 299)*

10 sec double-leg cone jump

4 × 10-foot shuttle run

4 × 10-foot shuttle run

4 × 10-foot shuttle run

3 × 4-count zigzag line jump *(page 306)*

3 × 4-count zigzag line jump

3 × 4-count zigzag line jump

DAY 35

AEROBIC: REST

AGILITY/STRENGTH: REST

WEEK FIVE SHOPPING LIST

BREAD/CEREALS/GRAINS

- ☐ 3 whole grain bagels
- ☐ 2 slices whole grain bread
- ☐ 1 whole wheat pita
- ☐ 2 whole wheat tortillas (8" each)

NUTS/SEEDS/LEGUMES

- ☐ ⅛ cup black beans
- ☐ ⅛ cup kidney beans
- ☐ ⅛ cup pinto beans

FRUIT

- ☐ 1 Granny Smith apple
- ☐ ¼ avocado
- ☐ 3 medium bananas
- ☐ 2½ cups fruit salad of choice
- ☐ ½ melon
- ☐ 2 peaches
- ☐ 2 plums
- ☐ 1 medium pear
- ☐ ¾ cup strawberries
- ☐ 2 cups unsweetened applesauce
- ☐ 2 navel oranges
- ☐ 1 red grapefruit
- ☐ ¼ cup dried cranberries
- ☐ 1 teaspoon orange zest

VEGETABLES

- ☐ 1 red bell pepper
- ☐ 1 green bell pepper
- ☐ 2 cups broccoli
- ☐ 4 small ribs celery
- ☐ 1¼ cups mushrooms
- ☐ 1 medium white or yellow onion
- ☐ 1 small red onion
- ☐ 1 head romaine lettuce
- ☐ 4 cups mixed greens
- ☐ 4¼ cups spinach
- ☐ 1 pound 2 ounces kale
- ☐ 1 cup green beans
- ☐ 1 medium tomato
- ☐ 2 cups vegetables of choice
- ☐ 3 cups cherry tomatoes
- ☐ 1 small cucumber
- ☐ ¼ cup corn

DAIRY/EGGS

- ☐ 8 eggs
- ☐ 2 containers (6 ounces each) fat-free yogurt (any flavor)
- ☐ 6 ounces feta cheese
- ☐ 1 slice low-fat cheese
- ☐ ⅛ cup low-fat shredded cheese
- ☐ 3¾ cups fat-free milk
- ☐ 1 ounce mozzarella string cheese
- ☐ ¼ cup low-fat blue cheese crumbles
- ☐ 2 tablespoons low-fat cream cheese

MEAT/POULTRY/FISH

- ☐ 1 pound 4 ounces chicken breast
- ☐ 4 ounces salmon
- ☐ 3 ounces canned water-packed tuna
- ☐ 7 ounces cod
- ☐ 12 ounces skirt steak
- ☐ 4 ounces pork loin
- ☐ 4 ounces turkey sausage
- ☐ 8 ounces sliced smoked turkey

WEEK FIVE MEAL PLAN

Day 29—1,722 Calories

BREAKFAST

Peaches, Oatmeal, and "Cream"

- ½ cup rolled oats (dry)
- 1 cup fat-free milk
- 2 peaches, sliced
- 2 teaspoons cinnamon
- 2 tablespoons chopped pecans

SNACK

½ whole grain bagel
1 tablespoon 100% fruit spread

LUNCH

Southwestern Salad

- 2 cups greens of choice
- ¼ cup chopped tomatoes
- 2 ounces leftover chicken
- ¼ avocado
- ¼ cup black beans
- ¼ cup low-fat cheese
- ¼ cup salsa

1 medium banana

SNACK

½ whole grain bagel
1 tablespoon natural peanut butter
1 tablespoon ground or milled flaxseed

DINNER

4 ounces grilled chicken*
1 serving Warm Black-Eyed Pea Salad with Kale (page 199)

**Leftovers will be used in tomorrow's lunch. Just in case you need to make extra, check tomorrow's menu to see what is needed.*

Quick Cuts

How to Cut 200 to 300 Calories on This Day

- **Breakfast: Have ½ cup milk, 1 peach, and 1 tablespoon chopped pecans.**
- **Afternoon snack: Eliminate the flaxseed.**
- **Dinner: Have 3 ounces chicken.**

Day 30—1,726 Calories

BREAKFAST

1½ cups whole grain cereal
1 cup fat-free milk
1 orange

SNACK

1 apple
2 tablespoons natural peanut butter

LUNCH

1 serving Pasta Salad with Chicken and Pesto (page 194)

SNACK

Strawberries and Cream Wrap

- 1 whole wheat tortilla
- 2 tablespoons low-fat cream cheese
- ½ cup sliced strawberries

DINNER

4 ounces cod*
1 cup brown rice
1 cup steamed broccoli
1 cup fat-free milk

**Leftovers will be used in tomorrow's lunch. Just in case you need to make extra, check tomorrow's menu to see what is needed.*

Quick Cuts

How to Cut 200 to 300 Calories on This Day

- **Breakfast: Eat 1 cup cereal with ⅔ cup milk.**
- **Morning snack: Have 1 tablespoon peanut butter.**
- **Dinner: Have 3 ounces cod with ⅔ cup milk.**

WEEK FIVE MEAL PLAN

Day 31–1,751 Calories

BREAKFAST

Banana Burrito

- 1 whole wheat tortilla
- 2 tablespoons natural peanut butter
- 1 medium banana

SNACK

6 ounces fat-free yogurt (any flavor)

LUNCH

Fish Pita

- 1 whole wheat pita
- 3 ounces leftover cod
- 2 tablespoons light cream cheese
- 2 tomato slices
- ¼ cup spinach

1 cup unsweetened applesauce

1 pear

SNACK

7 whole wheat crackers

½ cup salsa

DINNER

1 serving Steak over Wheat Berries and Greens* (page 206)

**Leftovers will be used in tomorrow's lunch. Just in case you need to make extra, check tomorrow's menu to see what is needed.*

Quick Cuts

How to Cut 200 to 300 Calories on This Day

» **Breakfast: Have ½ banana.**

» **Lunch: Eat 2 ounces cod and skip the applesauce.**

» **Afternoon snack: Have 4 crackers.**

Day 32–1,695 Calories

BREAKFAST

¾ cup rolled oats (dry)

¾ cup fat-free milk

1 plum

2 teaspoons cinnamon

SNACK

6 ounces fat-free yogurt (any flavor)

1 peach

LUNCH

1 serving Greek Salad (page 198)

SNACK

1 whole grain bagel

2 tablespoons low-fat cream cheese

DINNER

Chicken Pasta Salad

- 4 ounces cooked chicken
- 1½ cups whole wheat pasta, prepared according to package directions
- 2 teaspoons olive oil
- 1 tablespoon balsamic or red wine vinegar
- 1 cup finely chopped veggies of choice

Quick Cuts

How to Cut 200 to 300 Calories on This Day

» **Breakfast: Eat ½ cup oats with ½ cup milk.**

» **Dinner: Have 3 ounces chicken with 1 cup pasta.**

WEEK FIVE MEAL PLAN

Day 33—1,802 Calories

BREAKFAST

PB&J Bagel

- 1 whole grain bagel
- 1 tablespoon 100% fruit spread
- 1 tablespoon natural peanut butter

SNACK

¼ melon

LUNCH

1 serving: Green Salad with Wheat Berries, Almonds, and Citrus (page 197)

SNACK

5 whole wheat crackers

3 ounces tuna

DINNER

4 ounces broiled pork loin with
1 tablespoon hoisin sauce

1 cup buckwheat noodles

1 cup steamed mixed veggies

Quick Cuts

How to Cut 200 to 300 Calories on This Day

- **Breakfast: Substitute a whole wheat English muffin for the bagel.**
- **Dinner: Have 3 ounces pork.**

Day 34—1,796 Calories

BREAKFAST

1 serving Baked Eggs with Turkey Sausage, Peppers, and Feta Cheese (page 191)

1 cup fat-free milk

SNACK

1½ cups chopped mixed fresh fruit

LUNCH

Three-Bean Pasta Salad

- 1½ cups whole wheat pasta, prepared according to package directions
- ⅛ cup each black, kidney, and pinto beans
- ¼ cup corn
- 2 teaspoons olive oil
- 1 tablespoon red wine vinegar

SNACK

1 cup fat-free milk

3 whole wheat fig cookies
(like Fig Newmans)

DINNER

4 ounces grilled salmon

1 cup quinoa

1 cup steamed green beans

1 tablespoon shredded Parmesan cheese

Quick Cuts

How to Cut 200 to 300 Calories on This Day

- **Lunch: Have 1 cup pasta.**
- **Afternoon snack: Eat 2 fig cookies.**
- **Dinner: Have 3 ounces salmon and ½ cup quinoa.**

Day 35–1,706 Calories

BREAKFAST

Egg Sandwich

- 2 slices whole grain toast
- 2 egg whites and 1 whole egg (prepared with cooking spray)
- 1 slice low-fat cheese

1 medium banana

SNACK

1 cup unsweetened applesauce

2 tablespoons chopped walnuts

LUNCH

1 serving Roast Turkey Breast, Spinach, and Endive Salad* (page 193)

SNACK

1 cup chopped fresh fruit of choice

DINNER

Chicken-Broccoli Stir-Fry

- 4 ounces cooked chicken
- 1 cup chopped broccoli
- ¼ cup teriyaki sauce
- 1 cup wild rice

**Leftovers will be used in tomorrow's lunch. Just in case you need to make extra, check tomorrow's menu to see what is needed.*

Quick Cuts

How to Cut 200 to 300 Calories on This Day

- **Breakfast: Eliminate the whole egg.**
- **Morning snack: Have 1 tablespoon chopped walnuts.**
- **Dinner: Have 3 ounces chicken, 2 tablespoons teriyaki sauce, and ⅔ cup wild rice.**

WEEK SIX WORKOUTS

DAY 36

AEROBIC WORKOUT
40 MINUTES

- 5 min Range 1
- 5 min Range 3
- 10 min Range 2
- 5 min Range 1
- 5 min Range 3
- 10 min Range 2

STRENGTH WORKOUT
25 MINUTES

REST PERIODS: 45 SECONDS BETWEEN EACH EXERCISE

- 20 sec overhead medicine ball pass *(page 282)*
- 8 medicine ball solo twists *(page 279)*
- 8 curl and presses *(page 272)*
- 20 sec overhead medicine ball pass
- 8 medicine ball solo twists
- 8 curl and presses
- 12 squat and pauses with cord *(page 291)*
- 15 bench dips *(page 269)*
- 8 windshield wipers *(page 295)*
- 10 lateral arm raises *(page 274)*
- 20 sec side core bridge *(per side)* *(page 271)*
- 20 squat and pauses with cord
- 15 bench dips
- 8 windshield wipers
- 10 lateral arm raises
- 20 sec side core bridge *(per side)*

DAY 37

AEROBIC WORKOUT
30 MINUTES

- 5 min Range 1
- 15 min Range 2
- 5 min Range 3
- 5 min Range 2

AGILITY WORKOUT
15 MINUTES

REST PERIODS: 60 SECONDS BETWEEN EACH EXERCISE

- 3 × square drill *(page 305)*
- 3 × square drill
- 3 × square drill
- 20 sec alternating box-top foot taps *(page 297)*
- 20 sec alternating box-top foot taps
- 20 sec alternating box-top foot taps
- 20 sec speed skaters *(page 304)*
- 20 sec speed skaters
- 20 sec speed skaters

DAY 38

AEROBIC: REST

AGILITY/STRENGTH: REST

DAY 39

AEROBIC WORKOUT
40 MINUTES

- 5 min Range 1
- 10 min Range 2
- 5 min Range 3
- 5 min Range 1
- 10 min Range 2
- 5 min Range 3

STRENGTH WORKOUT
20 MINUTES

REST PERIODS: 45 SECONDS BETWEEN EACH EXERCISE

- 50 jump-rope jumps *(page 273)*
- 12 squat and pauses with cord
- 8 reverse medicine ball lunges *(per leg)* *(page 288)*
- 50 jump-rope jumps
- 12 squat and pauses with cord
- 8 reverse medicine ball lunges *(per leg)*
- 15 squat and presses *(page 290)*
- 10 medicine ball solo twists
- 10 reverse medicine ball lunges *(per leg)*
- 15 squat and presses
- 10 medicine ball solo twists
- 10 reverse medicine ball lunges *(per leg)*

(continued)

WEEK SIX WORKOUTS

DAY 40

AEROBIC WORKOUTS
40 MINUTES

5 min Range 2
5 min Range 3
5 min Range 2
5 min Range 3
5 min Range 2
5 min Range 3
5 min Range 2
5 min Range 3

AGILITY WORKOUT
20 MINUTES

REST PERIODS: 60 SECONDS BETWEEN EACH EXERCISE

3 × 4-count zigzag line jump *(page 306)*
3 × 4-count zigzag line jump
3 × 4-count zigzag line jump
3 × 4-count zigzag line jump
4 × 10-foot shuttle run *(page 296)*
4 × 10-foot shuttle run
4 × 10-foot shuttle run
20 sec speed skaters
20 sec speed skaters
20 sec speed skaters

DAY 41

AEROBIC WORKOUT
60 MINUTES TOTAL

5 min Range 1
5 min Range 2
5 min Range 3
5 min Range 1
5 min Range 2
5 min Range 3
5 min Range 1
5 min Range 2
5 min Range 3
5 min Range 1
5 min Range 2
5 min Range 3

STRENGTH WORKOUT
20 MINUTES

REST PERIODS: 45 SECONDS BETWEEN EACH EXERCISE

15 squat and presses
8 medicine ball solo twists
8 curl and presses
15 squat and presses
8 medicine ball solo twists
8 curl and presses
12 squat and pauses with cord
15 bench dips
8 windshield wipers
8 curl and presses
15 bench dips
8 windshield wipers
20 sec side core bridge *(per side)*

DAY 42

AEROBIC: REST

AGILITY/STRENGTH: REST

WEEK SIX SHOPPING LIST

BREAD, CEREALS, GRAINS

- ☐ 2 whole grain bagels
- ☐ 6 slices whole grain bread
- ☐ 2 whole wheat hamburger buns
- ☐ 2 whole wheat pitas
- ☐ 1 whole wheat tortilla (8")

FRUIT

- ☐ 1 avocado
- ☐ 3 medium bananas
- ☐ 1½ cups fruit of choice
- ☐ 1 cup grapes
- ☐ 3 medium peaches
- ☐ 2 plums
- ☐ ½ cup pineapple
- ☐ ½ grapefruit
- ☐ 2 boxes (0.5 ounce each) raisins
- ☐ 2½ cups strawberries, sliced
- ☐ 2 kiwifruits
- ☐ 1 cup dried cranberries
- ☐ ½ cup golden raisins
- ☐ 4 dried figs, chopped
- ☐ 1 apple, any variety
- ☐ 2 Granny Smith apples
- ☐ 2 lemons
- ☐ 1 lime
- ☐ 1 medium pear

VEGETABLES

- ☐ 8–10 spears asparagus
- ☐ 1 red bell pepper
- ☐ 2 green bell peppers
- ☐ 2 sweet potatoes
- ☐ 2 plum (Roma) tomatoes
- ☐ 1 cup broccoli
- ☐ 1 medium cucumber
- ☐ ½ pound fresh green beans
- ☐ 2 cups mixed greens
- ☐ ½ cup mushrooms
- ☐ ½ onion
- ☐ 1 leaf romaine lettuce
- ☐ 2 small scallions
- ☐ 3¾ cups spinach
- ☐ 1 medium tomato
- ☐ ½ cup vegetable of choice
- ☐ ¾ cup chopped parsley
- ☐ ¼ cup shredded carrots
- ☐ 1 clove garlic
- ☐ 1 jalapeño pepper

DAIRY/EGGS

- ☐ 2 eggs
- ☐ 6 containers (6 ounces each) fat-free yogurt (any flavor)
- ☐ 1 cup plain fat-free yogurt
- ☐ 2 slices Gruyère cheese
- ☐ 6 slices low-fat cheese
- ☐ ¾ cup low-fat mozzarella cheese
- ☐ 1 tablespoon low-fat sour cream
- ☐ 5½ cups fat-free milk
- ☐ 5 tablespoons light cream cheese
- ☐ ½ cup butter

MEAT/POULTRY

- ☐ 1 pound 3 ounces chicken breast
- ☐ 7 ounces tilapia
- ☐ 7 ounces beef tenderloin
- ☐ 7 ounces sirloin
- ☐ 8 ounces chopped buffalo meat
- ☐ 3 tablespoons hummus
- ☐ 8 ounces tofu

WEEK SIX MEAL PLAN

Day 36—1,754 Calories

BREAKFAST

¾ cup rolled oats (dry)
¾ cup fat-free milk
1 cup sliced strawberries

SNACK

1 medium banana

LUNCH

Turkey, Spinach, and Endive Sandwich
- 1 whole wheat pita
- ¾ cup leftover turkey, spinach, and endive mixture

10 whole wheat crackers
3 tablespoons hummus

SNACK

6 ounces fat-free yogurt (any flavor)
1 tablespoon ground or milled flaxseed
½ cup whole grain cereal

DINNER

4 ounces grilled chicken
1¼ cups Buckwheat Tabbouleh (page 201)
1 sweet potato, sliced and grilled*
2 teaspoons olive oil
2 teaspoons cinnamon

**Leftovers will be used in tomorrow's lunch. Just in case you need to make extra, check tomorrow's menu to see what is needed.*

Quick Cuts

How to Cut 200 to 300 Calories on This Day

» **Breakfast: Eat ½ cup oats with ½ cup milk.**
» **Lunch: Eliminate the hummus.**
» **Dinner: Have 3 ounces chicken.**

Day 37—1,705 Calories

BREAKFAST

1½ cups whole grain cereal
1 cup fat-free milk
1 medium peach, sliced

SNACK

1 serving Kiwifruit Smoothie (page 211)

LUNCH

Veggie Wrap
- 1 whole wheat tortilla
- ½ cup chopped leftover grilled sweet potatoes
- ½ cup spinach
- 1 teaspoon olive oil
- ¼ cup shredded carrots

1 mini box raisins

SNACK

Cheese and Avocado Pita
- 1 whole wheat pita
- 1 slice low-fat cheese
- ½ avocado

DINNER

4 ounces beef tenderloin*
1 cup brown rice
1 cup steamed broccoli

**Leftovers will be used in tomorrow's lunch. Just in case you need to make extra, check tomorrow's menu to see what is needed.*

Quick Cuts

How to Cut 200 to 300 Calories on This Day

» **Breakfast: Eat 1 cup cereal with ⅔ cup milk.**
» **Dinner: Have 3 ounces beef with ⅔ cup rice.**

WEEK SIX MEAL PLAN

Day 38–1,763 Calories

BREAKFAST

1 whole grain bagel
2 tablespoons light cream cheese
½ cup sliced strawberries

SNACK

1 individual bag 94% fat-free popcorn

LUNCH

Beef Pita
- 1 whole wheat pita
- 3 ounces leftover beef tenderloin
- 1 tablespoon light sour cream
- 2 slices tomato
- ¼ cup spinach
- ¼ avocado

1 pear

SNACK

6 ounces fat-free yogurt (any flavor)
1 medium banana, sliced
1 tablespoon ground or milled flaxseed
½ cup whole grain cereal

DINNER

Turkish-Style Chicken Skewers (page 205)
1 cup steamed whole wheat couscous

Quick Cuts

How to Cut 200 to 300 Calories on This Day

» **Lunch: Have 2 ounces leftover beef.**
» **Afternoon snack: Eliminate the cereal.**
» **Dinner: Have ⅔ cup couscous.**

Day 39–1,768 Calories

BREAKFAST

Fruit and Yogurt Parfait
- 6 ounces fat-free yogurt (any flavor)
- ½ cup whole grain cereal
- 1 medium peach
- 1 tablespoon ground or milled flaxseed

SNACK

2 plums

LUNCH

Chicken Sandwich
- 2 slices whole wheat bread
- 3 ounces cooked chicken breast
- 1 slice low-fat cheese
- Tomato slices
- Romaine lettuce leaf

1 apple

SNACK

4 Maple, Oat, and Fig Cookies (page 209)

DINNER

2 beef kebabs (4 ounces sirloin, with peppers, mushrooms, onion, and pineapple)
1 cup wild rice
1 cup fat-free milk

Quick Cuts

How to Cut 200 to 300 Calories on This Day

» **Breakfast: Have ¼ cup cereal.**
» **Morning snack: Have 1 plum.**
» **Afternoon snack: Have 2 cookies.**

WEEK SIX MEAL PLAN

Day 40—1,795 Calories

BREAKFAST

¾ cup rolled oats (dry)
¾ cup fat-free milk
½ grapefruit

SNACK

6 ounces fat-free yogurt (any flavor)

LUNCH

Steak Salad
- 2 cups mixed greens
- 3 ounces cooked sirloin
- ¼ avocado
- 2 tablespoons chopped walnuts
- 2 tablespoons light dressing of choice

SNACK

1 whole grain bagel
2 tablespoons low-fat cream cheese

DINNER

1 Buffalo Burger (page 203)
Side Salad
- 1 cup spinach
- 1 mini box raisins
- ½ cup veggies of choice
- 1 tablespoon low-fat dressing of choice

Quick Cuts

How to Cut 200 to 300 Calories on This Day

» **Breakfast: Eat ½ cup oats with ½ cup milk.**
» **Morning snack: Have ½ banana.**
» **Lunch: Have 2 ounces sirloin.**
» **Dinner: Have 3 ounces chicken.**

Day 41—1,706 Calories

BREAKFAST

1½ cups whole grain cereal
1 cup fat-free milk
1 cup sliced strawberries

SNACK

1 cup grapes

LUNCH

1 serving Thai Tofu Salad (page 195)

SNACK

6 ounces fat-free yogurt (any flavor)
1 sliced peach
1 tablespoon ground or milled flaxseed

DINNER

Grilled Chicken Marinara Sandwich
- 2 slices whole wheat toast
- 4 ounces grilled chicken breast
- ¼ cup low-fat mozzarella cheese
- 2 tablespoons marinara sauce

2 whole wheat fig cookies (like Fig Newmans)

Quick Cuts

How to Cut 200 to 300 Calories on This Day

» **Breakfast: Eat 1 cup cereal with ⅔ cup milk.**
» **Dinner: Have 3 ounces chicken and 1 fig cookie.**

Day 42–1,744 Calories

BREAKFAST

1 cup Cranberry Cashew Granola* (page 192)

6 ounces fat-free yogurt (any flavor)

SNACK

1½ cups sliced fresh fruit of choice

LUNCH

Tomato Soup and Grilled Cheese
- 2 cups tomato soup
- 2 slices whole wheat bread
- 2 slices low-fat American cheese

7 whole wheat crackers

SNACK

3 leftover Maple, Oat, and Fig Cookies

1 cup fat-free milk

DINNER

4 ounces grilled tilapia**

¼ cup mango salsa

1 cup quinoa

8–10 asparagus spears, steamed

**Used as a breakfast on more than 1 day. Look ahead; you may want to make extra.*

***Leftovers will be used in tomorrow's lunch. Just in case you need to make extra, check tomorrow's menu to see what is needed.*

Quick Cuts

How to Cut 200 to 300 Calories on This Day

- **Lunch: Eat 1½ cups soup with half a sandwich made with 1 slice bread and 1 slice cheese.**
- **Afternoon snack: Have 2 cookies.**

»Breakfasts

SWEET POTATO HASH WITH CHICKEN AND POACHED EGGS

This great new twist on hash packs a serious nutritional punch. Sweet potatoes are rich in beta-carotene and a good source of protein and carbohydrate. To save time, you can make extra hash (without the eggs) and keep it in the refrigerator for up to 2 days.

MAKES 2 SERVINGS

ACTIVE TIME: 25 MINUTES

TOTAL TIME: 25 MINUTES

1 tablespoon extra-virgin olive oil
1 small sweet potato, scrubbed and cut into ½" cubes
1 small red onion, chopped
1 green bell pepper, seeded and chopped
Salt
Freshly ground black pepper
1 boneless, skinless chicken breast (6 ounces), cut widthwise into ½"-thick slices
1 teaspoon white vinegar
2 large eggs
Hot-pepper sauce (optional)

1. Heat the oil in a medium nonstick skillet over medium-high heat. Add the potato, onion, bell pepper, and a pinch each of salt and black pepper. Cook, tossing, for 5 minutes, or until the potato begins to brown. Add the chicken, reduce the heat to medium, cover, and cook, stirring occasionally, for 8 to 10 minutes, or until no longer pink.

2. While the chicken is cooking, add 1½" water to a small skillet. Add the vinegar and bring to a low simmer. Crack the eggs into a bowl, and gently slide one at a time into the water. Cook at a low simmer for 4 minutes, or until the whites set and the yolks are still soft and runny. Remove them from the water with a slotted spoon.

3. Season the hash to taste with the salt and pepper, and serve hot with eggs and hot-pepper sauce, if desired.

CALORIES/ SERVING	CARBS (G)	PROTEIN (G)	FAT (G)	SAT FAT (G)	SODIUM (MG)	FIBER (G)
297	17	28	13	3	144	3

»Breakfasts

BAKED EGGS WITH TURKEY SAUSAGE, PEPPERS, AND FETA CHEESE

This is a rich, hearty recipe with a bit of sweetness from the peppers and natural saltiness from the feta cheese. Look for packaged mini bell peppers in the grocery store; they're a great way to get more nutrient-rich red and yellow peppers for less money.

MAKES 2 SERVINGS

ACTIVE TIME: 15 MINUTES

TOTAL TIME: 25 MINUTES

1 teaspoon extra-virgin olive oil

1 link (4 ounces) turkey sausage, removed from casing and crumbled

1 red bell pepper, seeded and cut into strips

1 green bell pepper, seeded and cut into strips

2 large whole eggs and 2 egg whites

¼ cup low-fat feta cheese, crumbled

1. Preheat the oven to 375°F. Add the oil to a medium ovenproof nonstick skillet and heat over medium-high heat. Add the sausage and cook, stirring frequently, for 2 to 3 minutes, or until browned. Add the red and green bell peppers, cover, and cook for 5 to 10 minutes, or until beginning to soften. Remove from the heat and arrange the sausage and peppers to evenly cover the bottom of the pan.

2. Carefully crack the eggs over the sausage and peppers. Place the skillet in the oven and bake until the eggs are cooked to your liking: about 5 minutes for soft-cooked; 10 minutes for firmer yolks.

3. Using a thick oven mitt, remove the skillet from the oven, transfer the eggs to plates, and sprinkle with the cheese.

CALORIES/ SERVING	CARBS (G)	PROTEIN (G)	FAT (G)	SAT FAT (G)	SODIUM (MG)	FIBER (G)
287	7	22	19	7	870	1

»Breakfasts

CRANBERRY CASHEW GRANOLA

You can make a lot of this granola mix at once and store it in an airtight container for up to a month. It's great to serve with yogurt or either hot or cold with fat-free milk. You can also sprinkle it over a bowl of fresh fruit or simply eat it alone as a snack. To make this recipe sweeter, add more cranberries, coconut, and raisins. To make it less sweet and more salty, add more nuts. This will change the nutritional information from what's listed, but not by very much.

MAKES 7 SERVINGS (7 CUPS TOTAL)

ACTIVE TIME: 20 MINUTES

TOTAL TIME: 55 MINUTES

3 cups rolled oats
1½ cups shredded sweetened coconut
1 cup sliced almonds
1 cup roughly chopped unsalted cashews
1 cup (4 ounces) dried cranberries, chopped
½ cup golden raisins
¼ cup sunflower seeds
⅓ cup canola oil
¼ cup honey
1½ teaspoons cinnamon
½ teaspoon salt

1. Preheat the oven to 325°F. In a large bowl, combine the oats, coconut, almonds, cashews, cranberries, raisins, sunflower seeds, oil, honey, cinnamon, and salt. Stir to coat the oats and nuts with the honey and oil.

2. Spread the mixture on a baking sheet and bake, stirring occasionally, for 35 minutes, or until the oats and nuts are golden brown. Cool on the baking sheet, stirring occasionally. Store in an airtight container.

CALORIES/ SERVING	CARBS (G)	PROTEIN (G)	FAT (G)	SAT FAT (G)	SODIUM (MG)	FIBER (G)
643	60	13	39	3	11	9

ROAST TURKEY BREAST, SPINACH, AND ENDIVE SALAD

The combination of flavors in this nutritious salad will have your tastebuds dancing. There's the richness of blue cheese; the tart sweetness of the Granny Smith apple; the nutty flavor of toasted walnuts; and the crisp, refreshing crunch of endive. Above all, there's quality protein from the turkey, heart-healthy fat from walnuts and olive oil, and iron and fiber from the spinach and endive.

MAKES 2 SERVINGS

ACTIVE TIME: 15 MINUTES

TOTAL TIME: 20 MINUTES

¼ cup walnut pieces
4 packed cups baby spinach
1 thick slice (8 ounces) roast turkey breast, cut into cubes
1 medium head endive, chopped
1 Granny Smith apple, sliced
¼ cup (1 ounce) crumbled low-fat blue cheese
2 tablespoons extra-virgin olive oil
2 teaspoons red wine vinegar
Salt
Freshly ground black pepper

1. Preheat the oven to 275°F. Spread the walnuts on a baking sheet and cook for 10 minutes, or until fragrant and lightly golden. Transfer to a plate to cool.

2. In a large bowl, combine the spinach, turkey, endive, apple, and walnuts.

3. In a small bowl, whisk together the blue cheese, oil, and vinegar. Add the dressing to the salad, toss to coat the leaves, season with the salt and pepper to taste, and serve.

CALORIES/ SERVING	CARBS (G)	PROTEIN (G)	FAT (G)	SAT FAT (G)	SODIUM (MG)	FIBER (G)
534	23	43	30	6	320	12

»Lunches

PASTA SALAD WITH CHICKEN AND PESTO

This quick and easy lunch travels well and is great served either hot or cold. You can vary the amount of fat and calories greatly if you use more pesto, which is high in unsaturated fat from the pine nuts, Parmesan cheese, and olive oil. You can save time by making the chicken in advance; it'll keep for a few days in a sealed container. For variety, serve the pasta on a bed of lightly dressed greens.

MAKES 2 SERVINGS (5 CUPS TOTAL)

ACTIVE TIME: 15 MINUTES

TOTAL TIME: 30 MINUTES

2 cups whole wheat fusilli (spiral-shaped pasta)
1 boneless, skinless chicken breast (8 ounces), cut across the grain into ½"-thick slices
¼ cup jarred basil pesto
1 pint grape tomatoes, halved
Salt
Freshly ground black pepper

1. Bring a large pot of salted water to a boil. Cook the fusilli according to package directions. Add the chicken to the boiling pasta water for the last 5 minutes of cooking.

2. Drain the pasta and chicken and transfer to a mixing bowl. Toss with the pesto and tomatoes. Season with the salt and pepper to taste, and serve warm or at room temperature.

CALORIES/ SERVING	CARBS (G)	PROTEIN (G)	FAT (G)	SAT FAT (G)	SODIUM (MG)	FIBER (G)
413	30	35	17	3	300	2

»Lunches

THAI TOFU SALAD

The ingredients for this recipe could be a bit different than what you're used to buying—especially the fish sauce—but you should be able to find them in your local supermarket. This recipe will make you love tofu, because it's combined in a refreshing salad that has some crunch as well as some sweetness mixed with the heat of jalapeño chile peppers. (If you want even more heat, leave the pepper seeds in the salad.)

MAKES 2 SERVINGS

ACTIVE TIME: 20 MINUTES

TOTAL TIME: 25 MINUTES

8 ounces green beans, trimmed
2½ tablespoons lime juice
2 tablespoons creamy natural peanut butter
1 tablespoon honey
1 tablespoon fish sauce
1 jalapeño chile pepper, seeded and minced
1 scallion, sliced (greens only)
1 medium cucumber, peeled, seeded, and thinly sliced
2 packed cups baby spinach
8 ounces extra-firm tofu, cut into ¾" cubes
1 cup mung beans
Crushed peanuts

1. Fill a medium mixing bowl with ice and water. Bring a medium pot of salted water to a boil. Add the green beans and cook 1 to 2 minutes, or until bright green and still very crisp. Drain and submerge in the ice bath for 1 minute. Drain and set aside.

2. In a large bowl, combine the lime juice, peanut butter, honey, fish sauce, jalapeño chile pepper, and scallion. Stir to combine. Add the reserved green beans and toss to coat.

3. Add the cucumber, spinach, tofu, and mung beans to the bowl. Stir gently, so as not to break up tofu. Divide between two plates. For added crunch, sprinkle crushed peanuts over the top before serving.

CALORIES/ SERVING	CARBS (G)	PROTEIN (G)	FAT (G)	SAT FAT (G)	SODIUM (MG)	FIBER (G)
587	65	39	19	3	757	18

»Lunches

HEARTY VEGETABLE AND BARLEY SOUP

Soups are great recovery foods because they combine energy, fluid, and an electrolyte (sodium) in one bowl. This soup is also filling without being very high in calories, so you'll feel satisfied and full even though you're still losing weight. Meat eaters can substitute chicken broth for a slightly different flavor or add shredded chicken breast to up the protein. Go ahead and double or triple the recipe, if you have a pot big enough, and freeze batches in airtight containers.

MAKES 4 SERVINGS (8 CUPS TOTAL)

ACTIVE TIME: 15 MINUTES

TOTAL TIME: 60 MINUTES

1 small sweet potato, quartered lengthwise and cut into ¼"-thick slices
1 medium onion, chopped
1 medium carrot, peeled and cut into ¼"-thick slices
1 rib celery, sliced
5 ounces cremini mushrooms, quartered
½ cup pearl barley
1 bay leaf
Salt
4 cups low-sodium vegetable broth
2 packed cups chopped spinach
½ cup frozen baby green peas
Freshly ground black pepper

1. Place the potato, onion, carrot, celery, mushrooms, barley, bay leaf, and a pinch of salt in a medium saucepan. Cover with the broth and bring to a boil. Reduce to a simmer and cook until the barley is tender, about 45 minutes.

2. Stir in the spinach and peas. Return the soup to a simmer, season with the salt and pepper to taste, and serve hot.

CALORIES/ SERVING	CARBS (G)	PRO (G)	FAT (G)	SAT FAT (G)	SODIUM (MG)	FIBER (G)
193	40	6	1	0	121	8

»Lunches

GREEN SALAD WITH WHEAT BERRIES, ALMONDS, AND CITRUS

Fortunately, there are many more ways to eat whole grains than just in breads or side dishes. Wheat berries and almonds lend a great crunch and nutty flavor to this green salad, while the orange adds a refreshing sweetness. You can find wheat berries in the grain section of the supermarket or in Middle Eastern markets. They're available hard and soft; hard berries work best in this recipe.

MAKES 2 SERVINGS

ACTIVE TIME: 25 MINUTES

TOTAL TIME: 1 HOUR 15 MINUTES

½ cup hard wheat berries
3 tablespoons sliced almonds
2 packed cups mixed baby greens
2 medium navel oranges, peeled and sliced (reserve juice)
1 medium red seedless grapefruit, peeled and sliced (reserve juice)
4 ribs celery, sliced
¼ cup dried cranberries
1 tablespoon extra-virgin olive oil
Salt
Freshly ground black pepper

1. Cook the wheat berries in a medium pot of unsalted boiling water, uncovered, until tender, 50 minutes to 1 hour. (If you're using soft wheat berries, decrease the cooking time 10 minutes.) Drain and cool.

2. Meanwhile, heat the oven or toaster oven to 275°F. Place the almonds on a baking sheet and toast for 10 to 12 minutes, or until golden brown. Transfer to a plate and set aside.

3. In a large bowl, combine the greens, wheat berries, oranges, grapefruit, 1 tablespoon of the citrus juice, celery, cranberries, reserved almonds, and oil. Season with the salt and pepper to taste. Serve immediately.

CALORIES/ SERVING	CARBS (G)	PROTEIN (G)	FAT (G)	SAT FAT (G)	SODIUM (MG)	FIBER (G)
473	79	11	13	2	96	12

STRENGTHEN PERIOD RECIPES

»Lunches

GREEK SALAD

This classic Greek salad is both rich and refreshing, and it's packed with heart-healthy nutrition, thanks to the unsaturated fat from the olives and olive oil. The first step in this recipe is perhaps the most important: Soaking the onion in ice water mellows it so it doesn't overwhelm the other flavors.

MAKES 2 SERVINGS

ACTIVE TIME: 25 MINUTES

TOTAL TIME: 25 MINUTES

1 small red onion, thinly sliced
¼ cup extra-virgin olive oil
1 cup (4 ounces) low-fat feta cheese, crumbled
1½ tablespoons red wine vinegar
½ teaspoon dried oregano
1 pound (1 head) romaine lettuce, chopped
1 small cucumber, halved lengthwise and thinly sliced
7½ ounces canned chickpeas
1 cup cherry tomatoes, halved
⅓ cup pitted kalamata olives
Salt
Freshly ground black pepper

1. Soak the onion in ice water for 15 minutes. Drain and set aside.

2. Whisk together the oil, cheese, vinegar, and oregano and stir to combine. Add the romaine, cucumber, chickpeas, tomatoes, olives, and reserved onion. Toss to combine.

3. Divide the salad between two plates. Season with the salt and pepper to taste.

CALORIES/ SERVING	CARBS (G)	PROTEIN (G)	FAT (G)	SAT FAT (G)	SODIUM (MG)	FIBER (G)
386	48	17	14	11	1,014	12

WARM BLACK-EYED PEA SALAD WITH KALE

From the standpoint of weight loss and nutrient density, you can't beat kale; yet most of us have no idea what to do with it. This quick and simple salad can serve as a great introduction to this versatile vegetable, plus it packs a lot of vitamin A, lutein, and fiber into your day.

MAKES 2 SERVINGS (3 CUPS)

ACTIVE TIME: 15 MINUTES

TOTAL TIME: 25 MINUTES

1 tablespoon extra-virgin olive oil
2 cloves garlic, sliced
4 packed cups sliced kale (1 small bunch, leaves removed from stem, cut into 1½" ribbons)
½ cup water
Salt
1 can (15 ounces) black-eyed peas, rinsed and drained

1. Heat the oil in a medium skillet over medium-high heat. Add the garlic and tilt the pan so that the garlic is completely submerged in the oil; cook for 1 minute, continuing to hold the pan. (Do not let the garlic brown).

2. Add the kale (be careful, as the oil may sputter), water, and salt to taste. Cover, reduce the heat to medium, and cook for 12 minutes, until the kale softens but is still bright green.

3. Add the peas, cover, and cook for 2 minutes, or until warmed through.

CALORIES/ SERVING	CARBS (G)	PROTEIN (G)	FAT (G)	SAT FAT (G)	SODIUM (MG)	FIBER (G)
340	56	11	8	1	560	13

»Sides

SPICY PARSNIP OVEN FRIES

If french fries are one of your vices, try this alternative to fast-food or frozen types. Look for large, bulbous parsnips; they're the easiest to cut into wedges. Adjust the amounts of cumin, cayenne, and salt according to your taste.

MAKES 2 SERVINGS

ACTIVE TIME: 10 MINUTES

TOTAL TIME: 30 MINUTES

½ teaspoon cumin
¼ teaspoon cayenne
½ teaspoon salt
2 tablespoons extra-virgin olive oil
1 pound parsnips, peeled and cut into ¾"-thick wedges

1. Preheat the oven to 400°F. In a medium bowl, combine the cumin, cayenne, ¼ teaspoon of the salt, and the oil.

2. Toss the parsnips with the oil mixture to coat well.

3. Place the parsnips on a baking sheet and cook, stirring midway, for 20 to 25 minutes, or until browned on the edges and cooked through. Sprinkle with the remaining ¼ teaspoon salt.

CALORIES/ SERVING	CARBS (G)	PROTEIN (G)	FAT (G)	SAT FAT (G)	SODIUM (MG)	FIBER (G)
275	41	3	11	2	605	11

»Sides

BUCKWHEAT TABBOULEH

Buckwheat, or kasha, is a unique and underutilized whole grain with a nutty flavor, a slightly crunchy texture, and a truckload of minerals. Tabbouleh is typically made with bulgur, and this variation with buckwheat yields an even nuttier and heartier flavor. You can typically find whole-kernel buckwheat with the rice and couscous in the grocery store.

MAKES 2 SERVINGS (2½ CUPS)

ACTIVE TIME: 15 MINUTES

TOTAL TIME: 20 MINUTES

1 large egg white
½ cup roasted buckwheat, dry
1 cup water
¾ cup chopped parsley
2 plum tomatoes, seeded and chopped
1½ teaspoons lemon zest
1½ tablespoons lemon juice
1 tablespoon extra-virgin olive oil
Salt
Freshly ground black pepper

1. In a small bowl, combine the egg white and buckwheat. Stir to coat.

2. Place the mixture in a medium saucepan over medium heat and stir with a wooden spoon for 2 to 4 minutes, or until the kernels brown and separate. Add the water, bring to a boil, reduce the heat to low, cover, and cook for 10 minutes.

3. While the buckwheat is cooking, combine the parsley and tomatoes in a medium bowl. Add the lemon zest, lemon juice, oil, and cooked buckwheat. Toss together and season with the salt and pepper to taste.

CALORIES/ SERVING	CARBS (G)	PROTEIN (G)	FAT (G)	SAT FAT (G)	SODIUM (MG)	FIBER (G)
139	14	5	7	1	45	3

»Dinners

HALIBUT WITH SESAME-GINGER BOK CHOY

Like other types of cabbage, bok choy is an excellent source of beta-carotene and fiber. It is also rich in folate, which has been shown to reduce heart-disease risk by lowering the blood levels of homocysteine. (If you can't find bok choy in the grocery store, you can substitute another form of cabbage or kale.) Then there's the halibut, which provides omega-3 fatty acids for improved heart and brain health.

MAKES 2 SERVINGS

ACTIVE TIME: 20 MINUTES

TOTAL TIME: 20 MINUTES

2 halibut fillets (4 ounces each), about 1" thick, skin removed
Salt
4 teaspoons vegetable oil
1 piece (1") fresh ginger, cut into very thin matchsticks
1 pound baby bok choy, quartered lengthwise
1 tablespoon rice wine vinegar
¼ cup vegetable broth or water
½ teaspoon dark sesame oil

1. Preheat the oven to 400°F. Pat the halibut dry and season with the salt.

2. Heat 2 teaspoons of the vegetable oil in a small ovenproof nonstick skillet over medium-high heat. Add the fish, flesh-side down, and cook until browned. Turn the fillets over and bake for 5 minutes, or until cooked through.

3. While the fish is in the oven, heat the remaining 2 teaspoons of oil in a medium skillet over medium heat. Add the ginger and cook for 1 minute. Add the bok choy, vinegar, and broth. Cover and simmer for 5 minutes, or until the bok choy is bright green and tender. Remove from the heat and add the sesame oil. Serve the halibut on a warm bed of bok choy.

CALORIES/ SERVING	CARBS (G)	PROTEIN (G)	FAT (G)	SAT FAT (G)	SODIUM (MG)	FIBER (G)
266	8	27	14	2	400	2

»Dinners

BUFFALO BURGERS

Ground buffalo is typically leaner than ground beef, and it's richer in iron, as well. But to make a really great burger from buffalo, it's important to add ingredients that bring out the flavor in the meat. To reduce the calories in this recipe, you can substitute low-fat Cheddar or American cheese for the Gruyère.

MAKES 2 SERVINGS

ACTIVE TIME: 20 MINUTES

TOTAL TIME: 20 MINUTES

½ pound chopped buffalo meat
1 small scallion, chopped
1½ teaspoons Worcestershire sauce
½ teaspoon soy sauce
⅛ teaspoon salt
2 slices (¾ ounce) Gruyère cheese
2 whole wheat hamburger buns
1 tablespoon low-fat mayonnaise
2 tablespoons olive or canola oil
Sliced red onion, sliced avocado, sliced beefsteak tomatoes, and lettuce for garnish

1. In a medium bowl, combine the buffalo, scallion, Worcestershire sauce, soy sauce, and salt. Form into 2 patties.

2. Heat the oil in a medium nonstick skillet. Add the burgers and cook 2½ minutes per side. Add the cheese for the last minute of cooking. Remove from the skillet and let rest for 5 minutes.

3. Place the buns, cut-side down, in the same skillet over medium heat and cook for 1 to 2 minutes, or until toasted. Smear the buns with mayonnaise and serve the hamburgers with onion, avocado, tomato, and lettuce.

CALORIES/ SERVING	CARBS (G)	PROTEIN (G)	FAT (G)	SAT FAT (G)	SODIUM (MG)	FIBER (G)
381	27	30	17	4	612	5

»Dinners

SPICY BLACK BEAN BURRITOS

For portability and nutritional power, it's hard to beat a burrito. One of my coaches likes this recipe so much that he and his wife prepare big batches to refrigerate and freeze. For an even bigger protein boost, substitute black soybeans (found in health-food stores) for the black beans. With the combination of sweet potato and chipotle pepper, these burritos have a unique smoky and sweet flavor with a spicy kick.

MAKES 2 SERVINGS

ACTIVE TIME: 25 MINUTES

TOTAL TIME: 30 MINUTES

1 tablespoon extra-virgin olive oil
1 small red onion, sliced (1 cup)
1 small sweet potato (8 ounces), cut into ¼" cubes
Salt
1 can (15 ounces) black beans, rinsed and drained
2 packed cups baby spinach
1 chipotle with adobo sauce (from a can), minced
2 teaspoons roasted sunflower seeds
2 whole wheat tortillas (10" diameter)
½ cup shredded low-fat Cheddar cheese

1. Heat the oil in a medium skillet over medium-high heat. Add the onion and sweet potato, season with salt to taste, and toss to coat the vegetables with oil. Cover. Reduce the heat to medium and cook, stirring occasionally, for 7 to 8 minutes, or until heated through.

2. Add the beans, spinach, and chipotle, cover, and cook, stirring, for 3 minutes, or until the spinach has wilted and the beans are heated through. Sprinkle with sunflower seeds and remove from heat.

3. Heat the tortillas according to the package directions. Divide the filling between the tortillas, sprinkle with the cheese, and roll each into a burrito. Serve warm.

CALORIES/ SERVING	CARBS (G)	PRO (G)	FAT (G)	SAT FAT (G)	SODIUM (MG)	FIBER (G)
736	115	33	16	3	860	26

»Dinners

TURKISH-STYLE CHICKEN SKEWERS

When you don't want to bother with dishes but still want a great meal, fire up the grill. The only thing that really takes any time with this recipe is letting the skewers sit in the yogurt marinade, but if you're in a rush, just brush the marinade on the skewers right before grilling. And let me save you from having to look up lemon zest in a cookbook: It's finely grated lemon peel, and you can incorporate it into a wide variety of marinades to add a hint of tart lemon flavor.

MAKES 2 SERVINGS (4 SKEWERS TOTAL)

ACTIVE TIME: 20 MINUTES

TOTAL TIME: 1 HOUR 45 MINUTES (INCLUDES MARINATING TIME)

1 red bell pepper, seeded and cut into 1" squares
1 green bell pepper, seeded and cut into 1" squares
1 small red onion, cut into ¾" wedges
1 boneless, skinless chicken breast (8 ounces), cut into 1" pieces
½ cup low-fat plain yogurt
2 teaspoons ground cumin
1 clove garlic, chopped
1½ teaspoons lemon zest
¼ teaspoon salt
4 bamboo or metal skewers

1. Divide the red and green bell peppers, onion, and chicken among 4 skewers. Leave ⅛" space between each item for even cooking.

2. In a small bowl, whisk together the yogurt, cumin, garlic, lemon zest, and salt. Brush the skewers with the yogurt marinade until completely coated. Refrigerate for 1 hour or overnight. Let sit at room temperature 15 minutes before cooking.

3. Cook on a hot grill, turning, for 8 to 10 minutes, or until charred at the edges and no longer pink. Serve warm or at room temperature.

CALORIES/ SERVING	CARBS (G)	PROTEIN (G)	FAT (G)	SAT FAT (G)	SODIUM (MG)	FIBER (G)
206	15	32	2	5	420	3

»Dinners

STEAK OVER WHEAT BERRIES AND GREENS

With kale, wheat berries, and sunflower seeds, this recipe provides a powerful mixture of vitamins, minerals, and antioxidants, including beta-carotene. The relatively high fiber content and the high-quality protein (from the steak) make it a filling, satisfying meal that's great for recovery.

MAKES 2 SERVINGS

ACTIVE TIME: 20 MINUTES

TOTAL TIME: 35 MINUTES

½ pound skirt steak, ¾"–1" thick
Salt
Freshly ground black pepper
1 tablespoon extra-virgin olive oil
1 medium onion, chopped
6 cups chopped kale, thick stems removed (about one 10-ounce bunch)
⅓ cup water
1 cup cooked wheat berries*
2 teaspoons roasted unsalted sunflower seeds
1 teaspoon cider vinegar
1 teaspoon orange zest (optional)

1. Preheat the broiler. Line a baking sheet with aluminum foil and place 6" from flame. Heat for 10 minutes. Season the steak with the salt and pepper. Place on the baking sheet, fat-side down. Cook for 7 to 8 minutes, or until browned on top. Turn and continue cooking for 4 to 5 minutes for medium-rare. Let rest for 10 minutes before slicing.

2. While the steak is cooking, heat the oil in a medium skillet over medium-high heat. Add the onion and cook, stirring, for 3 minutes, or until the onion begins to brown. Add the kale and water. Reduce the heat to medium, cover, and cook, stirring occasionally, for 12 minutes, or until softened.

3. Stir in the wheat berries, sunflower seeds, vinegar, and orange zest, if using. Cook, stirring, for 2 to 3 minutes, or until the wheat berries are warmed through. Serve hot with sliced steak.

*WHEAT BERRY PREPARATION INSTRUCTIONS

½ cup roasted wheat berries, dry
1 cup water

Bring water to a boil, add wheat berries, reduce the heat to low, cover, and cook until the water is absorbed, about 30 minutes.

CALORIES/ SERVING	CARBS (G)	PROTEIN (G)	FAT (G)	SAT FAT (G)	SODIUM (MG)	FIBER (G)
671	62	45	27	7	179	10

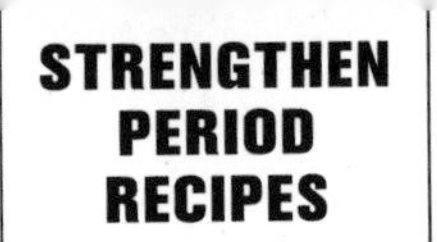

»Dinners

SOBA NOODLE SOUP WITH CHICKEN

Japanese soba noodles are made with a combination of buckwheat and regular wheat flours for a bigger nutrient kick, but without the mealy texture some whole wheat pastas can have. You'll find them in the pasta or ethnic foods section of your supermarket. This recipe sounds complicated, but you'll be surprised by both how easy and how satisfying it is.

MAKES 2 SERVINGS (6 CUPS)

ACTIVE TIME: 30 MINUTES

TOTAL TIME: 30 MINUTES

1 tablespoon canola oil
2 cloves garlic, minced
1 tablespoon minced ginger
1 scallion, sliced, greens and whites separated
3½ ounces shiitake mushrooms, stems removed and caps sliced ¼" thick
4 cups low-sodium chicken broth
1 boneless, skinless chicken breast (6 ounces), sliced into ½"-thick pieces
3 ounces soba noodles
½ cup frozen baby peas

1. Heat the oil, garlic, ginger, and scallion whites in a saucepan over medium-high heat for 2 minutes, or until softened. Add the mushrooms and stir to coat. Add the broth, cover, and bring to a boil.

2. Add the chicken and noodles. Return to a boil, reduce the heat, and simmer gently, uncovered, for 4 minutes. Add the peas and return to a boil. Remove from the heat.

3. Divide the soup between two bowls. Serve hot.

CALORIES/ SERVING	CARBS (G)	PROTEIN (G)	FAT (G)	SAT FAT (G)	SODIUM (MG)	FIBER (G)
443	47	39	11	2	614	3

»Snacks

MAPLE, OAT, AND FIG COOKIES

Substituting whole wheat flour for refined white flour makes most cookie recipes taste funny, but this recipe was specifically designed to be prepared with whole wheat. The maple syrup, figs, and oats keep these cookies moist and tasty.

MAKES 26 (NUTRITION INFORMATION BASED ON 1 COOKIE; TYPICAL SERVING SIZE IS 4 COOKIES)

ACTIVE TIME: 15 MINUTES

TOTAL TIME: 30 MINUTES

½ cup unsalted butter, at room temperature
½ cup dark brown sugar
¼ cup maple syrup
1 large egg
¼ teaspoon vanilla extract
½ cup whole wheat flour
½ teaspoon baking soda
Pinch salt
1 cup rolled oats
⅔ cup chopped dried figs

1. Preheat the oven to 350°F. Lightly coat a baking sheet with cooking spray.

2. In a medium bowl, combine the butter and sugar. Using a handheld mixer, beat for 3 minutes, or until light. Add the syrup, egg, and vanilla and continue to blend. Sprinkle with the flour, baking soda, and salt and mix until just combined. Add the oats and figs and incorporate.

3. Drop the batter onto the sheet by the tablespoonful, 1½" apart. Bake for 12 to 14 minutes, or until the bottoms have browned. Transfer to a rack to cool. Serve warm or at room temperature.

CALORIES/ COOKIE	CARBS (G)	PROTEIN (G)	FAT (G)	SAT FAT (G)	SODIUM (MG)	FIBER (G)
76	9	1	4	2	37	1

»Snacks

DAIRY-FREE MAPLE, OAT, AND FIG COOKIES

This version of Maple, Oat, and Fig Cookies is for people who choose not to eat dairy products. In addition to swapping butter for canola oil, this recipe calls for more figs and more flour, giving it a more cakelike flavor and texture.

MAKES 28 (NUTRITION INFORMATION BASED ON 1 COOKIE; TYPICAL SERVING SIZE IS 4 COOKIES)

ACTIVE TIME: 15 MINUTES

TOTAL TIME: 30 MINUTES

2 large eggs
⅓ cup maple syrup
¼ cup canola oil
1¼ cups rolled oats
¾ cup whole wheat flour
½ teaspoon baking powder
¼ teaspoon salt
¼ teaspoon cinnamon
1 cup chopped dried figs

1. Preheat the oven to 350°F. Lightly coat a baking sheet with cooking spray.

2. In a medium bowl, combine the eggs, syrup, and oil and whisk to combine. Add the oats, flour, baking powder, salt, cinnamon, and figs. Stir to combine.

3. Drop the dough onto the baking sheet by the tablespoonful, 1½" apart. Bake for 12 minutes, or until browned on the bottom. Cool on a rack and serve warm or at room temperature.

CALORIES/ COOKIE	CARBS (G)	PROTEIN (G)	FAT (G)	SAT FAT (G)	SODIUM (MG)	FIBER (G)
79	11	2	3	0	33	1

»Snacks

KIWIFRUIT SMOOTHIE

Some smoothies are just too sweet to handle, but this one has a refreshingly tart bite from the kiwifruit and Granny Smith apple. You can also make this shake without peeling the apples for convenience and more fiber, but you might have trouble drinking it with a straw. The added flaxseed oil makes the smoothie rich and provides omega-3 fatty acids for heart and brain health. For an added kick, add a pinch of ground ginger to the recipe.

MAKES 2 SERVINGS (2 CUPS TOTAL)

ACTIVE TIME: 10 MINUTES

TOTAL TIME: 10 MINUTES

2 kiwifruits, peeled
1 Granny Smith apple, peeled, cored, and roughly chopped
1 tablespoon flaxseed oil
½ cup low-fat plain yogurt
¾ cup ice
2 teaspoons honey

Place the kiwifruit, apple, oil, yogurt, ice, and honey in a blender and blend for 20 seconds, or until smooth. Divide between two glasses and serve.

CALORIES/ SERVING	CARBS (G)	PROTEIN (G)	FAT (G)	SAT FAT (G)	SODIUM (MG)	FIBER (G)
203	31	4	7	1	37	6

»Snacks

COCOA–PEANUT BUTTER SMOOTHIE

Whereas the Kiwifruit Smoothie is light, tart, and refreshing, this one is as creamy and indulgent as it sounds—definitely a must-have for anyone who enjoys chocolate and peanut butter. The carbohydrate and protein make it great for either a postworkout recovery shake or an energizing preworkout snack. While a reasonably high percentage of the calories come from fat, it's mostly the heart-healthy unsaturated kind, and the recipe contains no cholesterol.

MAKES 2 SERVINGS

ACTIVE TIME: 5 MINUTES

TOTAL TIME: 5 MINUTES

1 small banana
2 tablespoons natural creamy peanut butter
3 tablespoons unsweetened cocoa
1 cup fat-free milk
¾ cup ice
1 tablespoon honey

Place the banana, peanut butter, cocoa, milk, ice, and honey in a blender and blend for 20 seconds, or until smooth. Divide between two glasses and serve.

CALORIES/ SERVING	CARBS (G)	PROTEIN (G)	FAT (G)	SAT FAT (G)	SODIUM (MG)	FIBER (G)
257	33	10	9.5	2	112	5

WEEK SEVEN WORKOUTS

DAY 43

AEROBIC WORKOUT
45 MINUTES

- 5 min Range 1
- 5 min Range 2
- 5 min Range 3
- 5 min Range 2
- 5 min Range 1
- 5 min Range 2
- 5 min Range 3
- 5 min Range 2
- 5 Min Range 1

STRENGTH WORKOUT
20 MINUTES

REST PERIODS: 45 SECONDS BETWEEN EXERCISES

- 50 jump-rope jumps *(page 273)*
- 15 overhead squats *(page 284)*
- 10 lateral arm raises *(page 274)*
- 50 jump-rope jumps
- 15 overhead squats
- 10 lateral arm raises
- 12 reverse medicine ball lunges *(per leg) (page 288)*
- 30 sec side core bridge *(per leg) (page 271)*
- 12 reverse medicine ball lunges *(per leg)*
- 30 sec side core bridge *(per side)*

DAY 44

AEROBIC WORKOUT
45 MINUTES

- 5 min Range 1
- 5 min Range 2
- 5 min Range 3
- 5 min Range 1
- 5 min Range 2
- 5 min Range 3
- 5 min Range 2
- 5 min Range 3
- 5 min Range 1

AGILITY WORKOUT
20 MINUTES

REST PERIODS: 60 SECONDS BETWEEN EXERCISES

- 15 sec double-leg cone jump *(page 299)*
- 15 sec double-leg cone jump
- 15 sec double leg cone jump
- 4 × six-cone sidestep *(page 302)*
- 4 × six-cone sidestep
- 4 × six-cone sidestep
- 3 × 4-count zigzag line jump *(page 306)*
- 3 × 4-count zigzag line jump
- 3 × 4-count zigzag line jump
- 3 × 4-count zigzag line jump

DAY 45

AEROBIC: REST

AGILITY/STRENGTH: REST

DAY 46

AEROBIC WORKOUT
50 MINUTES

- 5 min Range 1
- 5 min Range 3
- 5 min Range 2
- 5 min Range 3
- 5 min Range 2
- 5 min Range 3
- 5 min Range 1
- 5 min Range 3
- 5 min Range 2
- 5 min Range 3

AGILITY WORKOUT
20 MINUTES

REST PERIODS: 60 SECONDS BETWEEN EACH EXERCISE

- 15 sec double-leg cone jump
- 15 sec double-leg cone jump
- 15 sec double-leg cone jump
- 4 × six-cone sidestep
- 4 × six-cone sidestep
- 4 × six-cone sidestep
- 3 × 4-count zigzag line jump
- 3 × 4-count zigzag line jump
- 3 × 4-count zigzag line jump
- 3 × 4-count zigzag line jump

(continued)

WEEK SEVEN WORKOUTS

DAY 47

AEROBIC WORKOUT
60 MINUTES

- 5 min Range 1
- 5 min Range 2
- 5 min Range 3
- 10 min Range 2
- 10 min Range 1
- 5 min Range 2
- 10 min Range 1
- 10 min Range 2

STRENGTH WORKOUT
20 MINUTES

REST PERIODS: 45 SECONDS BETWEEN EACH EXERCISE

- 50 jump-rope jumps
- 15 overhead squats
- 10 lateral arm raises
- 50 jump-rope jumps
- 15 overhead squats
- 10 lateral arm raises
- 12 reverse medicine ball lunges *(per leg)*
- 30 sec side core bridge *(per side)*
- 12 reverse medicine ball lunge *(per leg)*
- 30 sec side core bridge *(per side)*

DAY 48

AEROBIC WORKOUT
60 MINUTES

- 5 min Range 1
- 10 min Range 2
- 5 min Range 3
- 5 min Range 1
- 10 min Range 2
- 5 min Range 3
- 5 min Range 1
- 10 min Range 2
- 5 min Range 3

AGILITY WORKOUT
10 MINUTES

REST PERIODS: 60 SECONDS BETWEEN EACH EXERCISE

- 3 × square drill *(page 305)*
- 3 × square drill
- 3 × square drill
- 4 × 10-foot shuttle run *(page 296)*
- 4 × 10-foot shuttle run

DAY 49

AEROBIC: REST

AGILITY/STRENGTH: REST

WEEK SEVEN SHOPPING LIST

BREAD/CEREALS/GRAINS

- ☐ 2 whole wheat English muffins
- ☐ 11 slices whole grain bread
- ☐ 2 whole wheat pitas
- ☐ 1 whole wheat dinner roll

NUTS/SEEDS/LEGUMES

- ☐ 7 tablespoons hummus
- ☐ 6 ounces tempeh

FRUIT

- ☐ ¼ avocado
- ☐ 3 medium bananas
- ☐ 2 apples
- ☐ 1 Granny Smith or Golden Delicious apple
- ☐ 2 oranges
- ☐ 1¾ cups green grapes
- ☐ 1 cup raspberries
- ☐ 1 cup strawberries, halved
- ☐ ½ cup prunes
- ☐ 1 miniature box (0.5 ounce) raisins
- ☐ 2 cups dried cranberries
- ☐ 1 cup dried apricot halves
- ☐ ½ cup dried pear halves
- ☐ 1½ cups unsweetened applesauce
- ☐ 2 tangerines

VEGETABLES

- ☐ 20 large baby carrots
- ☐ ½ cup squash
- ☐ ½ cup zucchini
- ☐ 1 small red onion
- ☐ 8–10 asparagus stalks
- ☐ 2 cups spinach
- ☐ 1 medium tomato
- ☐ 2 sweet potatoes
- ☐ 1 red potato
- ☐ 3¾ cups veggies of choice
- ☐ ½ cup broccoli
- ☐ ½ cup cauliflower
- ☐ 10 ounces Swiss chard (1 bunch)
- ☐ 2 cloves garlic
- ☐ 2 plum tomatoes
- ☐ 2 ounces arugula
- ☐ 1 roasted red pepper (from a jar)

DAIRY/EGGS

- ☐ 5 eggs
- ☐ 3 containers (6 ounces each) fat-free yogurt (any flavor)
- ☐ 2 slices low-fat cheese of choice
- ☐ 7 cups fat-free milk
- ☐ 1 tablespoon low-fat cream cheese
- ☐ ½ cup low-fat cottage cheese
- ☐ 2 ounces low-fat goat cheese

MEAT/POULTRY/FISH

- ☐ 8 ounces chicken breast
- ☐ 3 ounces water-packed canned tuna
- ☐ 4 ounces salmon
- ☐ 4 ounces turkey cutlets
- ☐ 8 ounces roast turkey
- ☐ 7 ounces eye of round roast
- ☐ 4 ounces pork loin

WEEK SEVEN MEAL PLAN

Day 43—1,752 Calories

BREAKFAST

1 cup Cranberry Cashew Granola (leftover)

½ cup fat-free milk

SNACK

2 leftover Maple, Oat, and Fig Cookies

LUNCH

Fish Pita

- 1 whole wheat pita
- 3 ounces leftover tilapia
- 2 tablespoons low-fat mayonnaise
- ½ cup veggies of choice (cucumber, spinach, red bell peppers, tomato, mushrooms, etc.)

1 mini box raisins

1 orange

SNACK

6 ounces fat-free yogurt (any flavor)

1 cup sliced strawberries

1 tablespoon wheat germ

½ cup whole grain cereal

DINNER

4 ounces turkey cutlets

1 serving Nutty Wild Rice and Grains* (page 243)

1 cup steamed broccoli and cauliflower

**Leftovers will be used in tomorrow's lunch. Just in case you need to make extra, check tomorrow's menu to see what is needed.*

Quick Cuts

How to Cut 200 to 300 Calories on This Day

» **Morning snack: Have 1 cookie.**

» **Lunch: Have 1 tablespoon mayonnaise.**

» **Afternoon snack: Skip the cereal.**

» **Dinner: Have 3 ounces turkey.**

Day 44—1,760 Calories

BREAKFAST

1½ cups whole grain cereal

1 cup fat-free milk

SNACK

1 cup sliced raw veggies

3 tablespoons hummus

LUNCH

1 serving Roast Turkey Salad with Grapes, Grains, and Cashews (page 241)

SNACK

1 medium banana

1 tablespoon natural peanut butter

DINNER

4 ounces pot roast (eye of round)*

1 cup veggies and potatoes roasted with the beef (such as baby carrots, red potatoes, or sliced sweet potatoes)

1 whole wheat dinner roll

**Leftovers will be used in tomorrow's lunch. Just in case you need to make extra, check tomorrow's menu to see what is needed.*

Quick Cuts

How to Cut 200 to 300 Calories on This Day

» **Breakfast: Have 1 cup cereal.**

» **Dinner: Have 3 ounces pot roast and half of the roll.**

WEEK SEVEN MEAL PLAN

Day 45—1,794 Calories

BREAKFAST

6 ounces fat-free yogurt (any flavor)
½ cup raspberries

SNACK

1 cup grapes

LUNCH

Barbecue Beef Sandwich
  2 slices whole grain bread
  3 ounces leftover pot roast
  2 tablespoons barbecue sauce
1 apple
10 large baby carrots

SNACK

Veggie/Hummus Pita
  1 whole wheat pita
  1 cup veggies of choice
  2 tablespoons hummus
  1 slice low-fat cheese

DINNER

1 serving Pasta with Swiss Chard, Red Onion, and Parmesan* (page 250)

**Leftovers will be used in tomorrow's lunch. Just in case you need to make extra, check tomorrow's menu to see what is needed.*

Quick Cuts

How to Cut 200 to 300 Calories on This Day

» **Breakfast: Have ½ cup granola.**

Day 46—1,764 Calories

BREAKFAST

1 cup rolled oats (dry)
1 cup fat-free milk
1 cup blackberries
1 cup low-fat granola

SNACK

6 ounces fat-free yogurt (any flavor)
1 medium banana
1 tablespoon ground or milled flaxseed

LUNCH

2 cups leftover pasta

SNACK

1 serving Snack Mix with Toasted Pecans, Sesame Seeds, Flaxseeds, and Dried Fruit (page 254)

DINNER

4 ounces grilled salmon
1 cup quinoa
8 asparagus spears, steamed

Quick Cuts

How to Cut 200 to 300 Calories on This Day

» **Breakfast: Have ½ cup oats and ½ cup milk.**

» **Lunch: Have 1½ cups pasta.**

WEEK SEVEN MEAL PLAN

Day 47—1,736 Calories

BREAKFAST

1 Pecan Apple Muffin (page 234)

1 cup fat-free milk

1 medium banana

SNACK

20 large baby carrots

LUNCH

Spinach Salad

- 2 cups spinach
- ¼ avocado
- 2 sliced tangerines
- ⅓ cup dried cranberries
- 2 tablespoons light dressing

Half PB&J

- 1 slice whole grain bread
- 1 tablespoon natural peanut butter
- 1 tablespoon 100% fruit spread

SNACK

1 whole wheat English muffin

1 tablespoon low-fat cream cheese

DINNER

4 ounces grilled chicken breast

1 cup wild rice

1 cup steamed squash and zucchini slices

1 cup fat-free milk

Quick Cuts

How to Cut 200 to 300 Calories on This Day

- **Breakfast: Have ½ banana.**
- **Afternoon snack: Have 6 whole wheat crackers instead of the English muffin and cream cheese.**
- **Dinner: Have 3 ounces chicken and ½ cup wild rice.**

Day 48—1,721 Calories

BREAKFAST

2 egg whites and 1 whole egg (scrambled with cooking spray)

¼ cup chopped veggies

1 slice whole grain toast with 2 tablespoons 100% fruit spread

SNACK

1 apple

6 whole wheat crackers
with 2 tablespoons hummus

LUNCH

Seared Tempeh, Goat Cheese, Arugula, and Roasted Red Pepper Sandwich (page 239)

SNACK

1 cup mixed berries

1 cup fat-free milk

DINNER

4 ounces pork loin

1 cup unsweetened applesauce

1 sweet potato, baked or sliced and grilled

2 teaspoons olive oil (or olive oil spread)

2 teaspoons brown sugar

2 teaspoons cinnamon

Quick Cuts

How to Cut 200 to 300 Calories on This Day

- **Breakfast: Have 2 egg whites and no whole egg, 1 slice toast, and 1 tablespoon fruit spread.**
- **Lunch: Skip the roll and olive oil spread.**
- **Dinner: Have 3 ounces pork loin.**

WEEK SEVEN MEAL PLAN

Day 49–1,746 Calories

BREAKFAST

1 serving Steel-Cut Oatmeal with Stewed Fruit (page 236)

SNACK

6 ounces fat-free yogurt (any flavor)

LUNCH

Grilled Tuna Melt

- 2 slices whole grain bread
- 3 ounces water-packed canned tuna
- 2 teaspoons low-calorie mayonnaise
- 1 slice low-fat cheese

SNACK

1 orange, sliced

1 tomato, sliced

½ cup low-fat cottage cheese

DINNER

Chicken and Veggies Pasta Marinara

- 1 cup whole wheat pasta*, prepared according to package directions
- 1 cup chopped veggies of choice (red, green, or yellow bell peppers; eggplant; onion; mushrooms; broccoli; cauliflower; plum tomatoes; zucchini; squash...)
- ¾ cup marinara sauce
- 4 ounces cooked chicken*

**Leftovers will be used in tomorrow's lunch. Just in case you need to make extra, check tomorrow's menu to see what is needed.*

Quick Cuts

How to Cut 200 to 300 Calories on This Day

- **Lunch: Have half a sandwich made with 1 slice of bread and 2 ounces of tuna.**
- **Dinner: Have ½ cup pasta, ½ cup marinara sauce, and 3 ounces chicken.**

WEEK EIGHT WORKOUTS

DAY 50

AEROBIC WORKOUT
30 MINUTES

- 10 min Range 2
- 10 min Range 3
- 10 min Range 2

STRENGTH WORKOUT
20 MINUTES

REST PERIODS: 45 SECONDS BETWEEN EACH EXERCISE

- 50 jump-rope jumps *(page 273)*
- 20 squat and presses *(page 290)*
- 20 bench dips *(page 269)*
- 50 jump ropes
- 20 squat and presses
- 20 bench dips
- 8 reverse medicine ball lunges *(per leg) (page 288)*
- 10 lateral arm raise *(page 274)*
- 10 alternating forward shoulder raises *(page 267)*
- 8 reverse medicine ball lunges *(per leg)*
- 10 lateral arm raises
- 10 alternating forward shoulder raises

DAY 51

AEROBIC WORKOUT
30 MINUTES

- 5 min Range 1
- 5 min Range 3
- 5 min Range 1
- 5 min Range 2
- 5 min Range 1
- 5 min Range 2

AGILITY WORKOUT
30 MINUTES

REST PERIODS: 60 SECONDS BETWEEN EACH EXERCISE

- 2 × six-cone crossover *(page 303)*
- 2 × six-cone crossover
- 2 × six-cone crossover
- 2 × six-cone sidestep *(page 302)*
- 2 × six-cone sidestep
- 2 × six-cone sidestep
- 10 × box jump drill *(page 298)*
- 10 × box jump drill
- 10 × box jump drill
- 3 × square drill *(page 305)*
- 3 × square drill
- 3 × square drill

DAY 52

AEROBIC: REST

AGILITY/STRENGTH: REST

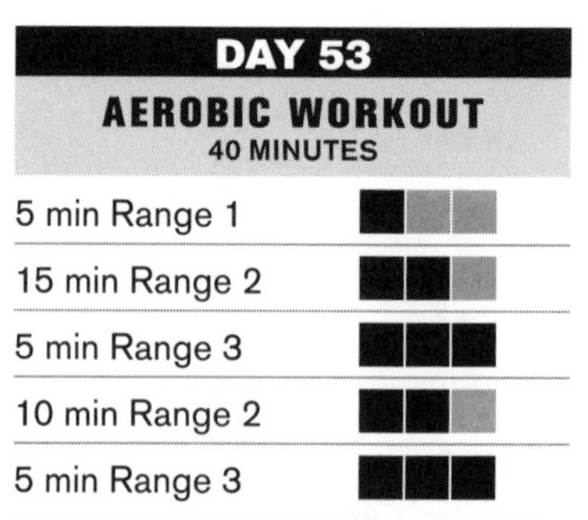

DAY 53

AEROBIC WORKOUT
40 MINUTES

- 5 min Range 1
- 15 min Range 2
- 5 min Range 3
- 10 min Range 2
- 5 min Range 3

AGILITY WORKOUT
30 MINUTES

REST PERIODS: 60 SECONDS BETWEEN EACH EXERCISE

- 2 × six-cone crossover
- 2 × six-cone crossover
- 2 × six-cone crossover
- 2 × six-cone sidestep
- 2 × six-cone sidestep
- 2 × six-cone sidestep
- 10 × box jump drill
- 10 × box jump drill
- 10 × box jump drill
- 3 × square drill
- 3 × square drill
- 3 × square drill
- 20 sec speed skaters *(page 304)*
- 20 sec speed skaters

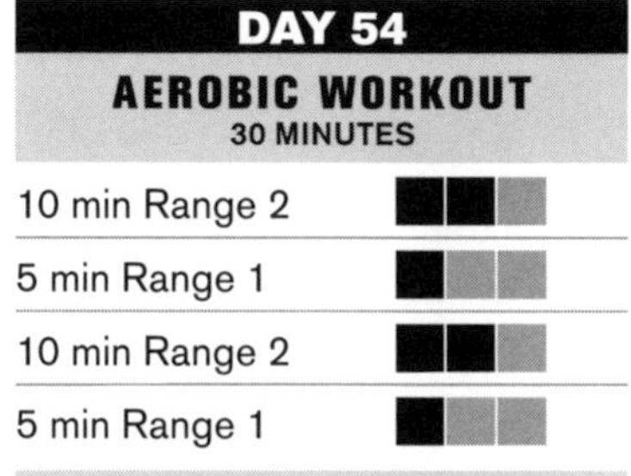
DAY 54

AEROBIC WORKOUT
30 MINUTES

10 min Range 2	■■□
5 min Range 1	■□□
10 min Range 2	■■□
5 min Range 1	■□□

STRENGTH WORKOUT
20 MINUTES

REST PERIODS: 45 SECONDS BETWEEN EACH EXERCISE

- 50 jump-rope jumps
- 20 squat and presses
- 20 bench dips
- 50 jump-rope jumps
- 20 squat and presses
- 20 bench dips
- 8 reverse medicine ball lunges *(per leg)*
- 10 lateral arm raises
- 10 alternating forward shoulder raises
- 8 reverse medicine ball lunges *(per leg)*
- 10 lateral arm raises
- 10 alternating forward shoulder raises

DAY 55

AEROBIC WORKOUT
40 MINUTES

10 min Range 1	■□□
10 min Range 2	■■□
10 min Range 3	■■■
10 min Range 2	■■□

NO AGILITY/STRENGTH WORKOUT

DAY 56

AEROBIC: REST

AGILITY/STRENGTH: REST

WEEK EIGHT SHOPPING LIST

BREAD/CEREALS/GRAINS

- ☐ 1 whole grain bagel
- ☐ 6 slices whole grain bread
- ☐ 1 medium whole wheat dinner roll
- ☐ 2 whole wheat hamburger buns
- ☐ 1 whole wheat pita
- ☐ 4 whole wheat tortillas (8" each)
- ☐ 4 corn tortillas (6" each)
- ☐ 2 whole wheat English muffins

NUTS/SEEDS/LEGUMES

- ☐ 3 tablespoons hummus
- ☐ 8 ounces silken tofu

FRUIT

- ☐ 1 cup strawberries
- ☐ 1½ cups blueberries
- ☐ 1 cup raspberries
- ☐ 1 container (6 ounces) blackberries
- ☐ 1 cup grapes
- ☐ 1 mango
- ☐ 1 Granny Smith or Golden Delicious apple
- ☐ 1 apple
- ☐ ¾ avocado
- ☐ 3 medium bananas
- ☐ 6 cups fruit of choice
- ☐ ¼ cup dried cranberries
- ☐ 1½ cups dried apricots
- ☐ 1 cup shredded coconut

VEGETABLES

- ☐ 1 red bell pepper
- ☐ 1 green bell pepper
- ☐ 40 large baby carrots
- ☐ 1 cup broccoli
- ☐ 2 medium onions
- ☐ 1 cup romaine lettuce
- ☐ 1 medium carrot
- ☐ 2 cups mixed greens
- ☐ 3¼ cups spinach
- ☐ 1 medium tomato
- ☐ ½ cup cherry tomatoes
- ☐ 2 cups vegetable of choice
- ☐ 2 ribs celery
- ☐ 1 cup fresh parsley
- ☐ 7 cloves garlic
- ☐ 1 small head cauliflower
- ☐ ¾ cup frozen baby peas
- ☐ 1 pound broccoli raab (1 bunch)
- ☐ ⅛ cup fresh basil
- ☐ 1 can (14 ounces) diced tomatoes
- ☐ 1 cup alfalfa sprouts
- ☐ ½ cup broccoli
- ☐ 1 small potato

DAIRY/EGGS

- ☐ 1 container (6 ounces) fat-free yogurt (any flavor)
- ☐ 3 tablespoons crumbled feta cheese
- ☐ 2 slices low-fat cheese of choice
- ☐ 4 slices low-fat Cheddar cheese
- ☐ ¾ cup low-fat shredded cheese of choice
- ☐ ½ cup low-fat cottage cheese
- ☐ 6 cups fat-free milk
- ☐ 6 tablespoons low-fat cream cheese

MEAT/POULTRY/FISH

- ☐ 12 ounces chicken breast
- ☐ 4 ounces cod
- ☐ 6 ounces skirt steak
- ☐ 8 ounces ground white-meat chicken
- ☐ 2 ounces roast turkey
- ☐ 6 ounces sliced deli turkey
- ☐ 4 ounces 90% lean (or leaner) ground beef

WEEK EIGHT MEAL PLAN

Day 50–1,710 Calories

BREAKFAST

1½ cups whole grain cereal
½ cup blueberries
1 cup fat-free milk

SNACK

1 cup grapes

LUNCH

Pasta Salad
- 1½ cups leftover pasta
- 2 ounces leftover chicken
- ½ cup finely chopped broccoli
- 2 tablespoons fat-free Italian dressing

1 apple

SNACK

10 large baby carrots
2 large ribs celery with 2 tablespoons natural peanut butter

DINNER

1 serving Soft Steak Tacos with Mango Chimichurri* (page 252)

**Leftovers will be used in tomorrow's lunch. Just in case you need to make extra, check tomorrow's menu to see what is needed.*

Quick Cuts

How to Cut 200 to 300 Calories on This Day

- **Breakfast: Have 1 cup cereal and ⅔ cup milk.**
- **Lunch: Have 1 cup pasta.**

Day 51–1,801 Calories

BREAKFAST

1 whole grain bagel
2 tablespoons low-fat cream cheese

SNACK

1 cup fresh chopped mixed fruit (use leftover mango if you have any)

LUNCH

Steak Salad
- 2 cups greens of choice
- 2 ounces leftover steak
- 3 tablespoons crumbled low-fat feta cheese
- 2 tablespoons sunflower seeds
- 2 tablespoons light dressing

2 whole wheat fig cookies (like Fig Newmans)

SNACK

6 ounces fat-free yogurt (any flavor)
½ cup whole grain cereal
½ cup blueberries

DINNER

1 serving Curried Cauliflower and Chickpea Stew (page 248)
1 whole wheat roll with 2 teaspoons olive oil spread

Quick Cuts

How to Cut 200 to 300 Calories on This Day

- **Breakfast: Have 1 tablespoon cream cheese.**
- **Lunch: Have 1 tablespoon feta and 1 fig cookie.**
- **Dinner: Have half the roll with 1 teaspoon olive oil spread.**

WEEK EIGHT MEAL PLAN

Day 52—1,754 Calories

BREAKFAST

1½ cups mixed fruit
1 whole wheat English muffin
1 tablespoon natural peanut butter
1 cup fat-free milk

SNACK

1 cup chopped raw veggies
3 tablespoons hummus

LUNCH

Turkey Pita
- 1 whole wheat pita
- 2 ounces deli turkey
- 2 teaspoons mustard
- 2 tomato slices
- ¼ cup spinach

2 whole wheat fig cookies (like Fig Newmans)

SNACK

Berry Roll-Up
- 1 whole wheat tortilla
- 2 tablespoons low-fat cream cheese
- ¾ cup mixed berries
- 2 tablespoons ground or milled flaxseed

DINNER

4 ounces cod
1 cup brown rice
1 serving Sautéed Broccoli Raab, Red Peppers, and Garlic* (page 245)

**Leftovers will be used in tomorrow's lunch. Just in case you need to make extra, check tomorrow's menu to see what is needed.*

Quick Cuts

How to Cut 200 to 300 Calories on This Day

- **Breakfast: Have ⅔ cup milk.**
- **Lunch: Have 1 fig cookie.**
- **Afternoon snack: Use 1 tablespoon cream cheese.**
- **Dinner: Have 3 ounces cod and ⅔ cup rice.**

Day 53—1,723 Calories

BREAKFAST

1 cup rolled oats (dry)
1 cup fat-free milk
½ cup raspberries
2 tablespoons chopped walnuts

SNACK

10 whole wheat crackers
½ cup salsa

LUNCH

Leftovers Wrap
- 1 whole wheat tortilla
- 1 slice low-fat cheese
- 1 cup leftover sauté

SNACK

1 serving Blackberry Banana Smoothie (page 253)

DINNER

Grilled Chicken Sandwich
- 4 ounces grilled chicken breast*
- 1 whole wheat bun
- 1 tablespoon light mayonnaise
- Romaine lettuce and tomatoes for toppings

Side Salad
- 1 cup romaine or greens of choice
- ½ cup chopped vegetables of choice
- 1 tablespoon low-fat dressing of choice

**Leftovers will be used in tomorrow's lunch. Just in case you need to make extra, check tomorrow's menu to see what is needed.*

Quick Cuts

How to Cut 200 to 300 Calories on This Day

- **Breakfast: Have ½ cup oats and ½ cup milk.**
- **Morning snack: Have 7 crackers.**
- **Dinner: Have 3 ounces chicken.**

WEEK EIGHT MEAL PLAN

Day 54–1,806 Calories

BREAKFAST

1 Banana-Pecan Breakfast Bar (page 235)
1 cup fat-free milk

SNACK

10 baby carrots

LUNCH

Strawberry Spinach Salad
- 2 cups spinach
- ¼ avocado
- 2 ounces leftover cooked chicken breast
- ¼ cup dried cranberries
- 1 cup sliced strawberries
- 2 tablespoons light dressing of choice

SNACK

1 cup sliced fruit of choice
½ cup low-fat cottage cheese

DINNER

Cheeseburger
- 4 ounces lean (90% or leaner) ground beef
- 1 slice low-fat cheese
- 1 whole grain hamburger bun
- Veggie toppings (lettuce, tomato, onion, etc.), ketchup, and mustard

Pasta Salad
- 1 cup whole wheat pasta, prepared according to package directions
- 1 cup each basil, finely chopped broccoli, and halved cherry tomatoes
- 2 teaspoons olive oil
- 1 tablespoon vinegar of choice, if desired

Quick Cuts

How to Cut 200 to 300 Calories on This Day

» **Breakfast: Have ⅔ cup milk.**

» **Dinner: Have a 3-ounce hamburger patty and ⅔ cup pasta, and use fat-free Italian dressing on the salad instead of olive oil and vinegar.**

Day 55–1,705 Calories

BREAKFAST

1½ cups whole grain cereal
1 cup fat-free milk
½ cup blueberries

SNACK

1½ cups chopped mixed fresh fruit

LUNCH

1 serving Tex-Mex Chicken Chili (page 237)
5 crushed whole wheat crackers

SNACK

1 whole wheat English muffin
1 tablespoon 100% fruit spread

DINNER

Veggie Quesadilla
- 2 whole wheat tortillas
- 1 cup chopped veggies of choice (mushroom, bell peppers, onion, etc.)
- ¾ cup shredded low-fat cheese
- ½ avocado
- ½ cup salsa

Quick Cuts

How to Cut 200 to 300 Calories on This Day

» **Breakfast: Have 1 cup cereal and ⅔ cup milk.**

» **Dinner: Have 1 tortilla.**

WEEK EIGHT MEAL PLAN

Day 56–1,761 Calories

BREAKFAST

2 slices whole grain toast

2 tablespoons 100% fruit spread

1 medium banana

1 cup fat-free milk

SNACK

6 ounces fat-free yogurt (any flavor)

1 tablespoon ground or milled flaxseed

LUNCH

Turkey Cheddar Melt with Apple and Sprouts (page 238)

SNACK

5 whole wheat crackers topped with a dollop of light cream cheese and about 3 blueberries

DINNER

Chicken/Veggie Pasta

1½ cups whole wheat pasta*, prepared according to package directions

4 ounces cooked chicken

1 cup chopped veggies of choice

¾ cup marinara sauce

**Leftovers will be used in tomorrow's lunch. Just in case you need to make extra, check tomorrow's menu to see what is needed.*

Quick Cuts

How to Cut 200 to 300 Calories on This Day

- **Breakfast: Have 1 slice toast and 1 tablespoon fruit spread.**
- **Dinner: Have 3 ounces chicken and ½ cup marinara sauce.**

WEEK NINE WORKOUTS

DAY 57

AEROBIC WORKOUT
20 MINUTES

5 min Range 1	
10 min Range 2	
5 min Range 3	

STRENGTH WORKOUT
20 MINUTES

REST PERIODS: 45 SECONDS BETWEEN EACH EXERCISE

- 20 squat and presses *(page 290)*
- 20 upright rows *(page 293)*
- 10 leg and hip raises *(page 275)*
- 20 squat and presses
- 20 upright rows
- 10 leg and hip raises
- 15 walking overhead lunges *(per leg)* *(page 294)*
- 25 pushups *(pages 286–87)*
- 8 windshield wipers *(page 295)*
- 15 walking overhead lunges *(per leg)*
- 25 pushups
- 8 windshield wipers

DAY 58

AEROBIC WORKOUT
20 MINUTES

5 min Range 1	
5 min Range 3	
5 min Range 1	
5 min Range 3	

AGILITY WORKOUT
30 MINUTES

REST PERIODS: 60 SECONDS BETWEEN EACH EXERCISE

- 2 × six-cone crossover *(page 303)*
- 2 × six-cone crossover
- 2 × six-cone crossover
- 2 × six-cone sidestep *(page 302)*
- 2 × six-cone sidestep
- 2 x six-cone sidestep
- 10 × box jump drill *(page 298)*
- 10 × box jump drill
- 10 × box jump drill
- 3 × square drill *(page 305)*
- 3 × square drill
- 20 sec speed skaters *(page 304)*
- 20 sec speed skaters

DAY 59

AEROBIC: REST

AGILITY/STRENGTH: REST

DAY 60

AEROBIC WORKOUT
60 MINUTES

5 min Range 1	
15 min Range 2	
5 min Range 3	
10 min Range 2	
5 min Range 3	
15 min Range 2	
5 min Range 3	

AGILITY WORKOUT
30 MINUTES

REST PERIODS: 60 SECONDS BETWEEN EACH EXERCISE

- 2 × six-cone crossover
- 2 × six-cone crossover
- 2 × six-cone crossover
- 2 × six-cone sidestep
- 2 × six-cone sidestep
- 2 × six-cone sidestep
- 10 × box jump drill
- 10 × box jump drill
- 10 × box jump drill
- 3 × square drill
- 3 × square drill
- 3 × square drill

(continued)

WEEK NINE WORKOUTS

DAY 61

AEROBIC WORKOUT
40 MINUTES

5 min Range 1

10 min Range 2

5 min Range 3

5 min Range 1

10 min Range 2

5 min Range 3

STRENGTH WORKOUT
20 MINUTES

REST PERIODS: 45 SECONDS BETWEEN EACH EXERCISE

20 squat and presses

20 upright rows

10 leg and hip raises

20 squat and presses

20 upright rows

10 leg and hip raises

15 walking overhead lunges *(per leg)*

25 pushups

8 windshield wipers

15 walking overhead lunges *(per leg)*

25 pushups

8 windshield wipers

DAY 62

AEROBIC WORKOUT
60 MINUTES

5 min Range 1

10 min Range 2

5 min Range 3

5 min Range 1

10 min Range 2

5 min Range 3

5 min Range 1

10 min Range 2

5 min Range 3

AGILITY/STRENGTH: REST

DAY 63

AEROBIC: REST

AGILITY/STRENGTH: REST

WEEK NINE SHOPPING LIST

BREAD/CEREALS/GRAINS

- ☐ 2 whole grain bagels
- ☐ 7 slices whole grain bread
- ☐ 2 whole wheat rolls
- ☐ 1 whole wheat English muffin
- ☐ 1 whole wheat tortilla

NUTS/SEEDS/LEGUMES

- ☐ 5 tablespoons hummus

FRUIT

- ☐ 1 avocado
- ☐ 2 medium bananas
- ☐ 1 small banana
- ☐ 1 cup fruit of choice
- ☐ 1 cup grapes
- ☐ 2 cups strawberries, sliced
- ☐ 2 apples
- ☐ 1 Granny Smith or Golden Delicious apple
- ☐ ½ cup raspberries
- ☐ 1 cup blueberries
- ☐ 3 oranges
- ☐ 1 mango
- ☐ ¼ cup golden raisins
- ☐ 1 miniature box (0.5 ounce) raisins
- ☐ ¼ cup dried cranberries

VEGETABLES

- ☐ 1 sweet potato
- ☐ 8 plum (Roma) tomatoes
- ☐ 2½ medium tomatoes
- ☐ 1 cup broccoli
- ☐ 1 cup fresh green beans
- ☐ 2 cups mixed greens of choice
- ☐ ¼ cup mushrooms
- ☐ 4 medium onions
- ☐ 2 ribs celery
- ☐ 3 leaves romaine lettuce
- ☐ 4 scallions
- ☐ 2⅓ cups spinach
- ☐ 1½ cups vegetable of choice
- ☐ 1½ cups chopped parsley
- ☐ 10 large baby carrots
- ☐ 8 ounces brussels sprouts
- ☐ 5 cloves garlic

DAIRY/EGGS

- ☐ 3 eggs
- ☐ 3 containers (6 ounces each) fat-free yogurt (any flavor)
- ☐ 4 ounces plain fat-free yogurt
- ☐ 3 slices low-fat cheese of choice
- ☐ ¾ cup low-fat shredded cheese of choice
- ☐ 2 tablespoons low-fat sour cream
- ☐ 3¼ cups fat-free milk
- ☐ ½ cup light cream cheese

MEAT/POULTRY/FISH

- ☐ 1 pound 3 ounces chicken breast
- ☐ 7 ounces tilapia
- ☐ ¼ pound large shrimp
- ☐ ¼ pound sea or bay scallops
- ☐ ¼ pound mussels
- ☐ 2 ounces sliced deli turkey
- ☐ 8 ounces salmon fillet
- ☐ 1 ounce smoked salmon
- ☐ 12 ounces pork chops (bone in)
- ☐ 4 ounces lean ground beef

WEEK NINE MEAL PLAN

Day 57–1,769 Calories

BREAKFAST

¾ cup rolled oats (dry)
¾ cup fat-free milk
1 box mini raisins
1 tablespoon chopped walnuts
½ medium banana

SNACK

1 cup grapes

LUNCH

Spinach and Pasta Salad
- 1 cup spinach
- 1 cup leftover pasta
- 2 teaspoons olive oil
- 1 tablespoon vinegar of choice
- 2 tablespoons shredded Parmesan cheese

SNACK

Half PB & Banana
- 1 slice whole wheat bread
- 1 tablespoon natural peanut butter
- ½ medium banana

DINNER

1 serving Salmon with Brussels Sprouts and Chestnuts (page 246)
1 cup steamed wild rice

Quick Cuts

How to Cut 200 to 300 Calories on This Day

- **Breakfast: Eat ½ tablespoon walnuts.**
- **Lunch: Have ⅔ cup pasta and 1 tablespoon Parmesan.**
- **Afternoon snack: Have ½ tablespoon peanut butter.**
- **Dinner: Have ½ cup wild rice.**

Day 58–1,744 Calories

BREAKFAST

1½ cups whole grain cereal
1 cup fat-free milk
½ cup raspberries

SNACK

6 ounces fat-free yogurt (any flavor)
1 tablespoon ground or milled flaxseed
½ cup blueberries

LUNCH

Turkey Sandwich
- 2 slices whole grain bread
- 2 ounces deli turkey
- 1 slice low-fat cheese
- 2 leaves romaine lettuce
- 4 tomato slices
- ½ avocado
- 1 tablespoon hummus

1 apple

SNACK

1 serving Salmon Mousse with Whole Grain Crackers* (page 255)

DINNER

4 ounces grilled chicken breast**
1 cup brown rice pilaf
1 cup steamed fresh green beans
1 whole wheat roll with 2 teaspoons olive oil spread

**Used as a snack on another day this week*

***Leftovers will be used in tomorrow's lunch. Just in case you need to make extra, check tomorrow's menu to see what is needed.*

Quick Cuts

How to Cut 200 to 300 Calories on This Day

- **Breakfast: Eat 1 cup cereal with ⅔ cup milk.**
- **Lunch: Have ¼ avocado.**
- **Dinner: Have 3 ounces chicken with ⅔ cup rice pilaf.**

WEEK NINE MEAL PLAN

Day 59—1,762 Calories

BREAKFAST

1 whole wheat English muffin

1 tablespoon 100% fruit spread

1 cup sliced mixed fruit

SNACK

2 ribs celery with 2 tablespoons natural peanut butter

LUNCH

Grilled Chicken Wrap

- 1 whole wheat tortilla
- 2–3 ounces leftover grilled chicken
- 1 slice low-fat cheese
- 3–4 slices tomatoes
- ¼ avocado
- ¼ cup spinach

7 whole wheat crackers

SNACK

6 ounces fat-free yogurt (any flavor)

1 banana

DINNER

1 serving Spicy Shellfish Stew (page 251)

1 whole wheat roll with 2 teaspoons olive oil spread

Quick Cuts

How to Cut 200 to 300 Calories on This Day

- **Breakfast: Have ½ tablespoon fruit spread.**
- **Lunch: Eliminate the cheese and eat 4 crackers.**
- **Afternoon snack: Have ½ banana.**
- **Dinner: Eliminate the olive oil spread.**

Day 60—1,789 Calories

BREAKFAST

1 whole wheat bagel

2 tablespoons light cream cheese

½ cup blueberries or blackberries

SNACK

1 cup vegetable of choice

¼ cup hummus

LUNCH

PB&J

- 2 slices whole grain bread
- 1 tablespoon natural peanut butter
- 1 tablespoon 100% fruit spread

Side Salad

- 1 cup greens of choice
- ½ cup vegetable of choice
- ¼ cup low-fat cheese
- 1 tablespoon low-fat dressing of choice

SNACK

1 serving leftover salmon mousse

DINNER

4 ounces grilled tilapia*

Lentils, Bulgur, and Caramelized Onions (page 244)

**Leftovers will be used in tomorrow's lunch. Just in case you need to make extra, check tomorrow's menu to see what is needed.*

Quick Cuts

How to Cut 200 to 300 Calories on This Day

- **Lunch: Eat half a sandwich with 1 slice bread, ½ tablespoon peanut butter, and ½ tablespoon fruit spread.**
- **Afternoon snack: Have half a serving of salmon mousse.**

WEEK NINE MEAL PLAN

Day 61—1,760 Calories

BREAKFAST

¾ cup rolled oats (dry)
¾ cup fat-free milk
1 cup sliced strawberries
1 tablespoon flaxseed

SNACK

1 whole grain bagel
1 tablespoon low-fat cream cheese

LUNCH

Mango Fish Salad
- 2 cups spinach or greens of choice
- 3 ounces leftover tilapia
- ¾ cup sliced mango
- 2 tablespoons sliced almonds
- ¼ cup dried cranberries
- 2 tablespoons light vinaigrette

SNACK

½ whole grain bagel
1 tablespoon 100% fruit spread

DINNER

Ancho-Rubbed Pork Chops with Orange and Scallion Salsa (page 247)
1 cup steamed quinoa
1 cup steamed broccoli

Quick Cuts

How to Cut 200 to 300 Calories on This Day

» **Morning snack: Eat half a bagel.**
» **Lunch: Have 2 ounces tilapia.**
» **Dinner: Have ⅔ cup quinoa.**

Day 62—1,777 Calories

BREAKFAST

Breakfast Smoothie
- 6 ounces fat-free yogurt (any flavor)
- 1 tablespoon ground flaxseed
- 1 cup strawberries
- 1 small banana
- Leftover mango
- ½ cup fat-free milk
- Ice

SNACK

8 whole wheat crackers
1 tablespoon natural peanut butter

LUNCH

Curried Chicken and Rice Salad (page 242)

SNACK

10 large baby carrots
1 whole wheat English muffin
1 tablespoon 100% fruit spread

DINNER

Taco Salad
- 2 cups greens of choice
- 4 ounces seasoned lean ground beef
- ½ cup low-fat cheese
- ¼ cup diced tomatoes
- ¼ avocado
- 2 tablespoons light sour cream
- ¼ cup salsa

Quick Cuts

How to Cut 200 to 300 Calories on This Day

» **Breakfast: Have ¾ smoothie.**
» **Morning snack: Have 4 crackers.**
» **Dinner: Eat 2 ounces ground beef.**

WEEK NINE MEAL PLAN

Day 63–1,870 Calories

BREAKFAST

Egg and Cheese Sandwich

- 2 egg whites and 1 whole egg (scrambled with cooking spray)
- 1 slice low-fat cheese
- 2 slices whole grain bread, toasted
- 1 tablespoon olive oil spread

SNACK

1 apple

LUNCH

1 serving Sweet Potato Stew with Chickpeas and North African Spices (page 240)

SNACK

1 orange

DINNER

Chicken Pasta Salad

- 1 cup whole wheat pasta, prepared according to package directions
- 4 ounces cooked chicken
- 1 tablespoon olive oil
- 4 chopped plum tomatoes
- ¼ cup fresh mushrooms, sliced
- 2 tablespoons shredded Parmesan cheese

Quick Cuts

How to Cut 200 to 300 Calories on This Day

» **Breakfast: Eliminate the whole egg and olive oil spread.**

» **Dinner: Have 3 ounces chicken, ¾ cup pasta, and 1 tablespoon Parmesan.**

»Breakfasts

PECAN APPLE MUFFINS

Making these muffins at home saves you a massive number of calories and a truckload of fat, compared with what you'd get in a coffee shop or grocery store. With whole wheat flour, wheat germ, and pecans, they have the fiber, minerals, and clean-burning energy to get your morning started on the right foot. You can also substitute walnuts for pecans.

MAKES 12 (NUTRITION INFORMATION IS FOR 1 MUFFIN)

ACTIVE TIME: 15 MINUTES

TOTAL TIME: 40 MINUTES

½ cup chopped pecans
2 large eggs
⅔ cup fat-free milk
½ cup unsweetened applesauce
½ cup dark brown sugar
2 tablespoons honey
2 cups whole wheat flour
2 tablespoon wheat germ
1 tablespoon baking powder
½ teaspoon cinnamon
½ teaspoon salt
1 large Golden Delicious or Granny Smith apple, peeled and cut into small chunks

1. Preheat the oven to 275°F. Spread the pecans on a baking sheet and bake for 10 minutes, or until lightly golden and fragrant. Remove from the oven and cool.

2. Increase the oven temperature to 375°F. Lightly coat a muffin tin with cooking spray. In a medium bowl, whisk together the eggs, milk, applesauce, sugar, and honey.

3. In a small bowl, combine the flour, wheat germ, baking powder, cinnamon, and salt and whisk to combine. Gently whisk into the wet ingredients. Stir in the apple and pecans and divide the batter into the muffin cups.

4. Bake for 20 minutes, or until the muffins spring back when gently pressed. Cool on a rack. Serve warm or at room temperature.

CALORIES/ MUFFIN	CARBS (G)	PROTEIN (G)	FAT (G)	SAT FAT (G)	SODIUM (MG)	FIBER (G)
201	43	7	5	1	270	4

»Breakfasts

BANANA-PECAN BREAKFAST BARS

Here's an alternative to store-bought cereal bars that packs a whole lot more whole-food nutrition into the same small package. This recipe also contains ingredients that can help lower bad LDL cholesterol and promote heart health: flaxseeds (omega-3 fatty acids) and rolled oats and apricots (fiber). If you're not a fan of coconut, roll the bars in crushed nuts or toasted oats.

MAKES 4 (NUTRITION INFORMATION IS FOR 1 BAR)

ACTIVE TIME: 12 MINUTES

TOTAL TIME: 40 MINUTES

1 cup sweetened shredded coconut
1 cup pecans
2 tablespoons flaxseeds
1 cup rolled oats
1½ cups dried apricots
1 medium banana
2 teaspoons molasses
½ teaspoon salt

1. Preheat the oven to 350°F. Spread the coconut on a baking sheet and toast, stirring occasionally, for 15 minutes, or until golden brown. Transfer to a plate and set aside. Spread the pecans on the baking sheet and toast for 15 minutes, or until fragrant. Place in a food processor and cool slightly for 5 minutes.

2. Add the flaxseeds to the pecans and pulse for 20 to 30 seconds, or until finely ground. Add the oats, apricots, banana, molasses, and salt. Process for 30 seconds, or until a paste forms. You may need to stop and scrape down the sides to get an even paste or divide the mixture in half and process in batches.

3. Divide the mixture into 4 equal pieces and shape into bars. Roll the bars in the reserved coconut, pressing it into the bar so that it adheres. Wrap each bar in plastic wrap and refrigerate for 1 hour, or until firm. Keep chilled until ready to eat.

CALORIES/BAR	CARBS (G)	PROTEIN (G)	FAT (G)	SAT FAT (G)	SODIUM (MG)	FIBER (G)
536	62	9	28	8	304	12

»Breakfasts

STEEL-CUT OATMEAL WITH STEWED FRUIT

Start your day with this hearty and sweet yet still nutritionally powerful breakfast. In fact, this recipe provides more than half of the fiber you need in a day. In winter, make extra stewed fruit and freeze it.

MAKES 2 SERVINGS (2 CUPS OATMEAL AND 3 CUPS FRUIT TOTAL–ENOUGH FOR LEFTOVERS)

ACTIVE TIME: 10 MINUTES

TOTAL TIME: 35 MINUTES

4 cups water
Pinch of salt
½ cup steel-cut oatmeal
1 cup dried cranberries
⅔ cup dried apricot halves
4 dried pear halves, sliced in half
½ cup prunes
1 tablespoon honey
¼ teaspoon cinnamon
2 or 3 strips lemon zest
1 tablespoon lemon juice

1. In a small saucepan, bring 2½ cups of the water to a boil and add the salt. Slowly add the oatmeal and simmer over very low heat for 30 minutes. (Note: If the oatmeal simmers too quickly, you may need to add extra water.)

2. Meanwhile, in a medium saucepan, combine the remaining 1½ cups water and the cranberries, apricots, pears, prunes, honey, cinnamon, lemon zest, and lemon juice. Bring to a boil, reduce to a low simmer, partially cover, and cook, stirring occasionally, for 25 minutes, or until the fruit is plump and the liquid is reduced to ½ cup.

3. To serve, top 1 cup of hot oatmeal with ½ cup of warm stewed fruit.

CALORIES/ SERVING	CARBS (G)	PROTEIN (G)	FAT (G)	SAT FAT (G)	SODIUM (MG)	FIBER (G)
486	110	7	2	0	12	9

»Lunches

TEX-MEX CHICKEN CHILI

This version is packed with tomatoes to provide a lot of vitamin C and lycopene, an antioxidant that studies suggest plays a role in preventing several types of cancer. Enjoy it by the bowlful or, for an even heartier meal, ladle over a baked potato.

MAKES 4 SERVINGS (5½ CUPS TOTAL)

ACTIVE TIME: 20 MINUTES

TOTAL TIME: 30 MINUTES

2 tablespoons canola oil
1 medium green bell pepper, seeded and chopped
1 medium onion, chopped
2 cloves garlic, sliced
½ pound ground white-meat chicken
1½ tablespoons chili powder
1 can (15 ounces) low-sodium pinto or kidney beans, rinsed and drained
2 cups water or low-sodium chicken broth
1 can (14 ounces) diced tomatoes, drained
1 can (8 ounces) tomato sauce
1 small potato, cut into ¼" cubes
¾ teaspoon salt
1 bay leaf
Sliced scallions, shredded low-fat Cheddar cheese, low-fat sour cream, and finely chopped red onion (optional)

1. Heat the oil in a medium saucepan over medium-high heat. Add the pepper, onion, and garlic and cook for 3 minutes, or until beginning to soften. Add the chicken and chili powder and cook, breaking up the chicken with a wooden spoon, for 3 minutes, or until no longer pink.

2. Add the beans, water or stock, tomatoes, tomato sauce, potato, salt, and bay leaf. Bring to a boil, reduce the heat, and simmer, stirring occasionally, for 10 minutes, or until the chili has thickened. Garnish with the scallions, cheese, sour cream, and red onion, if desired, and serve hot.

CALORIES/ SERVING	CARBS (G)	PROTEIN (G)	FAT (G)	SAT FAT (G)	SODIUM (MG)	FIBER (G)
438	52	26	14	2	1,000	15

»Lunches

TURKEY CHEDDAR MELT WITH APPLE AND SPROUTS

Turkey sandwiches are always a good lunch, but they can get pretty boring after a while. Here's a good way to liven it up—and keep it interesting by trying different cheeses or whole grain rye or pumpernickel bread. Lightly butter the toasted bread if it's a bit drier than you'd like. One quick-cooking tip: Cover your broiler pan with aluminum foil to ensure faster cleanup.

MAKES 2 SERVINGS

ACTIVE TIME: 10 MINUTES

TOTAL TIME: 15 MINUTES

4 slices whole grain bread, cut ¼" thick
8 slices (¾ ounce each) turkey
1 Golden Delicious or Granny Smith apple, cored and very thinly sliced
1 cup alfalfa sprouts
4 slices (¾ ounce each) low-fat Cheddar cheese

1. Lightly toast the bread in a toaster.

2. Preheat the broiler and cover a baking sheet with aluminum foil. Place the toasted bread on the pan. Divide the turkey among the bread slices, cover with the apple and sprouts, and top with a slice of cheese.

3. Place the pan under the broiler and broil for 3 minutes, or until the cheese melts and begins to brown. Serve open-faced (2 slices of bread, total) or closed (4 slices of bread), as desired.

CALORIES/ SERVING	CARBS (G)	PROTEIN (G)	FAT (G)	SAT FAT (G)	SODIUM (MG)	FIBER (G)
367	36	40	7	3	525	5

»Lunches

SEARED TEMPEH, GOAT CHEESE, ARUGULA, AND ROASTED RED PEPPER SANDWICHES

Tempeh is a soybean product that typically comes in cakes and has a nutty, hearty flavor. This recipe can also be made with a big portobello mushroom, but you'll miss out on the complete protein and beneficial soy isoflavones from tofu. Tempeh comes in a variety of flavors, and "garden vegetable" works well because it complements the red pepper and arugula.

MAKES 2 SERVINGS

ACTIVE TIME: 15 MINUTES

TOTAL TIME: 20 MINUTES

6 ounces tempeh, cut in half widthwise
4 slices whole grain bread, toasted
2 ounces low-fat goat cheese
2 ounces arugula (1 small bunch), washed and trimmed
1 whole jarred roasted red pepper, cut in half lengthwise

1. Spray a medium skillet with cooking spray and place over medium-high heat. Add the tempeh and sear for 5 to 6 minutes, or until golden brown on both sides, turning once.

2. Place the toast on a flat surface and spread with the cheese. Layer two slices of bread with the tempeh, arugula, and peppers. Cover with the remaining toast. Slice in half and serve.

CALORIES/ SERVING	CARBS (G)	PROTEIN (G)	FAT (G)	SAT FAT (G)	SODIUM (MG)	FIBER (G)
327	22	26	15	5	280	3

»Lunches

SWEET POTATO STEW WITH CHICKPEAS AND NORTH AFRICAN SPICES

Make a large batch of this recipe's spice mix so it's handy for chicken or lamb. Sweet potatoes are absolutely fabulous from a nutrition standpoint. They provide a lot of antioxidants from beta-carotene, as well as protein and clean-burning carbohydrate. To reduce the fat and sodium in this recipe, look for fat-free vegetable broth.

MAKES 2 SERVINGS (4½ CUPS TOTAL)

ACTIVE TIME: 15 MINUTES

TOTAL TIME: 30 MINUTES

1 tablespoon extra-virgin olive oil
1 medium onion, chopped
1 large garlic clove, thinly sliced
¾ teaspoon salt
½ teaspoon ground cinnamon
½ teaspoon ground cumin
½ teaspoon ground ginger
¼ teaspoon cayenne
1 medium sweet potato, peeled and cut into ½" cubes
4 cups low-sodium vegetable broth
1 can (15 ounces) chickpeas
Toasted sliced almonds, chopped fresh cilantro, chopped fresh parsley, and low-fat plain yogurt (optional)

1. Heat the oil in a medium skillet over medium heat. Add the onion, garlic, salt, cinnamon, cumin, ginger, and cayenne. Cook for 3 minutes, or until the spices are fragrant and the onion begins to soften.

2. Add the sweet potato and broth. Bring to a simmer and cook over low heat, covered, for 15 minutes, or until the potatoes soften. Remove the cover and gently smash the potatoes with the back of a slotted spoon. Add the chickpeas and return to a simmer for 2 minutes, or until the chickpeas are heated through. Serve hot, garnished with the almonds, cilantro, parsley, and a dollop of yogurt, if desired.

CALORIES/ SERVING	CARBS (G)	PROTEIN (G)	FAT (G)	SAT FAT (G)	SODIUM (MG)	FIBER (G)
646	101	29	14	2	667	27

»Lunches

ROAST TURKEY SALAD WITH GRAPES, GRAINS, AND CASHEWS

This is an incredibly quick and easy salad to make, and it has a lot of flavor despite having few ingredients. You can also toss it with lightly dressed greens to make a bigger salad.

MAKES 2 SERVINGS

ACTIVE TIME: 10 MINUTES

TOTAL TIME: 10 MINUTES

1 thick (8 ounces) slice roast turkey breast, cut into cubes
1½ cups Nutty Wild Rice and Grains (page 243)
¾ cup sliced green grapes
⅓ cup chopped salted cashews

In a medium bowl, combine the turkey, rice, grapes, and cashews and stir well. Refrigerate until ready to serve.

CALORIES/ SERVING	CARBS (G)	PROTEIN (G)	FAT (G)	SAT FAT (G)	SODIUM (MG)	FIBER (G)
563	45	44	23	4	220	7

»Lunches

CURRIED CHICKEN AND RICE SALAD

Curry powder and yogurt give this variation on chicken salad a rich and exotic flavor that is very satisfying. This salad is perfectly suited to being stuffed into a whole wheat pita with baby spinach or some alfalfa sprouts. Add a handful of toasted walnuts for extra crunch and heart-healthy unsaturated fat.

MAKES 2 SERVINGS

ACTIVE TIME: 25 MINUTES

TOTAL TIME: 1 HOUR

1¾ cups water
½ teaspoon salt
½ cup brown rice
2 tablespoons canola oil
2 large scallions, chopped
2 teaspoons curry powder
8 ounces boneless, skinless chicken breast, cut into ½" cubes
½ cup low-fat plain yogurt
1 Golden Delicious or Granny Smith apple, cored and chopped
¼ cup golden raisins
½ cup chopped parsley

1. In a small saucepan, bring the water and ¼ teaspoon of the salt to a boil. Add the rice, return to a simmer, cover, and cook for 45 minutes over very low heat. Remove from the heat and let steam, covered, for 10 minutes.

2. Heat the oil in a medium skillet over medium-high heat. Add the scallions, curry powder, and the remaining ¼ teaspoon salt. Cook for 2 or 3 minutes, or until the scallions begin to soften. Add the chicken and cook, stirring, for 3 to 4 minutes, or until cooked through. Remove the skillet from the heat and stir in the yogurt to make a sauce. Add the apple, raisins, parsley, and rice and stir to combine. Let cool and serve salad warm or cold.

CALORIES/ SERVING	CARBS (G)	PROTEIN (G)	FAT (G)	SAT FAT (G)	SODIUM (MG)	FIBER (G)
538	68	35	14	2	1,000	6

»Sides

NUTTY WILD RICE AND GRAINS

You'll never go back to white rice after trying this recipe. Its nutty, hearty flavor will make you take a new look at whole grains. It's a very easy recipe to double and triple and goes great with fish, chicken, or beef. If you don't have to be concerned about your sodium intake, salt the water liberally to bring out more of the natural rice and grain flavors.

MAKES 2 SERVINGS

ACTIVE TIME: 7 MINUTES

TOTAL TIME: 60 MINUTES

Dash of salt
¼ cup wild rice
¼ cup barley
¼ cup bulgur
⅓ cup sliced almonds
2 teaspoons flaxseeds
1 tablespoon extra-virgin olive oil
1 teaspoon cider vinegar

1. Bring a large pot of salted water to a boil. Add the rice and boil 25 minutes. Add the barley and bulgur, and continue to boil for 20 minutes, or until the rice splits. Drain.

2. While the grains are cooking, preheat the oven to 275°F. Spread the almonds on a baking sheet and toast for 12 minutes, or until golden.

3. Toss the rice mixture with the almonds, flaxseeds, oil, and vinegar. Serve warm or at room temperature.

CALORIES/ SERVING	CARBS (G)	PROTEIN (G)	FAT (G)	SAT FAT (G)	SODIUM (MG)	FIBER (G)
422	53	12	18	2	86	12

»Sides

LENTILS, BULGUR, AND CARAMELIZED ONIONS

Packaged bulgur typically can be found in the grocery store near the rice and couscous; look for lentils by the dry beans. One serving of this recipe provides 20 grams of fiber to fill you up, keep you regular, and protect your arteries, plus a serious vitamin and mineral kick. The caramelized onions add some welcome sweetness and flavor.

MAKES 2 SERVINGS (ABOUT 2 CUPS TOTAL)

ACTIVE TIME: 25 MINUTES

TOTAL TIME: 45 MINUTES

1½ tablespoons extra-virgin olive oil
3 medium onions, sliced
¾ teaspoon salt
3 cups water
½ cup lentils
¼ cup bulgur
1½ teaspoons red wine vinegar
⅓ cup chopped parsley

1. Heat the oil in a medium skillet over medium-high heat. Add the onions and ¼ teaspoon of the salt and stir to coat. Cover and reduce the heat to medium-low. Cook for 15 minutes, or until the onions are soft. Remove the cover and cook, stirring occasionally, for 20 minutes, or until the onions caramelize.

2. Bring the water and the remaining salt to a boil in a small saucepan. Add the lentils, reduce the heat to low, and simmer, covered, for 5 minutes. Add the bulgur and simmer for 20 minutes, or until the lentils are firm but cooked through. Drain.

3. Add the lentil mixture to the onions and cook over very low heat until all the ingredients are warmed through. Add the vinegar and parsley and toss gently to incorporate. Adjust the seasoning to taste and serve warm.

CALORIES/ SERVING	CARBS (G)	PROTEIN (G)	FAT (G)	SAT FAT (G)	SODIUM (MG)	FIBER (G)
399	58	17	11	2	900	20

»Sides

SAUTÉED BROCCOLI RAAB, RED PEPPERS, AND GARLIC

Broccoli raab is different from your typical head of broccoli. With leaves and small clusters of buds attached to thin stalks, it's a green that you're likely to find in the produce section near the collards and cabbage. Like other greens, broccoli raab is high in fiber, folate, calcium, and the antioxidant beta-carotene. Blanching (dipping it in boiling water and then in ice water) takes the bitterness out. This recipe is great when added to an egg wrap made with a whole wheat tortilla.

MAKES 2 SERVINGS (4 CUPS TOTAL)

ACTIVE TIME: 20 MINUTES

TOTAL TIME: 30 MINUTES

1 bunch broccoli raab (1 pound), trimmed
2 tablespoons extra-virgin olive oil
2 large cloves garlic, thinly sliced
1 red bell pepper, seeded and cut into ¼" slices
Salt
Freshly ground black pepper

1. Fill a medium mixing bowl with ice and water.

2. In a medium, high-sided skillet, bring 1" salted water to a boil. Add the broccoli raab and return to a boil; remove after 1 minute, when the broccoli raab turns bright green and is still firm. Submerge it in ice water for 1 minute, drain, and pat dry.

3. Wipe the liquid from the skillet, add the oil, and heat over medium-high heat. Add the garlic and tilt the pan so that the garlic is submerged in the oil. Cook for 1 minute, or until the garlic has softened. Remove with a slotted spoon and set aside. Add the bell pepper, cover, and cook for 5 minutes, or until the pepper begins to soften and blacken on the edges.

4. Add the broccoli raab and reserved garlic to the skillet and cook for 2 minutes, or until heated through. Season with the salt and pepper to taste and serve warm or at room temperature.

CALORIES/ SERVING	CARBS (G)	PROTEIN (G)	FAT (G)	SAT FAT (G)	SODIUM (MG)	FIBER (G)
175	11	8	11	1.5	154	7

SALMON WITH BRUSSELS SPROUTS AND CHESTNUTS

This is a great recovery meal after a hard workout because it has a lot of high-quality protein, filling and heart-healthy unsaturated fat and omega-3 fatty acids, and almost the entire RDA for vitamin C.

MAKES 2 SERVINGS

ACTIVE TIME: 20 MINUTES

TOTAL TIME: 30 MINUTES

2 tablespoons + 1 teaspoon extra-virgin olive oil
½ pound brussels sprouts, trimmed and halved
Salt
Freshly ground black pepper
2 salmon fillets (4 ounces each), about 1" thick
1 teaspoon balsamic vinegar
15 roasted chestnuts, peeled and halved

1. Preheat the oven to 425°F. Heat 2 tablespoons of the oil in a medium ovenproof skillet over high heat. Add the brussels sprouts and season generously with the salt and pepper. Cook, stirring, for 1 minute, or until the brussels sprouts begin to sizzle. Place the skillet in the oven and roast, stirring occasionally, for 15 minutes, or until the brussels sprouts are browned and softened.

2. While the brussels sprouts are cooking, heat the remaining 1 teaspoon oil in a small skillet over medium-high heat. Season all sides of the salmon fillets with the salt and pepper and place in the skillet, skin-side down. Cook for 4 minutes, or until the skin is well browned and releases from the pan easily. Turn the salmon and place the hot skillet in the oven. Roast for 3 to 5 minutes, or until the salmon is cooked through.

3. Using a heavy oven mitt, return the brussels sprouts to the stovetop over medium heat (be careful—the skillet handle will be extremely hot). Add the vinegar and chestnuts and cook, stirring, for 1 to 2 minutes, or until the chestnuts are warmed through. Divide the salmon and brussels sprouts between two plates and serve warm.

CALORIES/ SERVING	CARBS (G)	PROTEIN (G)	FAT (G)	SAT FAT (G)	SODIUM (MG)	FIBER (G)
477	44	28	21	3	400	8

»Dinners

ANCHO-RUBBED PORK CHOPS WITH ORANGE AND SCALLION SALSA

Ancho chili powder lends a smoky richness, instead of the sharp and tangy heat you get from cayenne or habanero chili powders. You can also prepare these chops on the grill. The scallions in the salsa aren't just there for bite; the same compounds that give them their pungent odor and taste help keep arteries healthy and clear of fatty plaques.

MAKES 2 SERVINGS

ACTIVE TIME: 20 MINUTES

TOTAL TIME: 20 MINUTES

1 teaspoon ancho chili powder

½ teaspoon salt

1 tablespoon extra-virgin olive oil

2 bone-in center-cut pork chops (½" thick) (¾–1 pound total weight for both)

2 navel oranges, peeled and chopped

1 scallion, thinly sliced

1. Preheat the broiler. Line a broiler pan with aluminum foil and place under the heating broiler.

2. In a small bowl, combine the chili powder, ¼ teaspoon of the salt, and the oil. Brush both sides of the chops with the chili oil. Place the chops on the baking sheet and cook for 5 to 6 minutes, turning once. Remove from the oven and let rest 5 minutes.

3. Meanwhile, in a medium bowl, combine the oranges, scallion, and remaining ¼ teaspoon salt. Toss to combine.

4. Before serving, add any pork juices that accumulated while the pork was resting to the salsa. Spoon the salsa over the pork.

CALORIES/ SERVING	CARBS (G)	PROTEIN (G)	FAT (G)	SAT FAT (G)	SODIUM (MG)	FIBER (G)
428	20	33	24	7	1,240	4

»Dinners

CURRIED CAULIFLOWER AND CHICKPEA STEW

This rich, hearty meal is an excellent choice anytime but especially after a hard workout. It has a lot of carbohydrate for replenishing energy stores and protein for repairing muscle and speeding up the recovery process, and it's relatively high in sodium to replace the electrolytes you lost through sweating. You can use instant brown rice to reduce preparation time, and substitute broccoli if you don't like cauliflower.

MAKES 3 SERVINGS (5 CUPS STEW AND 1½ CUPS RICE TOTAL)

ACTIVE TIME: 30 MINUTES

TOTAL TIME: 1 HOUR

2¾ cups water
1¼ teaspoons salt
½ cup brown rice
2 tablespoons canola oil
1 medium onion, chopped
1 medium carrot, peeled and sliced ¼" thick
2 cloves garlic, minced
4 teaspoons curry powder
1 small head cauliflower (1¼ pounds), cut into bite-size pieces
2 cups low-sodium vegetable broth
1 can (15 ounces) chickpeas, rinsed and drained
¾ cup frozen baby peas
Freshly ground black pepper
Hot sauce

1. In a small saucepan, bring 1¾ cups of the water and ¼ teaspoon of the salt to a boil. Add the rice, return to a simmer, cover, and cook for 45 minutes over very low heat. Remove from the heat and let sit, covered, for 10 minutes.

2. Heat the oil in a medium saucepan over medium heat. Add the onion, carrot, garlic, curry powder, and the remaining 1 teaspoon salt. Cook, stirring, for 5 minutes, or until the onions begin to soften. Add the cauliflower and stir to coat. Add the broth and the remaining 1 cup water and bring to a boil. Cover and simmer for 15 minutes, or until the cauliflower has softened.

3. Meanwhile, place ½ cup of the chickpeas and ¼ cup hot cooking liquid (from the simmering stew) in a small bowl. Using a fork, mash the chickpeas into a paste.

4. When the cauliflower is done, add the chickpea paste, whole chickpeas, and baby peas to the stew. Return to a simmer and cook for 2 minutes, or until the peas are warmed through. Season generously with pepper and serve over the rice with hot sauce.

CALORIES/ SERVING	CARBS (G)	PROTEIN (G)	FAT (G)	SAT FAT (G)	SODIUM (MG)	FIBER (G)
454	64	18	14	1	1,100	17

PASTA WITH SWISS CHARD, RED ONION, AND PARMESAN

Swiss chard is in the same family as spinach and beets and can be found year-round with the greens in the produce section. Both the stems and leaves are edible and absolutely packed with nutrition. Swiss chard is high in fiber, filling, and low in calories. It's also very rich in nutrients, including vitamins A, C, and K, as well as muscle-building iron, magnesium, and manganese.

MAKES 2 SERVINGS (4 CUPS TOTAL)

ACTIVE TIME: 20 MINUTES

TOTAL TIME: 30 MINUTES

4 ounces whole wheat spaghetti
1 bunch (10 ounces) Swiss chard, leaves and stems separated
2 tablespoons extra-virgin olive oil
1 medium red onion, thinly sliced
2 garlic cloves, thinly sliced
¼ teaspoon salt + additional to taste
2 medium plum tomatoes, seeded and chopped
Salt
Freshly ground black pepper
¼ cup (½ ounce) grated Parmesan cheese

1. Prepare the pasta according to package directions.

2. While the pasta is cooking, slice the Swiss chard leaves 1½" wide and thinly slice the stems.

3. Heat the oil in a medium skillet over medium heat and add the onion, garlic, and ¼ teaspoon salt. Cover and cook for 4 minutes, or until softened. Add the stems, cover, and cook for 2 to 3 minutes, or until beginning to soften. Add the leaves, cover, and cook for 5 minutes, or until wilted. Remove from the heat and add the tomatoes.

4. Add the cooked pasta to the Swiss chard mixture and toss to combine. Season with the salt and pepper to taste and serve sprinkled with the cheese.

CALORIES/ SERVING	CARBS (G)	PROTEIN (G)	FAT (G)	SAT FAT (G)	SODIUM (MG)	FIBER (G)
418	58	15	14	3	501	4

SPICY SHELLFISH STEW

Shellfish stews were one of my favorite things about visiting the Mediterranean coasts of France, Spain, and Italy when I was racing in Europe. You can buy all the ingredients fresh, or you can use frozen peeled and deveined shrimp and frozen scallops. Shellfish are rich in muscle-building iron and zinc, and the tomatoes provide a lot of vitamin C and lycopene.

MAKES 2 SERVINGS

ACTIVE TIME: 25 MINUTES

TOTAL TIME: 25 MINUTES

2 tablespoons extra-virgin olive oil
4 cloves garlic, thinly sliced
¼ pound large shrimp, peeled and deveined
¼ pound bay or sea scallops
¼ to ½ teaspoon red pepper flakes
¼ pound mussels, scrubbed and beards removed
1 bottle (8 ounces) clam juice
4 medium plum tomatoes, seeded and chopped
¼ cup chopped parsley

1. Heat the oil in a medium skillet over medium heat. Add the garlic and tilt the pan so that the garlic is submerged in the oil, holding over the heat for 2 to 3 minutes, or until the garlic has softened and begun to turn a light golden brown. Remove with a slotted spoon and set aside.

2. Add the shrimp, scallops, and red pepper flakes to the skillet and cook, turning once, for 3 to 4 minutes, or until the shrimp and scallops have begun to brown. Remove the shellfish and set aside with the garlic. Add the mussels and clam juice. Use a wooden spoon to scrape up any browned bits from the bottom of the skillet. Simmer, stirring, for 4 to 5 minutes, or until the mussels have opened wide and the sauce has reduced.

3. Return the reserved shrimp, scallops, and garlic to the pan and add the tomatoes and parsley. Bring to a simmer and cook for 2 minutes, or until the sauce reduces a bit. Serve warm.

CALORIES/ SERVING	CARBS (G)	PROTEIN (G)	FAT (G)	SAT FAT (G)	SODIUM (MG)	FIBER (G)
350	26	30	14	2	792	2

SOFT STEAK TACOS WITH MANGO CHIMICHURRI

Chimichurri is a traditional sauce from Central America with many variations; this one uses fresh mango. You'll most likely end up with extra chimichurri, but save what you don't use—it's great over grilled meat, and you can even add a bit of oil to it and try it as a salad dressing.

MAKES 2 SERVINGS (1 GENEROUS CUP CHIMICHURRI PER SERVING)

ACTIVE TIME: 20 MINUTES

TOTAL TIME: 30 MINUTES

1 packed cup parsley leaves
¼ cup extra-virgin olive oil
2½ tablespoons red wine vinegar
1 clove garlic
1 mango, peeled and cut into cubes
6 ounces skirt steak
Salt
Freshly ground black pepper
4 corn tortillas
1 packed cup baby spinach

1. Preheat the broiler. Line a broiler pan with aluminum foil and heat 10 minutes.

2. In a blender or food processor, combine the parsley, oil, vinegar, and garlic. Blend or process for 30 seconds, or until the garlic and parsley are chopped. Transfer to a small serving bowl, add the mango, and stir to combine.

3. When the broiler has heated, season the steak well with the salt and pepper. Place on the prepared pan and cook for 6 minutes, or until browned. Flip and cook for 3 to 4 minutes, or until medium rare. Remove from the oven and let rest 5 minutes.

4. Heat the tortillas and place two on each of two plates. Divide the spinach among the tortillas, and layer the sliced steak on top of the spinach. Serve with the chimichurri.

CALORIES/ SERVING	CARBS (G)	PROTEIN (G)	FAT (G)	SAT FAT (G)	SODIUM (MG)	FIBER (G)
398	32	27	18	4	90	4

»Snacks

BLACKBERRY BANANA SMOOTHIE

Perhaps one of the best postworkout recovery smoothies you'll ever find, this powerful drink combines the complete protein of tofu with the potassium of bananas and the antioxidants of blackberries. In fact, the USDA recently ranked blackberries as one of the richest sources of antioxidant compounds. Blackberries also contain salicylic acid, the active ingredient in aspirin that's associated with reducing heart attack and stroke risk.

MAKES 2 SERVINGS

ACTIVE TIME: 5 MINUTES

TOTAL TIME: 5 MINUTES

8 ounces silken tofu
1 container (6 ounces) blackberries
1 medium banana, cut into chunks
½ cup ice cubes
1 teaspoon honey
¼ teaspoon cinnamon

In a blender, combine the tofu, blackberries, banana, ice, honey, and cinnamon. Blend until smooth. Divide between two glasses and serve cold.

CALORIES/ SERVING	CARBS (G)	PROTEIN (G)	FAT (G)	SAT FAT (G)	SODIUM (MG)	FIBER (G)
184	27	10	4	1	46	6

»Snacks

SNACK MIX WITH TOASTED PECANS, SESAME SEEDS, FLAXSEEDS, AND DRIED FRUIT

Toasting them in the oven brings out the natural and hearty flavors in the nuts and seeds, which are then complemented by the sweet and tart flavors of the cranberries and apricots. Throw a bag of this snack mix into your gym bag or briefcase for a delicious, filling, and energizing snack during the workday. You can also make it in bigger batches and store it in your pantry or freezer.

MAKES 2 SERVINGS

ACTIVE TIME: 5 MINUTES

TOTAL TIME: 40 MINUTES

¼ cup whole pecans
1 teaspoon sesame seeds
1 teaspoon flaxseeds
1 teaspoon honey
1 teaspoon vegetable oil
¼ teaspoon salt
¼ cup dried cranberries, roughly chopped
¼ cup dried apricots, sliced

1. Preheat the oven to 325°F. In a bowl, combine the pecans, sesame seeds, flaxseeds, honey, oil, and salt and stir until coated. Place on a small baking sheet and bake for 15 minutes, or until browned.

2. Transfer the mixture to a plate and let cool for 15 to 20 minutes. Toss with the cranberries and apricots. Serve cool.

CALORIES/ SERVING	CARBS (G)	PROTEIN (G)	FAT (G)	SAT FAT (G)	SODIUM (MG)	FIBER (G)
261	33	3	13	1	296	4

»Snacks

SALMON MOUSSE WITH WHOLE GRAIN CRACKERS

This indulgent snack is actually good for you. It's also a great way to impress guests, because it looks and tastes like you spent hours preparing it. With both salmon and dairy products, this snack provides high-quality protein, heart-healthy omega-3 fatty acids, and calcium from the milk and cream cheese. Serve on whole grain crackers or toast, or double the recipe so you have extra for spreading on bagels in the morning.

MAKES 2 SERVINGS

ACTIVE TIME: 10 MINUTES

TOTAL TIME: 10 MINUTES

4 ounces reduced-fat cream cheese
1 ounce smoked salmon, chopped
1 tablespoon fat-free milk
1 teaspoon chopped scallion greens or chives
Salt
4 long whole grain crackers (such as Wasa Crispbread)

1. In a medium bowl, combine the cream cheese, salmon, milk, and scallions or chives. Beat, using a fork, until the texture is light. Season to taste with the salt.

2. Divide the spread between the crackers (2 tablespoons per cracker) and serve.

CALORIES/ SERVING	CARBS (G)	PROTEIN (G)	FAT (G)	SAT FAT (G)	SODIUM (MG)	FIBER (G)
227	21	11	11	6	413	3

The Next Step

Staying on Top of Your Game

Over the course of this 9-week program, you have most likely dropped some weight; rediscovered strength you thought you had lost forever; and boosted your performance at home, at work, and at play. If you had any medical tests done at the beginning of the program and again at the end, you might have seen reduced blood pressure, lower levels of bad LDL cholesterol, and higher levels of good HDL cholesterol. However good the news, you're still in a very tenuous position; the positive changes you've made thus far can and will disappear quickly if you return to being a pork-rind-eating couch potato. On the other hand, if you continue to make the changes in this program part of your everyday life, your health, fitness, and performance will continue to improve for years to come.

As you've seen, the body can make some changes relatively quickly, whereas others take place gradually. For example, the strength training in this program will help increase bone mineral density and prevent loss of bone mass, but the difference won't be seen for several months or years. Similarly, making permanent changes to your lifestyle behaviors can lower your risk of developing chronic diseases and cancer, but you've got to make the changes from the past 9 weeks stick.

THE NEXT STEP

In my experience, people who continue following this program's dietary and exercise habits throughout the next 3 weeks stand the greatest chance of making permanent and positive changes in their lives. That, of course, raises the question, Why not make the program 12 weeks long? The truth is, it doesn't matter if I make the meal plan and exercise schedule 12, 16, 26, or 52 weeks. There's always going to be a crucial transition period when you move from following a written program to doing it on your own. Remember when you learned how to ride a bicycle? Eventually, your mother or father had to let go of the seat and let you balance on your own, and only then did you truly learn how to ride a bicycle.

Well, for the past 9 weeks, I've been holding on to the back of the seat, and I just let go. Now it's your turn to balance and steer. Don't worry—this book contains plenty of tools to help you stay upright. By going back to the preceding chapters, you can use the exercise programs and meal plans as guidelines, but you'll want to make some changes to keep them fresh and productive. I've laid out what I refer to as Next Step Principles to assist you.

A QUICK LOOK BACK—AND AHEAD

Before I talk about the Next Step Principles, it's important for you to recognize how far you have already come. If you're reading this after finishing the 9-week program, you're a different person than you were when you opened this book 3 months ago. If you're reading this before you start the program, you'll be a different person by the time you take the Next Step.

Over the course of 9 weeks, you:

- Became physically active on a regular basis
- Followed a sequential, progressive training program for developing muscular strength, endurance, and stability
- Challenged yourself with unfamiliar movement patterns
- Decreased your consumption of saturated and trans fats, as well as refined sugar
- Increased your consumption of whole grains, fruits, vegetables, low-fat dairy, fish, and lean meats
- Lost weight and inches from your waist
- Boosted your energy level so you're not exhausted by the time you get home in the evening
- Found the energy and focus to fully engage with your spouse, children, and friends again
- Reignited the passion in your love life
- Rediscovered your passion for your career

You've come a long way in 3 months, and if you don't believe me, just ask the people around you. When I talk to friends and families of clients who have been through the Carmichael Performance Program, they tell me that their friend, husband, brother, or cousin is more pleasant to be around, in a better mood, more attentive, more energetic, more enthusiastic about participating in games and sports, and generally more relaxed. This is you, right now. You have already made sweeping positive changes in your life and in the lives of those most important to you, and now you can use the Next Step Fitness Principles to make sure these positive changes stick.

» **Intensity:** To continue making progress, about 40 percent of your endurance training time (running, walking, swimming, cycling, snowshoeing, cross-country skiing, basketball) should be done at or above a 7 on a 1-to-10 intensity scale. Now that you can go faster than you could 9 weeks ago, don't just settle into your new comfortable pace—keep pushing. It'll help make your heart, lungs, muscles, and joints stronger and healthier. The same is true for strength training and agility movements: Increase the resistance or push yourself to go faster, and you'll keep your fitness level growing.

"Can I go back to the beginning?"

IF YOU CHOOSE TO GO through the program again, I recommend restarting with Week Four instead of repeating Weeks One through Three. With the progress you've already made, the workouts in the Commit Period are now too easy for you. When you restart at Week Four, you can keep the workout times as they are written, but be sure to push yourself to go faster during the endurance workouts and use more resistance during the strength workouts.

» **Frequency:** Aim to exercise four or five times each week—up to six if you're shooting for a major goal like your first half- or full marathon or a charity bike ride. I don't recommend training 7 days a week; 1 day of complete rest each week is essential for allowing the body to recover and become stronger. For most people who complete this 9-week program, I recommend continuing with four endurance, two strength, and two agility workouts in five total sessions each week: Combine endurance and strength, endurance and agility, and strength and agility workouts, and then include one endurance-only workout.

» **Duration:** Ideally, your endurance workouts get longer as you gain fitness, but that doesn't typically fit into most people's busy schedules. If you can't make your endurance workouts longer, make them harder. This means a faster overall pace or faster intervals (see "Intensity," page 261). Duration for strength training and agility doesn't need to increase; the resistance or speed does.

» **Individuality:** Different parts of this program resonate more strongly with different people. Some people fall in love with the endurance aspect, whereas others really enjoy the resistance exercises and the nutrition plan. It's important to maintain a balance among the endurance, strength, agility, and nutrition components of this program, but the truth is, if you concentrate on whatever element pleases you most at specific times, you're more likely to end up blending all of them into your life for many years to come. Change happens. We have children, get a new job, or move to a different state. The more flexible you can be with your approach to fitness and nutrition, the easier it'll be to maintain your healthy habits.

FITNESS NEEDS CHANGE WITH AGE

Everything changes with age. You know more now than you did on your first day at your first big job, you act differently in your current relationships than you did when you were 20, and your perspectives on the world have certainly changed as you've matured. Your fitness objectives need to change to reflect your age, as well. I'm not saying you need to sign up for aqua aerobics the same day you start receiving Social Security checks, though. I know men and women in their sixties and seventies who still participate in active sports like downhill skiing and snowboarding and compete in endurance competitions like Ironman triathlons, 100-mile mountain-bike races, and the Pikes Peak Marathon. There is no magic age at which you have to give away all your sports equipment and take up bridge or pinochle. Making simple, age-related adjustments to your fitness program can help ensure you're fit and trim when the retirement checks start rolling in.

Stay on Your Feet

As we get older, weight-bearing exercise becomes more important because it's instrumental in retaining bone mineral density, lean body mass, and joint integrity. For a long time now, weight-bearing exercise has been synonymous with running, because it is the easiest association to make. But any exercise you perform on your feet or with added weight supported by your skeleton counts as weight bearing. That means running and walking fit the bill, and so do cross-country and downhill skiing, racket sports, basketball, hockey, in-line skating, and even dancing. Resistance training, with weights or just with your body weight, can accomplish two objectives at once: It's a weight-bearing activity that also maintains your lean muscle mass.

In my heart, cycling will always be the sport and activity I'm most passionate about, but as I've grown older, I've replaced some of the time I used to spend riding with hiking, weight lifting, and skiing. If you're over 30 and your favorite exercise activity is not weight bearing (cycling, mountain biking, or swimming), you need to consider diversifying. You may be aerobically fit—you may even be a serious athlete—but unless you make changes soon, your short-term devotion to your sport is likely to impair your long-term health. Nutrition and activity choices play major roles in controlling calcium levels in your blood and bones, and consistent weight-bearing activity sends an important signal to your body that the calcium already in your bones needs to stay there.

Preserve Muscle to Keep Metabolism High

There is no age at which you cannot add more muscle mass. Although men lose an average of 3 percent of their lean muscle mass each decade starting at about age 50, age itself has almost nothing to do with the gradual loss of muscle and the subsequent slowing of metabolism that people tend to experience as they mature. Rather, you lose muscle mass because you're not exercising as much and not moving as much weight around (think kids or yard work) on a daily basis. The good news is that consistent strength training can elicit gains in lean body mass at any age.

Keep Joints Healthy

The human body is a great machine, but if there is one weakness in its design, it is that our joints are very vulnerable to damage. The two primary ways you can damage a joint are by accidentally tearing the ligaments, tendons, and menisci that hold it in proper alignment or by wearing out the cartilage and fluid that keep it moving smoothly. Both types of injuries happen more often in untrained individuals, compared with those who are even moderately trained.

Stronger and properly trained muscles lead to healthier and more stable joints. A stronger muscle needs a stronger tendon to attach it to your skeleton, and increased movement around a joint helps keep ligaments pliable and strong, as well. It's important to keep up the exercise diversity laid out in this book to maintain muscle balance and joint integrity.

Pick Your Battles

Andre Agassi played his first US Open in 1986, when Roger Federer was 5 years old, and yet the two men met in the finals of the 2005 US Open. At 35, Agassi was up against a man 11 years his junior, the number one tennis player in the world, and arguably the most dominating tennis champion of his generation. To earn the honor of walking onto center court that afternoon, they had each won six matches over the course of 2 weeks. Federer overpowered his opponents, whereas Agassi outfinessed them.

The biggest difference between Agassi's 20th appearance at the US Open and his earlier ones was the number of tournaments he played during the preceding months. As a younger man, he could play tennis week in and week out, month after month. At 35, he just couldn't perform at his absolute best as frequently as he could before. Rather than sacrifice his performance by playing every week, he learned to choose his battles and save his strength for the tournaments that mattered to him.

He also learned to use his age as a weapon rather than a hindrance. During his quarterfinal victory over a young and powerful James Blake, Agassi started slow and lost the first two sets. Smelling victory just one set away, Blake poured even more effort into his game. On the other end of the court, Agassi carefully orchestrated his returns and volleys to keep Blake on the run, just as he had during the two sets he had already lost. The tables turned during the third set because Agassi used his mastery of the game to exhaust a physically stronger opponent and take away his advantage. After winning sets three and four, the match came down to a tiebreaker in the fifth set, and Agassi's unexpected advancement to the semifinals drew people who don't watch tennis to their televisions for his next two matches.

The lesson here is that as we get older, athletic performance itself does not decline as fast as your ability to recover from it. When I coach Masters athletes (a competition category for athletes above age 30 to 35, depending on the sport) to win national championships or compete at the Ironman World Championships in Kona, Hawaii, they perform the same workouts I prescribe for men half their age. The big difference is how many hard workouts and interval sessions I put into a single week. Where the younger athlete may recover from a hard workout and be ready for another in 24 to 36 hours, a man in his forties or fifties typically needs at least 48 hours between similar training sessions.

Get Happy Feet

As we get older, opportunities to be nimble on our feet almost totally disappear. To be active and vital now and in the decades to come, your fitness program needs to enhance your balance, coordination, and agility.

The body adapts to movements you perform on a regular basis by mapping out commonly used neural pathways from your brain to muscles. When you first start a resistance-training program, the strength gains you see in the first several weeks are largely due to neuromuscular changes, not changes in muscle size. In response to the stimulus of exercise, your body reprograms the nerves supplying your muscles with information. To complete a particular movement like a squat or pushup, it increases the number of muscle fibers that are activated when you call for a muscle contraction and improves the coordination between all the muscles that are contracting. Keep challenging the body to respond to diverse motions and activities, and you'll find it acting in a more cohesive and integrated manner, whether you're walking across the living room or taking evasive action on the slopes to avoid an out-of-control skier.

GOOD NUTRITION BECOMES A WAY OF LIFE

As I said earlier, I don't want you to follow written meal plans for the rest of your life. Through this book's 9-week plan and the accompanying shopping lists, the contents of your cupboards and refrigerator most likely look completely different than they did 3 months ago. You may not have noticed, but your grocery-shopping habits have probably changed as well. You spend more time in the produce section, you visit the fish counter more often, and your trips down the snack and soda aisles are probably fewer and farther between. Over the next 3 weeks, during this critical transition between a structured program and doing it on your own, I want you to be especially mindful of the following Next Step Nutrition Principles. Over time, you'll find yourself adhering to them with little or no conscious effort.

Whole Foods First

Choose whole foods over processed whenever possible. This means more fresh or frozen fruits and vegetables than canned, more whole grains than bleached white flour or white rice, and as little fast food as you can get away with. Processed foods are convenient, but that convenience often comes at a price. Case in point: Manufacturing a low-fat version of a food typically means adding more sugar or salt—or both. Refining grains removes the bran containing most of the vitamins, minerals, and fiber. The more often you replace processed foods with whole ones, the higher your chances of successfully managing your weight, maintaining your health, and supporting your high-performance lifestyle.

Be Mindful of What You Eat

One of my primary goals with this program was to stir you from complacency and get you to take a more active role in your nutrition, fitness, performance, and health. Along those lines, it's important for you to continue being mindful of what, how much, and how often you're eating. Absentminded eating is one of the greatest threats to successful weight management and long-term health. It makes you much more likely to eat too many calories from high-fat, high-sugar, and high-sodium foods.

For Best Results, Water Frequently

The majority of the US population lives in a chronic state of dehydration. If you've followed the recommendations in this program, you're most likely consuming more fluids each day than you were 3 months ago. The changes you may have noticed as a result include less fatigue, fewer headaches, clearer skin, greater flexibility, and a better mood. I have often told clients that the first and best response to feeling "off" is to start drinking more fluids immediately. Hydration plays a big role in your enjoyment of life and how enjoyable you are to be around. Coworkers of one of my particularly cranky (and chronically dehydrated) employees hung a sign in his office that reads "For best results, water frequently."

Eat Fish Twice a Week

There are two reasons why I like this guideline. Number one, as I talked about at length earlier in this book, fish is packed with top-quality protein, as well as omega-3 and omega-6 fatty acids that can protect your heart and brain from damage and disease. I've also found—and this is the second reason—that for people who eat fish twice a week, the fish tends to displace at least one meal of poor-quality food. In other words, consciously choosing to eat fish twice a week gives you beneficial nutrients and, in many cases, takes the place of greasy fast food, a rich restaurant meal, or a high-fat and high-sodium frozen dinner.

Junk Food Happens

Let's face it, you're not going to abstain from junk food for the rest of your life, nor should you. It's obviously not a good idea to make junk food a staple, but trying to completely avoid it is unrealistic. There are times when junk food is part of life: Elephant ears and funnel cake are part of the county-fair experience, just like foot-long hot dogs at the baseball park. There are also times when it's the only realistic choice; for example, there might not be much else available when you're driving through a small town at 2 a.m. When you eat fast food or high-calorie comfort food once in a while, the impact is essentially the same as overeating on your nutrition program. You'll take in two normal meals' worth of fat, calories, and sodium, but as long as it's an occasional anomaly, it won't affect your weight or long-term health. It's not fast food that kills people, but the fact that people eat way too much of it.

Alternating Forward Shoulder Raise

❶ Stand on a resistance cord with your feet roughly hip-distance apart and equal lengths of cord on each side. Hold the handles at hip level so your palms face your thighs (Figure 1). There should be a slight bend in your knees.

❷ Keeping your back straight, chest high, and head up, smoothly raise your fully extended right arm to shoulder height in front of you (Figure 2). Slowly lower it to the starting position. Repeat with your left arm (Figure 3).

Back Extension

❶ Lie flat on your stomach with your hands behind your head, elbows bent, and your legs straight (Figure 1).

❷ Push your legs into the ground and use your back to lift your shoulders and chest 1 to 3 inches (Figure 2). Don't strain too hard to lift very high. Slowly lower your chest back to the floor. For an added challenge, extend your arms out to the sides or in front of you and lift them off the ground, as well.

Bench Dip

EASY:

❶ Sit on the edge of a chair or bench. Straighten your legs in front of you, then bend your knees, with your feet flat on the floor. Place your hands behind your hips and lift your body off the chair (Figure 1), shifting your hips forward.

❷ Slowly lower your hips toward the floor. If you get to the point where your elbows are bent at 90 degrees, that's great—stop there (Figure 2). If you feel pain in the front of your shoulders, don't lower any farther. Drive with your arms and shoulders to raise your body to the starting position.

DIFFICULT:

Instead of bending your knees, keep your legs straight, with your toes facing up and your heels on the ground (Figure 3). To make this exercise more difficult, elevate your legs on a second bench or chair (Figure 4). To add even more resistance, place a medicine ball in your lap or between your knees.

Body-Weight Squat

This is the same exercise you completed as part of the Carmichael Fitness Test. See page 114 for instructions.

Core Bridge

EASY:

❶ Lie on your left side with your legs, hips, and shoulders in a straight line. Prop yourself up on your left forearm so your elbow is directly under your shoulder. Lift your hips off the floor to create a straight line from your right shoulder to your right ankle. Place your top arm along your side (Figure 1). For added balance, place your right foot on the ground just in front of your left foot. Hold the position for the allotted time, then lower your hip to the ground. Alternate sides (Figure 2).

To do a **prone core bridge**, start by lying on your stomach instead of your side. Support your upper body with your elbows directly under your shoulders and your forearms flat on the ground. Hold your body in a straight line from your shoulders to your heels.

HARDER:

Instead of using your forearm(s) for support, place your hand(s) on the ground directly under your shoulder(s).

Curl and Press

❶ Stand on a resistance cord with your feet roughly hip-distance apart and equal lengths of cord on each side. Hold the handles so your palms face your thighs (Figure 1).

❷ Curl your arms to shoulder height (Figure 2).

❸ Press both hands overhead until your arms are fully extended, but don't lock your elbows (Figure 3). Slowly lower your hands to shoulder height, and then uncurl your arms to return to the starting position.

Jump Rope

❶ Hold one end of a jump rope in each hand, with the rope passing behind your heels (Figure 1).

❷ Swing the rope around your body and hop over it with both feet (Figure 2). If you can't polish off the number of jumps prescribed, break down the total number into sets, such as five sets of five jumps for a total of 25.

Lateral Arm Raise

❶ Stand on a resistance cord with your feet roughly hip-distance apart and equal lengths of cord on each side. Hold the handles at your sides (Figure 1).

❷ Keeping your back straight, chest high, and head up, simultaneously and smoothly raise both arms straight out to the side until they reach shoulder height (Figure 2). Slowly lower your hands to the starting position.

«1
«2

Leg and Hip Raise

❶ Lie flat on your back with your hands at your sides, palms on the floor, and legs straight (Figure 1).

❷ Raise your legs until they are perpendicular to the floor (Figure 2).

❸ Use your stomach muscles to slowly pull your hips off the floor and push your feet straight up toward the ceiling (Figure 3). Slowly lower your legs to the floor. To make this exercise more difficult, don't let your legs touch the floor before bringing them back up.

Medicine Ball Chest Pass

Your upper-body strength will determine whether you perform a lying or standing medicine ball chest pass.

EASIER:

❶ The lying medicine ball chest pass is good for people with less upper-body strength or without access to a solid wall. Lie flat on your back with your legs bent and feet flat on the floor. Hold a medicine ball on your chest with both hands (Figure 1).

❷ Push the ball straight up into the air by extending both arms completely (Figure 2), catch it with both hands, and lightly tap it on your chest. Be careful not to drop the ball on your head. Start by just barely letting it leave your fingers; as you get more comfortable catching the ball, push it up with more force so it gets more height. If you're uncomfortable tossing the ball at all, just lift it until your arms are fully extended, then lower it back to your chest.

ADVANCED:

❶ Stand no more than 3 feet from a solid wall with your feet shoulder-width apart. Hold a medicine ball with both hands at chest level (Figure 1).

❷ Throw the ball forcefully against the wall by pushing it straight out from your chest—think chest pass with a basketball (Figure 2). Catch the ball as it rebounds, and bring it back to your chest before throwing it again.

Medicine Ball Pick-Up

❶ Stand with your feet shoulder-width apart and a medicine ball next to the outside of your left foot. Lower into a squat and grasp the medicine ball with both hands (Figure 1), keeping your head up, back straight, and weight focused through your heels. You don't want your back and shoulders to round as you start to lift back up. To start rising, keep your arms straight and swing the ball forward so it's directly in front of you. At the same time, drive with your legs and hips to rise to a standing position.

❷ Keep the ball moving upward until it is extended straight overhead (Figure 2).

❸ Reverse the movement and squat down until you can tap the ball on the ground next to your right foot (Figure 3). One rep consists of lifting the ball from both sides.

«1

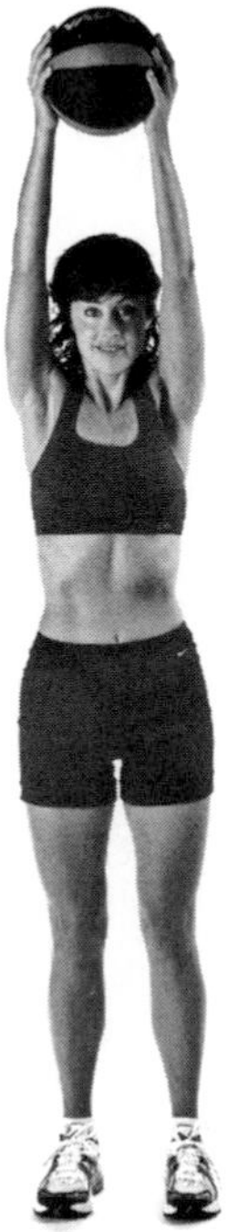

«2

«3

Medicine Ball Situp

«1

❶ Find a wall and lie down with your knees slightly bent, heels on the ground, and your toes touching the wall. Hold a medicine ball on your chest with both hands (Figure 1).

❷ Complete a situp by bringing your chest toward your knees (Figure 2). When you reach the top of the situp, extend your arms (ideally, you'll touch the ball to the wall), then bring the ball back to your chest and lower back to the starting position. To make this exercise more difficult, chest-pass the ball against the wall instead of extending your arms, and catch it before returning to start.

«2

Medicine Ball Solo Twist

❶ Sit on the floor with your legs bent at 45 degrees and your feet flat. Place a medicine ball directly behind you (Figure 1). Keeping your legs stationary, rotate your torso to the right, reach behind you, and pick up the ball.

❷ Grasp the ball and twist to the left as far as possible, keeping your torso upright and your sit bones on the floor (Figure 2). Tap the ball on the floor behind you as close as possible to its original starting position, then lift it and twist back to the right and tap the floor behind you. One repetition consists of one rotation to each side.

Medicine Ball Squat

❶ Stand with your feet slightly more than shoulder-width apart, and hold a medicine ball straight out in front of your body with your arms parallel to the ground (Figure 1). Keep your weight focused through your heels, and squeeze your shoulder blades together to engage the muscles in your upper back and bring your chest forward. Lower into a squat, being conscious to sit back into the movement instead of letting the weight roll you forward onto the balls of your feet.

❷ Lower yourself until your hips are as low as your knees or as close to that point as you can get, while keeping your arms parallel to the ground (Figure 2). Return to a standing position by driving upward with your legs and hips.

«1

«2

Medicine Ball Wall Touch

❶ Stand with your back against the wall and your heels roughly 6 inches from it, holding a medicine ball at chest level with your arms extended parallel to the ground (Figure 1).

❷ Keeping your hips still and facing forward, rotate to the right and lightly touch the medicine ball to the wall (Figure 2). Then rotate across the center and to the left, again lightly touching the ball to the wall. A touch on each side constitutes 1 rep. If you can't reach the wall at first, just go as far as you can. Your range of motion will increase with practice. If you have two medicine balls, use the heavier one for this exercise.

Overhead Medicine Ball Pass

❶ Hold a medicine ball in your right hand with your arms to the sides and parallel to the floor (Figure 1).

❷ Raise both hands overhead and pass the medicine ball from your right hand to your left hand (Figure 2).

❸ Lower both arms back to parallel with the floor, with the medicine ball now in your left hand (Figure 3). One repetition consists of passing the ball from right to left and back to right again.

Overhead Reverse Lunge and Press

❶ Stand with your feet shoulder-width apart and hold a medicine ball with both hands at your chest (Figure 1). Step back with your right foot and drop your hips until your left knee is bent at a 90-degree angle and positioned directly above your left ankle.

❷ As you step back, press the medicine ball overhead (Figure 2). Focus on keeping your chest high so you can press the ball upward instead of out in front of you.

❸ To return to the starting position, push off with your right foot and drive with your left leg while keeping the ball overhead (Figure 3). Return to a standing position, bringing the ball back down to your chest. The press challenges your ability to balance during the reverse lunge movement.

Overhead Squat

❶ Stand with your feet slightly more than shoulder-width apart while holding a stability ball or medicine ball overhead with both hands (Figure 1). Lower into a squat, sitting back into the movement to keep your weight focused through your heels.

❷ Keep your back straight, head up, and gaze forward. When your hips reach the same level as your knees or as close to that point as you can get, stop and hold for a count of 2 (Figure 2). Return to the starting position by driving with your legs and hips, being careful to keep the ball fully extended above you. Don't allow the ball to fall forward or your body to roll forward as you rise.

Reverse Crunch

❶ Lie on your back with your legs straight, feet together. Hold your arms at your sides against the floor, palms down (Figure 1).

❷ Bend your knees and bring them to your chest by tightening your abdominal muscles and curling your hips off the ground (Figure 2). Be careful to engage your abdominal muscles to produce the movement instead of relying on the muscles at the front of your hips and legs. When your knees reach your chest or as close to that point as you can get, curl back down and return to the starting position.

Pushup (with Variations)

EASIEST:

❶ Lie facedown on the floor with your hands even with your chest, just slightly more than shoulder-width apart. Keep your head, shoulders, and hips in a straight line and push your chest away from the floor so your weight is supported on your knees and hands. Push up until your arms are fully extended (Figure 1), but be careful not to lock your elbows.

❷ Slowly lower yourself until your chest barely touches the floor (Figure 2), then immediately push back up.

EASY:

❶ Find a box, bench, or chair. (Beginners should start with a higher bench or box and gradually move to a shorter one.) Place your hands on the box slightly more than shoulder-width apart, with your palms flat and your feet extended straight out behind you. Your weight should be propped on the tips of your shoes or curled toes. Keep your head, shoulders, butt, and legs in a straight line (Figure 1).

❷ Lower your upper body until your chest barely touches the edge of the box, and then push back up (Figure 2). Extend your arms fully, but be careful not to lock your elbows.

INTERMEDIATE:

Same as the easy version but without the box, bench, or chair. Place your hands on the floor, slightly more than shoulder-width apart, to start (Figures 1 and 2).

ADVANCED:

When a regular pushup is no longer challenging, put your feet on a box, bench, or chair (Figure 1) and complete your pushups (Figure 2).

Reverse Medicine Ball Lunge

«1

❶ Stand with your feet shoulder-width apart, holding a medicine ball extended in front of your chest with both hands (Figure 1).

❷ Step back with your left leg, keeping your torso as vertical as possible (focus on keeping your head and chest high) as you drop your hips until your right knee is bent at a 90-degree angle and positioned directly above your right ankle (Figure 2). To return to the starting position, push off with your left foot and drive with your right leg. Alternate legs with each lunge.

«2

Squat and Jump

❶ Stand with your feet slightly more than shoulder-width apart. With your arms at your sides, lower into a squat until your hips reach knee level, and bring your arms back (Figure 1).

❷ Explode straight up and jump as high as you can (Figure 2). As you begin to drive upward, swing your arms upward to generate momentum and more height. Bend your knees to absorb the impact as you land. Return to a standing position.

«1

«2

Squat and Press

❶ Lay a 4½- to 5-foot handled resistance cord on the ground. Find the center and mark it with tape or a marker. Step onto the cord with your feet slightly more than shoulder-width apart and equidistant from the mark. Lower into a squat and pick up a handle with each hand. Stand up straight, then curl the handles up to shoulder height. Hold the handles so your palms are facing each other with your elbows tucked at your sides (Figure 1).

❷ Lower yourself until your hips reach knee height by pushing your hips backward while keeping your head up and back straight (Figure 2). Focus your weight on your heels, and keep your knees from moving ahead of your toes. Drive with your legs and butt as you rise again.

❸ As you reach a standing position, immediately press your hands overhead until your arms are fully extended, but don't lock your elbows or knees (Figure 3). Lower your hands back to the starting position.

«1

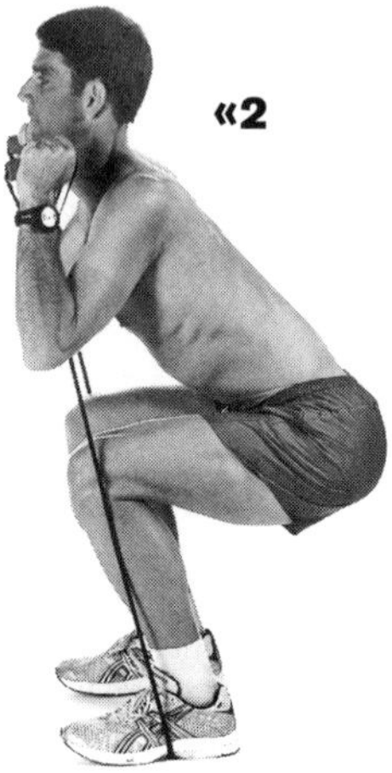

«2

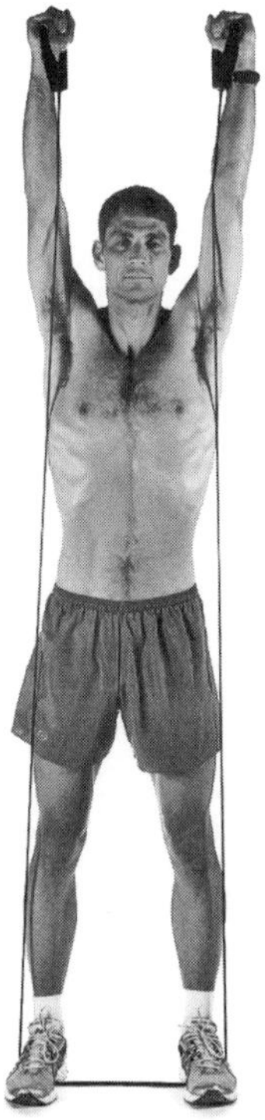

«3

Squat with Resistance Cord

❶ Lay a 4½- to 5-foot handled resistance cord on the ground. Find the center and mark it with tape or a marker. Step onto the cord with your feet slightly more than shoulder-width apart and equidistant from the mark. Lower into a squat and pick up a handle with each hand. Stand up straight, then curl the handles up to shoulder height. Hold the handles so your palms are facing each other with your elbows tucked at your sides (Figure 1).

❷ Using a controlled motion, squat down until your hips are at the same height as your knees, keeping your eyes and head up (Figure 2). Focus your weight on your heels, and keep your knees from moving ahead of your toes. Drive with your legs and butt as you rise to a standing position. Be careful not to lock your knees.

*Tip: To do the **Squat and Pause** with a resistance cord, simply pause for a 2-second count at the bottom of the movement, then drive with your legs and butt as you rise to a standing position.*

If you can't lower your hips to knee height without shifting your weight onto the balls of your feet or you feel your body rolling forward as you squat, just lower your hips as much as you can while keeping your weight focused over your heels.

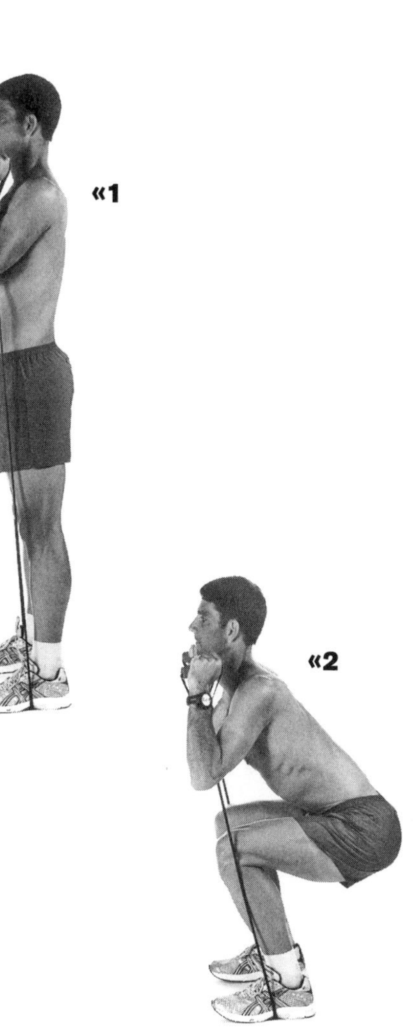

Up-Down

❶ Stand with your feet hip-width apart, arms at your sides (Figure 1).

❷ In one fluid motion, lower into a squat until you can place your palms flat on the floor on either side of your feet (Figure 2), ❸ and step or jump back into a classic pushup position with your head, hips, and legs in a straight line (Figure 3).

❹ Bring your knees back up under your body and return to a squat with your hands on the floor (Figure 4), ❺ and then drive upward, keeping your head and chest high, back to a standing position. Jumping your feet out behind you and then back up under your body is a more advanced version of this movement.

Upright Row

❶ Stand on a resistance cord with your feet roughly hip-distance apart and equal lengths of cord on each side. Hold the handles at hip level so your palms face your thighs (Figure 1). Keeping your back straight, chest high, and head up, pull up on the handles.

❷ Keep your hands close to your body and your elbows high as you bring the handles to midchest (Figure 2), then lower them to the starting position (hip level).

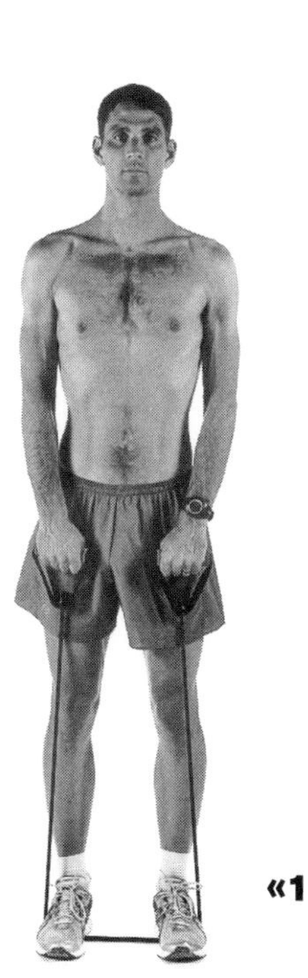

«1

«2

Walking Overhead Lunge

❶ Stand with your feet hip-distance apart while holding a stability ball overhead in both hands (Figure 1).

❷ Take a big step forward with your right leg, lowering your body until your hips are level with your right knee (Figure 2). Make sure the right knee doesn't travel ahead of your toes.

❸ Drive with your legs and hips to step forward to a standing position (Figure 3), then immediately lunge forward with your left leg while continuing to hold the ball overhead. The ball is not adding resistance as much as it is forcing you to engage muscles throughout your body for stabilization and balance.

Windshield Wiper

❶ Lie on your back with your legs together and arms extended perpendicular to your body. Lift your legs perpendicular to the floor (Figure 1).

❷ Keeping your arms and shoulders flat against the floor and your legs straight, lower your legs to the left (Figure 2).

❸ Raise your legs back to center, then lower them to the right (Figure 3). Lowering to both sides once completes 1 repetition.

«1

«2

«3

10-Foot Shuttle Run

Measure and mark out a distance of 10 feet. Start at one end and sprint to the other and back, touching a point (cone, T-shirt, can—whatever works) as you reach each end (Figures 1 through 5). Be sure to stand up completely as you move between the marks; don't just shuttle back and forth bent over. The motion of squatting down and reaching to touch the mark, then rising back up, is one of the important parts of this exercise.

«1

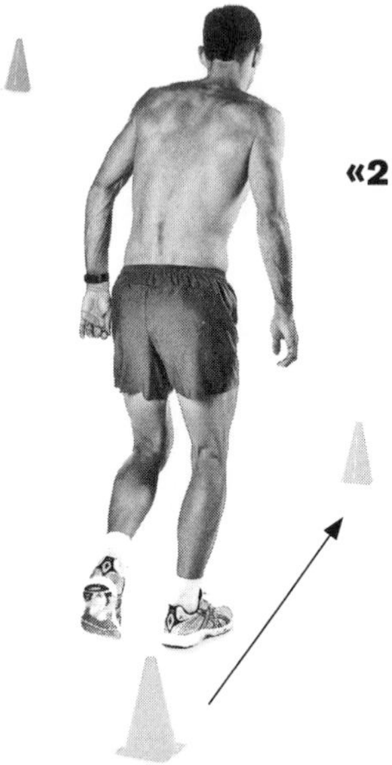

«2

«3

«4

«5

Alternating Box-Top Foot Taps

❶ Stand with your feet shoulder-width apart, facing a box or step 6 to 10 inches high (people with greater fitness can use a higher box, as illustrated in the accompanying figures). Place your right foot on top of the box to start (Figure 1).

❷ Simultaneously hop with your left leg and bring your right leg down, so you end up with your left leg on top of the box and your right foot on the ground (Figure 2). Immediately hop with your right foot and bring your left leg down to the ground. Continue alternating feet for the length of the interval. You should apply barely any weight to the box or step; your foot should only tap it.

Box Jump Drill

❶ Make a square on the floor of 1 or 2 square feet, using tape or chalk. Start in the center of the box and, without stopping, jump forward to the outside of the box (Figure 1), then jump back to the center.

❷ Then jump out to the right side of the box (Figure 2) and back to center.

❸ Now jump backward outside of the box (Figure 3), back to the center, ❹ out of the box to the left side (Figure 4), and, finally, back into the box to complete 1 repetition.

Double-Leg Cone Jump

❶ Stand next to a cone with your feet together and your arms at your sides (Figure 1).

❷ Bend your knees slightly and swing your arms up to chest level to generate momentum as you jump sideways over the cone while keeping your feet together (Figure 2).

❸ Bend your knees as you land to absorb the impact (Figure 3) and immediately jump back over the cone again. If you are using a T-shirt or can, be sure to jump at least 4 to 6 inches off the ground. Both height and moving from side to side are important in this exercise.

Double-Leg Line Jump

Mark out a 15-inch-long line on the floor. Stand next to the line with your feet parallel to it and your arms at your sides. Bend your knees slightly and bring your arms up to chest level as you jump over the line while keeping your feet together (Figures 1 and 2). Immediately upon landing, jump back to complete one repetition (Figure 3). Height is not important on this jump; just focus on moving from side to side.

Single-Leg Line Jump

❶ Stand on one foot next to a line with your arms at your sides. Bend your knee slightly and swing your arms up to your chest to generate momentum as you jump laterally over the line (Figure 1).

❷ Bend your knee as you land on the same foot, and then immediately jump back over the line to complete one repetition (Figure 2). Height is not important on this jump; just focus on moving from side to side.

Six-Cone Sidestep

Position six cones, spaced about 1 foot apart, in a straight line. Stand to the left of the first cone. Quickly step sideways to the right, lifting your feet over each cone, one foot at a time (Figures 1 through 4). Once you have stepped over the last cone, reverse the process by stepping sideways to the right, working your way back to the first cone. As you feel more comfortable with this exercise, increase your speed. If you are using T-shirts or cans, be sure to lift your knees as though stepping over an object at least 6 inches high.

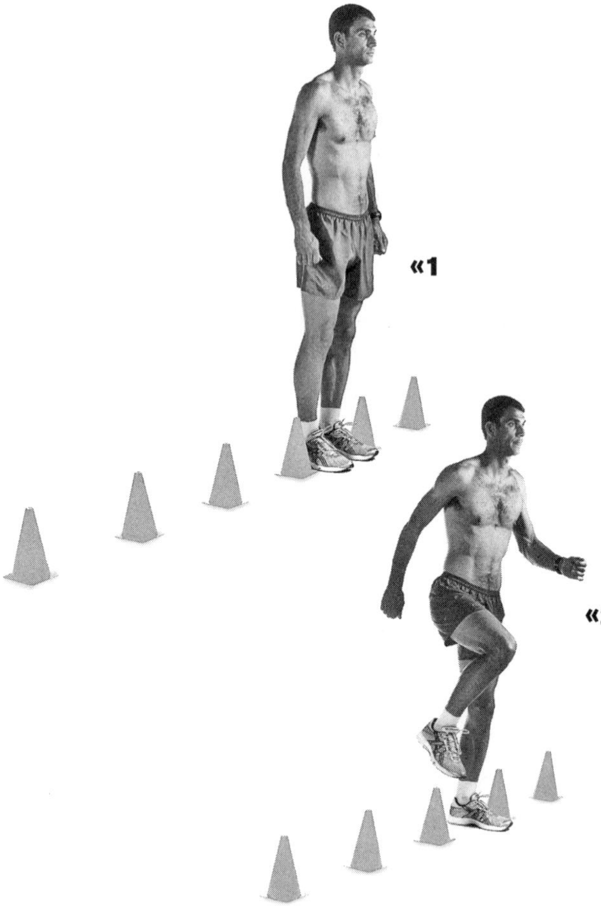

«1

«2

«3

«4

Six-Cone Crossover

❶ Position six cones, spaced about 1 foot apart, in a straight line. Stand to the right of the first cone. Cross your right leg over your left as you step over the cones (Figure 1).

❷ Bring your left leg around your right so both are between the cones (Figure 2). Repeat the process to the end of the cones, always crossing your right leg over your left. Reverse the exercise and work back to the first cone, this time crossing your left leg over your right and the cone. As you feel more comfortable with this exercise, increase your speed. If you are using T-shirts or cans, be sure to lift your knees as though stepping over an object at least 6 inches high.

Speed Skater

❶ Start in a standing position. To start the movement, kick your right foot back and to the side as you lower your body into a half-squat on your left leg (Figure 1). All of your weight should be on your left leg.

❷ Bring your right foot back up as you return to a standing position, and immediately lower into a half squat on your right leg (Figure 2) ❸ as you kick your left leg back and to the side (Figure 3). Continue for 20 seconds per set.

Square Drill

❶ Place four cones in a 5-by-5-foot square. Start by standing at one corner with a cone (cone 1) at your left foot, facing down one side of the square toward another cone (cone 2) (Figure 1).

❷ Run forward to cone 2 (Figure 2), ❸ and then shuffle sideways to your left to cone 3 (Figure 3).

❹ When you reach cone 3, run backward to cone 4.

❺ Shuffle sideways to your left to return to cone 1 (Figure 4).

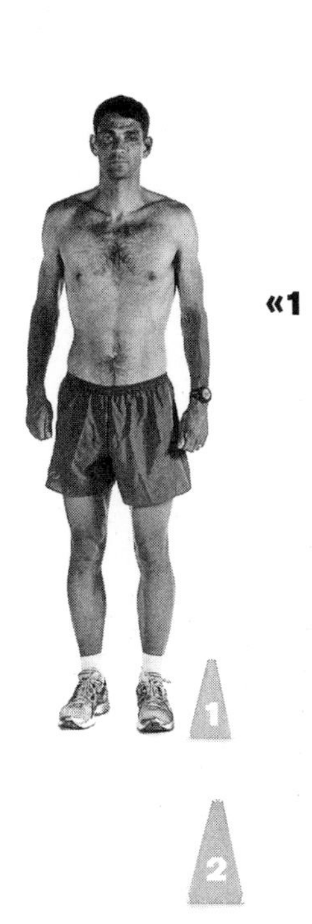

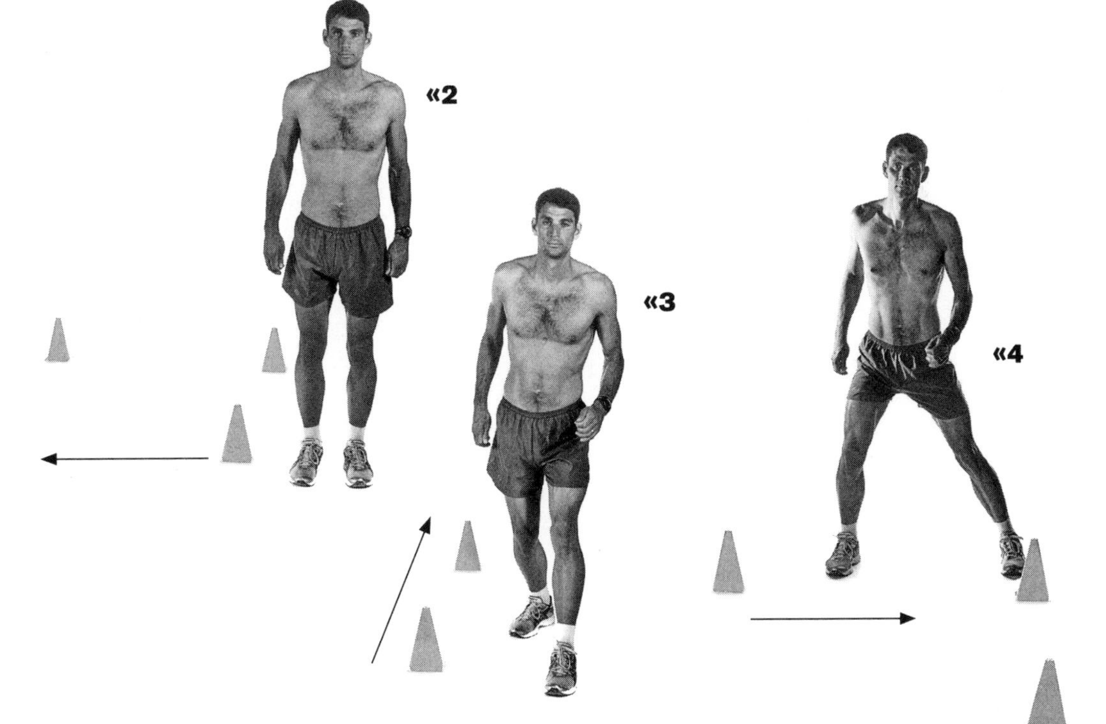

Zigzag Line Jump

❶ Make a line on the floor roughly 10 feet long, or use a line of grout in a tile floor or wood grain in a hardwood floor. Start by standing with your feet close together and the line extending in front of you on your right (Figure 1).

❷ In one motion, jump forward and to the right, over the line (Figure 2). Then jump again, forward and to the left. Every jump should be a forward motion, and every jump should propel your body over the line. One set consists of two 4-counts of jumps: Zigzag jump 1-2-3-4 down the line in one direction, turn around, and jump 1-2-3-4 back to the starting position.

INDEX

<u>Underscored</u> page references indicate boxed text and tables
Boldface references indicate photographs.

A

B

C

D

E

Q

R

S

T

U

V

W

Y

Z